Makan-lah!

The true taste of Malaysia

To Selva,

who taught me how to cook rice!

Makan-lah!

The true taste of Malaysia

Carol Selva Rajah

HarperCollinsPublishers

HarperCollins*Publishers*

First published in Australia in 1996
by HarperCollins*Publishers* Pty Limited

ACN 009 913 517
A member of the HarperCollins*Publishers* (Australia) Pty Limited Group

Copyright © Carol Selva Rajah

HarperCollins*Publishers*
25 Ryde Road, Pymble, Sydney NSW 2073, Australia
31 View Road, Glenfield, Auckland 10, New Zealand
77–85 Fulham Palace Road, London W6 8JB, United Kingdom
Hazelton Lanes, 55 Avenue Road, Suite 2900, Toronto, Ontario M5R 3L2
and 1995 Markham Road, Scarborough, Ontario M1B 5M8, Canada
10 East 53rd Street, New York NY 10032, USA

National Library of Australia Cataloguing-in-Publication data:

Selva Rajah, Carol.
Makan-Lah!: the true taste of Malaysia

   ISBN 0 7322 5762X.
   1. Cookery, Malaysian. I. Title.
   641.59595

Photography by Joe Filshie
Styling by Georgina Dolling

Printed in Hong Kong

7 6 5 4 3 2 1 96 97 98 99

Foreword

The aromas that fill my kitchen — the scents of coriander, cumin, fenugreek, candlenut, tamarind and fresh galangal — evoke the lush green spice islands of my past.

I grew up south of Kuala Lumpur, in Malaysia, where my parents were school teachers. Father and Mother were gregarious and loved to entertain, so we had many friends and relatives who visited and even some who stayed during times of crisis. The kitchen was a refuge for my thirsty soul — and a constant source of sustenance for my hungry stomach! Mother was not interested in cooking, so my Amah (nanny) would encourage me to help in the kitchen. What better place to hide out, where the choicest gossip could be gleaned and homework avoided?

Even as a schoolchild I was interested in knowing about food. I remember sitting through an English lesson on Tennyson, day-dreaming about the 'Lotus Eaters' and the description of a 'meadow set with slender galingale'. Father's book of botanical terms had taught me that galingale (galangal) was none other than the humble *lengkuas* that we used every day in our kitchen. When asked what I was musing on, I reported my finding to my teacher — a bright young lass fresh from England — and received her most righteous ire: 'And do you think Tennyson had nothing else to do but write about Malaysian herbs!'

Because of its position at the crossroads of Asia, Malaysia offers an appetising mix of cuisines: Malay, Singaporean, Nonya, Indonesian, Indian, Chinese and Sri Lankan, as well as Portuguese and Colonial. I have a special affinity with Sri Lankan and Nonya food because of close family ties: mother was of Indian descent but brought up by Hokkiens in Penang, while my father and husband were ethnically Sri Lankan.

Since moving to Australia, I have continued to infuse my cooking with the rich, spicy, soft and subtle flavours of Malaysian and Asian ingredients, along with wonderful Australian produce.

This fusion represents in many ways my own culinary journey through life.

Acknowledgements

This book has been a long time in the making. My husband Selva, who was always my teacher, official taster and harshest critic, fell ill soon after it began, but gamely continued to taste and advise. When Selva ate something with relish we knew it was good enough to end up in the book. I would like to acknowledge his help and encouragement throughout, sadly regretting he was unable to see its final completion.

I would also like to thank my friend, Cheong Liew the brilliant chef from Adelaide, whose recipe is featured here, and also Radha, Bawani and Hapsa for recipes they kindly provided.

To six special friends who have helped me along my culinary journey: Anne Shute in Canada, who goaded me into teaching cookery ; Annie Lee, who enthused about Nonya 30 years ago; Vijeya Rajendra, who insisted that I publish; Charlie Lockhart, who invited me to write for *Gourmet Traveller*; Ben Cardillo, for teaching me all that I know about cooking for television; and Max Lake, for opening my eyes to scents and flavours.

A million thanks to my little gumdrops: Jo Richardson, Rachel Mackay, Julie Ballard, Alex Deblasi, Linda Koreneff and Anushiya Selvarajah for shopping, testing, cooking for photography.

Thanks also to Liza Quddoos of Raffles Hotel, Singapore, for allowing me to use photographs of the hotel and for providing me with the recipe for Singapore Sling.

My thanks, also, to the following people and organisations: Australian Meat and Livestock Corporation, Balgowlah Heights Fruit & Flowers, Bertolli Olive Oils, Doffs Kitchen, Dulux Paints, Huon Herbs, National Dairies, Orson & Blake Collectables, Pontip Asian groceries, Porters Paints, Sydney Antique Centre, and Regina Walter.

My thanks to Joe Filshie and Georgina Dolling for making the food come alive with their photography and to Andy for the Roti Chanai photograph. Lastly, thanks to my friend Wendy Lloyd Jones, whose impeccable judgment has never failed me.

CONTENTS

Introduction

Picture a small town near a white sandy beach on the northern border of Malaysia; the season, pre-monsoon; the day, any one of a million. It is the weekly market day, a crowded kaleidoscope of colour. Amidst the bustle something strikes you as unusual: these markets are run wholly by women.

Diminutive women are sitting cross-legged on tiny kerchiefs of colour. They are surrounded by jade and brown vegetables, purple yams and magenta herbs, green leaves, orange pineapples, green and brown coconuts, yellow–green and gold bananas, and vivid red chillies. Over there, a wrinkled, tobacco-chewing old woman squats beneath a pyramid of aluminium woks and pans and coconut brooms.

Outside the town, a group of Chinese girls in school uniforms cycles past orderly rows of rubber trees. The cycles are wobbling, each girl trying to balance her slurpy pink ice-ball in one hand, while weaving around the sea of traffic heading into town after work.

In another town, along a dusty alley, an old Chinese hawker stands before a battered suitcase full of mystical charts, leopard oil and essence of snake. Close by, a woman fishes boiled noodles from a huge smoking cauldron. We watch as she spoons the delicate soup into bowls already piled high with bottle-green spinach and yellow nuggets of tofu. On the other side of the alley, an Indian man in a white dhoti, his forehead smeared in holy ash, makes up little cones of wok-roasted nuts for teatime snacks.

In the city, across the peninsula, it is late afternoon. The streets are wet from the daily downpour. Drivers slow down to pick up deep-fried battered bananas from a Malay vendor. Men play hockey and soccer in the local club, and office girls gather at the local YWCA for a satay-cooking class.

At a posh Tudor-style city club that could be anywhere in the Commonwealth, we see an assortment of Malay, Chinese, Indian, Eurasian, Punjabi and Portuguese people, in different styles of dress, sipping iced cocktails. They will dine on fried rice, stir-fried noodles and curried Laksa, at tables laid with starched white tablecloths, silver cutlery and gleaming glasses, and they will speak the common English which unites everyone in Malaysia.

Multiply this scene many times and the basic reality of Malaysia emerges: a mosaic of diverse communities, cultures and food with its origins in the 3rd and 4th centuries, when Malaysia and Indonesia made up the Hindu Javanese Empire, Srivijaya. Malaysia still bears the signs of that early Hindu culture, along with the later Chinese and Arabic influences.

In early times Malaysia was important because of its position halfway between India and China on the sea route and its pivotal position in the spice belt. The Straits of Melaka were a trading place for silks, spices and porcelain and sheltered many sailing ships during the monsoon season.

The indigenous Malays, who held animistic beliefs, adopted Buddhist and Hindu traditions from traders. In the 11th century, Indian Muslim converts brought Islam. It quickly gained popularity and overlaid the earlier religious and cultural traditions.

In the 13th century Marco Polo visited the 'Spice Islands' and listed the spices he saw, including pepper, nutmeg and cloves, and coconut, which he described as 'sweet but like milk'. At the time, Melaka, a rich trading port, was a haven of peace amidst other Asian waters rife with piracy, Europe was tired of paying high prices for spices, and Asia was about to be swamped by Western trading powers greedy for the wealth of the East.

The Portuguese, the first of these adventurous traders, arrived in 1511 and settled in, governing the city of Melaka for 100 years. Many other waves of migration followed. The Dutch were followed by the British who colonised and anglicised Malaya, leaving a sound educational and judiciary system, and medical and civil services. When tin mining and rubber tree cultivation became important industries in the late 18th and 19th centuries, there was a second wave of migration from China and India as people came to join the labour force. The British Colonials, who controlled these rubber plantations and tin mines and worked in government, led idyllic lives characterised by parties and nights at the club. Armies of cooks and amahs looked after their every need.

This colonial shangri-la ended with the Second World War. In 1963 the Federation of Malay States gained its independence from the British and became known as Malaysia, encompassing the Borneo States of Sabah and Sarawak. Today Malaysia is one of the fastest growing and most successful Asian nations with a population of 19 million people, mainly ethnic Malays, Indians, Chinese and Eurasians.

Malaysia can boast of some of the most exciting food styles in Asia, the dominant influences being Chinese and Indian. Malaysians are adventurous with their food. A typical meal may consist of a variety different cuisines: Malay, Indian, Chinese, Nonya and Portuguese — Eurasian.

In Malaysia today the selection, preparation and consumption of food is based on Confucian principles, Indian Vedic laws and Muslim taboos. Confucious's injunctions that 'rice could never be white enough, meat could never be chopped finely enough' and his advice to avoid 'fish that is not sound, meat that is high, anything overcooked or undercooked' are still paramount.

Spices have always been used in Malaysian cooking: ginger and pepper for heat, cloves, nutmeg and mace, and lemon grass and galangal to flavour meats and increase the body's wellbeing. Chilli was only introduced after the 15th century but soon found its way onto every table.

The traditional Malay kitchen was a small lean-to attached to the house. The old firewood stoves have since been replaced by the more sensible gas cooking. Woks called *kuali* are a part of the Malaysian kitchen repertoire, stirred with a wok *charn*, both utensils introduced to Malaya by the Chinese. The mortar and pestle, called the *batu tumbok* or *batu oelek*, and the grinding stone are still used to pulverise and grind spices. Many kitchens today also have blenders and mincers, refrigerators and microwave ovens.

The markets, called 'wet' markets because of the water used to hose down the vegetables (as compared to 'dry' Western-type supermarkets) are an important part of Malaysian life. Vegetables and fruit of every type imaginable, both local and imported, vie for space with flowers, seafood and meat. There are strict halal areas in the common markets to cater to Muslim dietary laws; meat stalls are segregated as pork is haram (prohibited) to Muslims.

There are many special services available in a Malaysian market that one could never find in a Western market. Chickens are slaughtered on the spot and bled in Muslim tradition, coconuts are freshly scraped and pulverised for creamy coconut milk, and spices are ground fresh and mixed tailor-made for the customer. People shop daily for produce, preferring to buy each item fresh rather than to freeze or refrigerate it. Markets are crowded all morning and deserted in the afternoon, except for the occasional satay vendor servicing the transition period from noon to evening, when the night markets — selling everything from designer clothes and watches through to prickly durian and chilli crab — commence.

Rice is eaten twice or even three times a day with soups, two curries and three or four simple vegetable stir-fries. Meals are finished off with the most exotic array of fruit in the world: rambutan, duku, langsat, starfruit, chicku or sapodilla, mangosteen and durian, considered heaven by Malaysians. Desserts, mainly eaten as teatime snacks, are usually starchy cakes made from glutinous rice, coconut milk and sugar.

In accordance with the old Confucian laws of texture, taste and flavour, and yin and yang principles, food should be well-balanced, combining crunchy and soft, rough and smooth, slippery and astringent. Bitter, sweet, sour, salty and pungent ingredients are combined, resulting in mouthwatering flavours, attractive colours and beautiful, subtle aromas.

Malays and Indians eat with the fingers of the right hand, the left being used for ablutions, while Chinese-style meals are eaten with chopsticks, and a porcelain spoon when soup is being served. If one is setting a Western-style table, forks and spoons are acceptable, but knives have traditionally been considered as a sign of aggression.

Malaysians are generous people who entertain whenever they have a chance. It is quite common to invite a person one has met casually home to dinner. Because of the ethnic and cultural mix, Malaysia celebrates more religious and cultural holidays than any other country in the region. There is always an excuse to party, to have a *kenduri* celebration or *selamatan*, a thanksgiving offering to God.

The recipes in this book have not been divided into their ethnic groups, but flow naturally as in real life. Above each recipe you will find a short note on its ethnic origin or cooking style.

Malaysian food is traditionally served with plain water, fruit juice or Chinese tea, but can also be served with chilled semi-dry or dry white wines and light beers. I find that a round and mellow red, such as a Cabernet Merlot, goes well with my richly spiced curries and soups.

So enjoy a cuisine that spans the ages and has successfully stood the test of time.

Selamat makan-lah!

Assam Laksa (recipe, page 14)

North Assam Laksa

Laksa, a curried noodle dish, is a blend of Chinese, Malay and Indian influences: the noodle from China, the curry from India and the coconuts from Malaysia itself. Northern Assam Laksa is similar to Thai tom yum soup.

Ingredients:

4 stalks lemon grass

4 centimetre (1½ in) length of galangal

6—8 red Asian onions or 1 Spanish (red) onion, blended in a food processor or finely chopped

1 tablespoon sambal oelek

1 centimetre (½ in) length of fresh turmeric root or ½ teaspoon turmeric powder

6 candlenuts, ground

500 grams (1 lb) fish fillets (Ling or Hake), diced

500 grams (1 lb) fresh prawns (shrimp), peeled and deveined or squid, cleaned and chopped

2 tablespoons oil

2 centimetre (¾ in) length of shrimp paste (belacan), dry roasted (see page 172)

4 cups (1 litre / 32 fl oz) fish or prawn (shrimp) stock

250 grams (8 oz) fishballs, cut into halves (see note)

4 cups (1 litre / 32 fl oz) water mixed with 2 tablespoons tamarind paste

4 pieces tamarind fruit slices (assam glugor)

1 tablespoon haekoe or rojak paste (black treacle-like shrimp paste)

50 grams (1½ oz) Vietnamese mint, chopped

500 grams (1 lb) dried, thin Chinese rice noodles (beehoon)

Garnish:

3 eggs, hard-boiled and cut into quarters

½ pineapple, thinly sliced

2 squares of tofu, shallow-fried and sliced paper-thin

100 grams (3½ oz) fresh bean sprouts, tails trimmed

30 grams (1 oz) mint, shredded

1 cucumber, skin only, finely shredded

2 limes, cut into quarters

Method:

Blend the lemon grass, galangal, onions, sambal oelek, turmeric and candlenuts together in a food processor or mortar and pestle.

Steam the fish and prawns (shrimp) or squid until the fish is opaque (about 2–3 minutes). Save any liquid and add it to the fish or prawn (shrimp) stock.

Heat the oil in a large saucepan and sauté the blended mixture of lemon grass, galangal, onions, sambal oelek, turmeric and candlenuts with the shrimp paste until they release their strong aroma (about 3–4 minutes).

Add the stock. When it starts boiling, add the fish and fishballs. Stir regularly on a medium heat. Add the tamarind liquid and tamarind fruit slices (assam glugor), then the haekoe or rojak paste.

When the spices smell cooked, add the 50 grams (1½ ounces) of Vietnamese mint and bring to the boil, stirring regularly.

Blanch the noodles in hot water for about 5 minutes.

Place the noodles in bowls, ladle the soup over the top and sprinkle over the garnish ingredients. Laksa should be served with a side dish of chilli sauce.

NOTE: You can buy ready-made fishballs in packets. If you prefer to make your own, see the recipe for Fishballs and Fishcakes on page 88.

North Assam Laksa is pictured on previous page.

Johore Laksa

Laksas vary according to the region of Malaysia they come from. Southern Laksas, such as this one from the Royal House of Johore, are the most creamy and flavoursome.

Ingredients:

1 cup (100 g / 3½ oz) grated fresh coconut or ½ cup (45 g / 1½ oz) desiccated coconut

3 stalks lemon grass

3 centimetre (1½ in) length of galangal

3 centimetre (1½ in) length of ginger

3 centimetre (1½ in) length of shrimp paste (belacan), dry roasted

2 tablespoons oil

1 kilogram (2 lb) fish fillets (Ling), chopped, or 700 grams chicken thigh fillets

500 grams (1 lb) fresh school prawns (small shrimp), peeled and deveined

2 tablespoons mixed Malaysian Fish Curry Powder (see note)

3 pieces tamarind fruit slices (assam glugor)

4 cups (1 litre / 32 fl oz) fish stock, or chicken stock if using chicken meat

3 cups (750 mL / 24 fl oz) thick coconut milk

salt and pepper, to taste

1 cup (250 mL / 8 fl oz) thick coconut cream

1 packet (200 g / 7 oz) rounded Chinese laksa noodles or thin Chinese rice noodles (beehoon)

1 tablespoon chilli powder

Garnish:

4 red Asian onions, finely sliced

6 limes or 1 lemon, quartered

1 cucumber, skin only, finely shredded

200 grams (7 oz) Vietnamese mint, chopped

100 grams (3½ oz) bean sprouts, tails trimmed

1 onion, finely sliced

50—80 grams (1½—2½ oz) crispy fried onions

2 tablespoons sambal oelek

Method:

Dry roast the coconut until it is golden (see page 172). Pound it in a mortar and pestle, or grind it in a coffee grinder, until it forms a dark paste (known as krisek).

Blend the lemon grass, galangal and ginger together using a food processor or mortar and pestle. Crumble the shrimp paste into the mixture. Heat the oil in a saucepan and fry the mixture until it releases its aroma.

Add the fish or chicken, and the prawns. Cook on a medium heat, stirring continuously, for about 5 minutes.

Add the curry powder, tamarind fruit slices (assam glugor), roasted coconut (krisek), stock and coconut milk and simmer uncovered for 20 minutes.

Stir in the coconut cream and add salt and pepper to taste.

Place the noodles in a large bowl, cover with hot water for about 5 minutes, then drain. Place the noodles in serving bowls, ladle the soup over and sprinkle with garnishes.

NOTE: Malaysian Fish Curry Powder is available from Asian food stores. If you prefer to make your own, see the instructions on page 172.

Spicy Chicken Soup
(Soto Jawa Timur)

While travelling in Bali I was able to taste a variety of soto, all served by tiny browned men riding rickety bicycles and balancing large pots of boiling hot soup. Standing between rice fields and watching ducks being driven across rice dams, I savoured a beautiful chicken soto, and felt this was the most fulfilling meal that one could have in a country that celebrates pure and simple tastes.

Ingredients:

500 grams (2 lb) chicken thigh fillets

3 cups (750 mL / 24 fl oz) chicken stock

3 centimetre (1½ in) length of ginger

2 cloves garlic

1 tablespoon oil

2 Spanish (red) onions

1 centimetre (½ in) length of fresh turmeric root, pounded or chopped finely, or ½ teaspoon turmeric powder

150 grams (5 oz) fresh school prawns (small shrimp), peeled and deveined

2 cups (500 mL / 16 fl oz) coconut milk

salt and pepper, to taste

2 packets (250 g / 8 oz) beanthread noodles

Garnish:

1 packet (200 g / 6½ oz) fried onions (or 10 small red Asian onions, sliced finely and fried)

2 limes, sliced into wedges

spring onions

coriander (cilantro), leaves only

Method:

Boil the chicken in the stock until it is just cooked. Remove the chicken from the stock, allow it to cool and then shred it. Reserve the stock for later.

Blend the ginger and garlic together in a food processor or mortar and pestle. Heat the oil in a wok or saucepan and sauté the ginger and garlic for 30 seconds. Add the onion and turmeric and fry until they release their aroma and the onion is golden (about 3–5 minutes).

Add the stock and cook on a medium heat for 10 minutes. Bring it to the boil, then reduce to a simmer. Add the shredded chicken and prawns (shrimp) and continue to simmer until the stock is flavoursome (about 10–15 minutes).

Add coconut milk and stir well. Simmer for 10 minutes. Add salt and pepper to taste.

Place the noodles in a large bowl, cover with boiling water for about 5 minutes. Drain the noodles in a colander and run cold water over to blanch them. Place the noodles in serving bowls, ladle over the boiling soup, and sprinkle over the garnish ingredients.

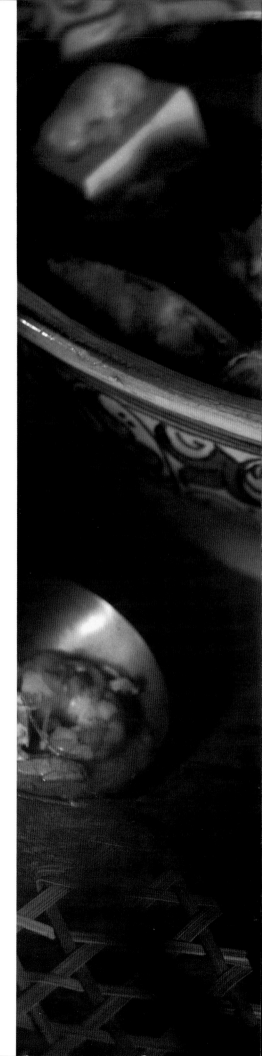

Back: Tofupok in Yongtahu Soup or Taucheo Sauce (recipe, page 100);
Front: Spicy Chicken Soup (Soto Jawa Timur)

Fishball Soup
(Ikan Dan Yongtahu Soup)

*The fishball-soup hawker heralded his arrival each night by
hitting two bamboo sticks together, so we called him the
'tok tok' man. Other hawkers would pass along our lane
in quick succession, selling kwonlo mee, lomai kai
(sticky rice chicken), and mamak murtabak
(roti stuffed with curried mince).*

Ingredients:

100 grams (3½ oz) beanthread noodles

1 tablespoon oil

5 cloves garlic, finely chopped

1 litre (32 fl oz) pork or chicken stock

fish sauce, to taste

pepper, to taste

1 tablespoon pickled radish (tangchai)

2 stalks spring onion (green part only), chopped

200 grams (7 oz) fishballs (see recipe for Fishballs
and Fishcakes, page 88)

½ cos lettuce, finely shredded

Garnish:

50 grams (1½ oz) crispy fried onions (see page 172)

Method:

Place the noodles in a medium-sized bowl and cover with hot
water for 5 minutes, then drain. When the noodles have cooled
down a little, cut them into 6 centimetre (2½ in) lengths.

Heat oil in a wok or saucepan and brown the garlic. Take the
wok off the heat, add the stock, fish sauce and pepper and return
to the heat. Bring it to the boil, then add the pickled radish,
spring onions, and the fishballs or stuffed vegetables. Simmer
until all the ingredients are heated through (about 10 minutes).
Add the noodles.

To serve, place a handful of shredded lettuce in each serving
bowl, ladle over the hot soup and garnish with crispy fried
onions (see page 172).

Mulligatawny
(Rassam or Pepper Water)

*This soup was originally known as 'Mulliga Thanni', the
literal translation of which is 'Pepper Water'. In an
Indian/Malaysian setting, it is served with rice as a second
course or as a digestive at the end of the meal. The British,
however, altered the recipe so that a whole meal could be
made of the soup.*

Ingredients:

1½ tablespoons coriander (cilantro) seeds

2 tablespoons cumin seeds

1 teaspoon black pepper

1 tablespoon oil

5 cloves garlic pounded roughly, skins left on

4 red Asian onions or 1 Spanish (red) onion,
halved then sliced thinly

3 dried chilli torn up into pieces

2 stalks curry leaves

1 litre (32 fl oz) thin tamarind juice

salt, to tase

Optional:

300 grams (9½ oz) chicken pieces on the bone
or 300 grams (9½ oz) dried anchovies (ikan bilis)

1 cup (250 mL / 8 fl oz) water

Method:

Dry roast the coriander (cilantro) seeds, cumin seeds and black
pepper. (For instructions on dry roasting, see page 172.) Grind
them together coarsely using a mortar and pestle.

Heat the oil in a saucepan and fry the garlic and onion till
golden. Add the chilli and the curry leaves and fry until they
release their aroma (about 2 minutes).

Add tamarind juice, the ground spices and salt. Bring to the
boil and cook for 10 minutes.

If you are using the optional chicken or dried anchovies, add
it to the saucepan and boil for 20 minutes, adding the cup of
water gradually as the soup reduces.

Mulligatawny should be served with a separate bowl of rice.

Lamb Soup
(Mutton Bif Sup or Sup Kambing)

Beef soup was a favourite of the British Colonials in Malaysia. When Indian Hindus, who came as traders to Malaysia, made the soup they used mutton instead of beef because of religious restrictions, but the name 'Bif Sup' (beef soup) remained.

Ingredients:

1 kilogram (2 lb) lamb, on the bone
1 teaspoon powdered turmeric
3 centimetre (1½ in) strip of ginger
3 onions
2 cloves garlic
300 grams (9½ oz) carrots, sliced diagonally
6 cups (1.5 litres/ 78 fl oz) water
4 cups (1 litre / 32 fl oz) beef stock, made from soup bones
2 cloves
5 peppercorns
3 cinnamon sticks
2 Spanish (red) onions, diced
½ cup (125 mL / 4 fl oz) oil
soy sauce, to taste
salt and freshly ground pepper, to taste
50 grams (1½ oz) fresh coriander (cilantro), leaves only

Method:

Coat the lamb in the turmeric and marinate in the refrigerator for 1 hour.

Blend together the ginger, onion and garlic in a food processor or mortar and pestle. Put this mixture, plus the carrots and the water into a saucepan and bring to the boil. Cook until the carrots are soft.

Then add the lamb, stock, cloves, peppercorns and cinnamon sticks and cook until the meat is soft (about 30–45 minutes). Top up with extra water if necessary.

While the soup is cooking, heat the oil in a pan and fry the onion until browned.

When the meat is soft, remove the cloves, peppercorns, cinnamon and ginger from the soup with slotted spoon.

Add the onion and soy (to taste) and cook on a low heat for 5–10 minutes.

Add salt and pepper and garnish with coriander (cilantro) leaves.

(If left to cool, the fat will solidify and can then be skimmed off.)

Spicy Breakfast Soup
(Bak Ku Teh)

This soup, reputedly the best cure for a hangover, was concocted by a Malaysian doctor as a tonic for his children who had poor appetites. Chinese herbs such as gankuo and dang xin are often added, turning the soup into a tonic. This version is more of a simple pick-me-up and is good not only for breakfast but for lunch and dinner as well.

Ingredients:

6 Chinese dried mushrooms
600 grams (1⅓ lb) meaty pork ribs (paikuat) or
600 grams (1⅓ lb) chicken pieces
200 grams (7 oz) pork neck strip, chopped
3.5 litres (7 pints) water
4 star anise, pounded roughly
2 cinnamon sticks
6-8 cloves
⅓ cup (80 mL / 2½ fl oz) light soy sauce
⅓ cup (80 mL / 2½ fl oz) dark soy sauce
⅓ cup (80 mL / 2½ fl oz) Shao Hsing rice wine
6 juliennes (100 g / 3½ oz) of sugared, preserved melon (tangkuey)
2 pieces dried mandarin peel
1½ tablespoons sugar
salt and pepper, to taste

Method:

Place the dried mushrooms in a small bowl and cover them with hot water for 10 minutes, then drain.

Place ribs (or chicken) and pork neck in water and bring to the boil in a large saucepan.

Place the star anise, cinnamon and cloves in a muslin bag. Add the bag to the saucepan, along with the light and dark soy sauce, rice wine, preserved melon, mushrooms and mandarin peel.

Simmer with the lid on until the meat is tender and almost falling off the bone. Add the sugar and season with salt and pepper to taste.

Place meat in serving bowls, ladle over the soup and serve hot with Chinese jasmine tea in small teacups.

Noodles, Rice and Bread

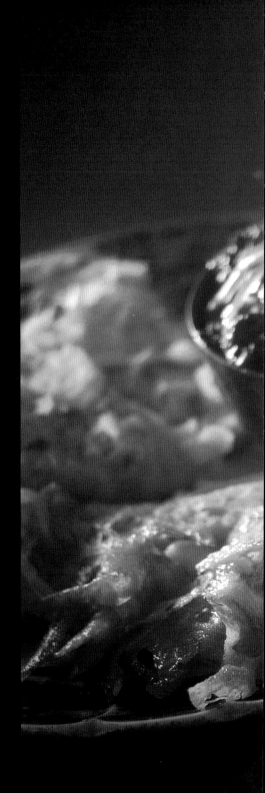

Clockwise from left: Lacy Pancakes (Roti Jala) (recipe, page 31),
Twenty Chilli Curry (recipe, page 71), Rainbow Fried Rice (recipe, page 33)
and Dark-fried Flat Chinese Noodles (Char Koeyteow) (recipe, page 22)

Dark-fried Flat Chinese Noodles
(Char Koeyteow)

Most towns in Malaysia have a resident Char Koeyteow man — he will have a huge wok in front of him and trays of fresh ingredients that dwindle quickly as the evening progresses. He works very fast, stirring, twisting and tossing the noodles in a blur of sound and movement and a cloud of delectable aromas.

Ingredients:

50 grams (2 oz) pork fat, cubed and ¼ cup (60 mL / 2 fl oz) water, or 2 tablespoons oil

4 Chinese sausages (lap cheong), finely sliced on a diagonal

100 grams (3½ oz) fresh school prawns (small shrimp), shelled and deveined

2 cloves garlic, finely chopped

2 tablespoons sambal oelek

2 tablespoons dark soy sauce (kecap manis)

1 tablespoon light soy sauce

1 kilogram (2 lb) fresh, flat rice noodles (koayteow)

1½ bunches garlic chives, chopped in 4 centimetre (1½ in) lengths

200 grams (7 oz) bean sprouts, tails trimmed

salt, to taste

Rendering the fat:

If you are using pork fat in this recipe, you will need to render it first. To do this, heat a wok on the highest heat and add the fat and water. Continue to heat it until the mixture begins to boil (do not stir), and boil it until the liquid evaporates.

(You will not need to use all of the rendered fat in this recipe; store the rest for use in other stir fries. It will keep in an airtight container for 2 weeks in the refrigerator, or longer if frozen.)

The crispy bits add flavour and texture to the noodles, and should be added to the dish towards the end of cooking.

Method:

Heat 2 tablespoons of pork fat, or 2 tablespoons of oil, in a wok. Add the sausages and prawns (shrimp) and cook until the sausages are browned and the prawns (shrimp) have reddened.

Make a well in the centre of the wok by pushing the sausages and prawns (shrimp) to the edge. Brown the garlic in the centre.

Add the sambal oelek and the dark and light soy sauce. Combine well with the sausages and prawns (shrimp).

Add the noodles a little at a time, stirring with two wok charns or ladles. Make sure the noodles are evenly coated with the sauce. Toss in the chives and bean sprouts (and crispy bits of fat if you cooked with rendered pork fat) and stir well to combine. Add salt to taste.

Pictured on previous page.

Makan-lah!

Seafood Lime Koayteow

This is a very subtle and delicate Nonya dish full of the flavours of mango, lime, seafood and plum. Seasonal vegetables can be substituted to make this dish colourful and fresh tasting at any time of the year.

Ingredients:

200 grams (7 oz) fresh, flat rice noodles (koayteow)

1 teaspoon of oil in 1 cup (250 mL / 8 fl oz) cold water

½ tablespoon sambal oelek

2 tablespoons teriyaki sauce

1 tablespoon plum sauce

2 teaspoons fish sauce (nam pla)

2 teaspoons palm sugar

1 tablespoon oil

3 centimetre (1 in) length of ginger, finely grated

3 cloves garlic, finely chopped

100 grams (3½ oz) fresh prawns (shrimp), shelled and deveined, tails left on

100 grams squid (3½ oz), cleaned, halved and scored with diamond shapes inside

1 medium-sized carrot, julienned

50 grams (2 oz) oyster mushrooms, thinly sliced

1 hard green mango (with skin), sliced in thin strips

½ bunch (50 g / 1½ oz) long-leaf coriander (saw leaf herb) leaves or normal coriander (cilantro) leaves

juice of 2 limes

Method:

Place the noodles in a bowl, pour over the oil–water mixture, and loosen the noodles with your fingers. Drain in colander. If the noodles have been refrigerated they may have become hard and could break on handling. This can be avoided by heating them in a microwave oven on medium for 3 minutes.

Mix the sambal oelek, teriyaki sauce, plum sauce, fish sauce and palm sugar together in a bowl. Set aside for later.

Heat the oil in a wok and saute the ginger and garlic on a high heat until they release their aroma (about 1 minute). Add the prawns (shrimp) and squid and cook on a high heat until the prawns (shrimp) start to turn red (about 2 minutes). Then add the carrots. When the carrots have soften, add the mushrooms. Maintaining a high heat, add the mango and coriander and toss everything together using two ladles or wok *cham*. You will need to work quickly so that the prawns (shrimp) do not overcook.

Add the noodles and the sauce mixture and toss, being careful not to break the noodles. Remove the wok from the heat. Pour in the lime juice and toss gently while the noodles are still hot. Serve at once.

Indian Mee Goreng

Indian Muslims who came from Kerala, one of India's most interesting food centres, were responsible for shaping much of Malaysia's cuisine, including the development of Indian Mee Goreng. This delicious dish can be sampled throughout Malaysia from the tiny portable kitchens of Mamak street stall vendors.

Ingredients:

1 bunch (250 g / 8 oz) choy sum

oil

100 grams (3½ oz) tofu, cut into 1 centimetre (½ in) cubes

3 eggs, lightly beaten

500 grams (1 lb) yellow hokkien noodles, fresh or dried

2 small Spanish (red) onions, sliced across then chopped finely

4 cloves garlic, finely chopped

2 centimetre (¾ in) length of ginger, grated

200 grams (7 oz) pork or lamb, cut into thin shreds

2 tablespoons sambal oelek

1 tablespoon chilli black bean paste

2 tomatoes, cubed

2 tablespoons light soy sauce

1 tablespoon dark soy sauce

2 tablespoons tomato puree

1 teaspoon chilli powder

150 grams (5 oz) bean sprouts, tails trimmed

Garnish

30—50 grams (1—1½ oz) coriander (cilantro) leaves

1 small lime, cut into 8—10 wedges

Method:

Cut the stems of the choy sum into 3 centimetre (1 in) lengths and coarsely shred the leaves. Set aside for later.

Fill a saucepan with enough oil to deep fry the tofu. Heat the oil. (To test whether the oil is sufficiently hot, insert a skewer; when bubbles appear around the skewer, the oil will be at the correct temperature.) Add the tofu and deep fry until it is golden. Remove the tofu from the oil, drain on paper towel and set aside.

Heat 1 tablespoon of oil in a fry pan and, on a high heat, add the eggs. Tilt the frypan to spread the eggs. This will result in a thin omelette. Remove the omelette, allow it to cool slightly then slice it into thin shreds.

If you are using dried noodles, place them in a large bowl and cover with warm water for 20 minutes. Drain and set aside. Fresh noodles need no soaking.

In a wok or a large frying pan, heat 1 tablespoon of oil and fry the onions until they are golden. Add the garlic, ginger, pork or lamb, sambal oelek and choy sum and fry on a high heat until the vegetables wilt (about 2 minutes), stirring continuously.

Add chilli black bean paste and tomatoes and fry until the tomatoes break down.

Toss in the noodles and fry for three minutes. Add the tofu, shredded omelette, light and dark soy sauce, tomato purée, chilli powder and bean sprouts. Heat through, tossing well.

Serve garnished with coriander (cilantro) and lime wedges.

Beanthread Pork Noodles

Beanthread noodles (also called glass noodles or suhoon) are used widely in all of Asia and have a special flavour and texture all of their own.

Ingredients:

30 grams (1 oz) beanthread noodles

200 grams (7 oz) belly pork with some fat on it, frozen

3 cloves garlic

3 dried chillis

2 tablespoons oil

1 tablespoon chilli bean garlic sauce

1 tablespoon dark soy sauce

2 teaspoons fish sauce

2 teaspoons palm sugar

½ teaspoon pepper, or to taste

Garnish:

1 leek, cut into thin feathery slices, deep-fried and drained on kitchen paper

oil, for deep-frying

Method:

Place the noodles in a large bowl, cover them with hot water and soak for 10–15 minutes. Drain the noodles in a colander and place them on kitchen paper.

Shred the pork into thin slivers with a very sharp knife. (If the pork is frozen it will be easier to shred.)

Roast the garlic well (either over a gas flame, or under a griller or in a dry wok). Roast the chilli. Blend the garlic and chilli together in a food processor or with a mortar and pestle.

Heat the oil in a wok or large frying pan and fry the garlic, chilli and chilli bean garlic sauce for a minute. Add the pork and stir-fry on a high heat until the pork is browned.

Add the noodles, dark soy sauce, fish sauce and palm sugar and toss well so that the noodles are evenly coated with the dark, caramelised sauce.

Serve garnished with the deep-fried leek.

Variation:

If pork is not to your liking, you can substitute it with the same amount of any other type of meat, seafood or tofu.

Nasi Ulam

This rice dish comes form the East Coast of Malaysia, where it is usually served cold during the fasting month with finely shredded herbs and aromatic leaves. It is said to aid the digestion, cleanse the blood and refresh the body.

Ingredients:

1 cup (250 mL/ 8 fl oz) vinegar

2 tablespoons and 1 teaspoon sugar

1 small Lebanese cucumber, sliced into rings

3 or 4 betel leaves (daun kaduk) or nasturtium leaves

water

50 grams (1½ oz) dried salted fish, finely cubed

2 Asian onions or 1 small Spanish (red) onion, finely sliced

4 tablespoons oil

1 turmeric leaf, preferably fresh (optional)

2 stems curry leaves, preferably fresh

1 centimetre (½ in) length of galangal finely diced or pureed

2 centimetre (¾ in) strip of ginger flower (bunga kantan) (optional), finely chopped

2 centimetre (¾ in) length of lemon grass (white part only), sliced very finely into rings

3 stems Vietnamese mint, finely chopped

6 rocket (arugula) leaves, finely chopped

3 stems Thai basil, finely chopped

3 stems mint, finely chopped

2 kaffir lime leaves

3 fresh bay leaves

1 small sprig fresh thyme, finely chopped

10 peppercorns

4½ cups (830 g/ 1¾ lb) cooked rice

1 teaspoon tamarind puree

3 tablespoons water

salt, to taste

Garnish:

1 salted duck egg, hard-boiled, peeled and chopped (see note)

Method:

Mix the vinegar with 2 tablespoons of sugar in a bowl. Soak the cucumber for 2 hours, then drain off the liquid.

In a small bowl, mix a little water (enough to cover the betel leaves) with 1 teaspoon of sugar. Soak the leaves for 2 hours.

Dry roast or grill the fish until a golden colour. To dry roast, put the fish into a frying pan (use no oil) and keep stirring over a medium heat until the fish is smelling strong. When the fish has cooled a little, flake the flesh with your fingers.

Heat the oil in a small frying pan and fry the onion until golden.

Place the rice in a large bowl and toss through the fish, herbs (including the betel leaves) and onions. Mix the tamarind puree and 3 tablespoons of water together and add gradually to the rice, mixing well. You may not need to add all of the tamarind liquid, as the aim is only to separate the rice into single grains, not to make it wet. Add salt to taste and garnish with the egg and cucumber. This dish goes well with pickled limes.

NOTE: Salted duck eggs are usually available from Chinese groceries. Hard-boiled hen's eggs are an acceptable alternative.

Nasi Ulam

Hawkers Mee Siam

This Nonya dish with Thai origins is cooked in three stages: the gravy, sauce and noodles. The gravy and sauce can be made earlier and refrigerated or frozen until needed, but should only be combined with the noodles immediately before serving.

Ingredients:

1 packet (200 g / 7 oz) dried, thin Chinese rice noodles (beehoon)

Gravy:

$\frac{1}{2}$ cup (60 g / 2 oz) salted black beans

4 cloves garlic, finely chopped

1 tablespoon oil

2 cups (500 mL / 16 fl oz) water or fish or prawn stock

Sauce:

2 tablespoons sambal oelek

1 tablespoon tamarind puree

2 cloves garlic, finely chopped

1 Spanish (red) onion or 5 Asian onions

500 grams (1 lb) fresh prawns (shrimp), shelled and deveined

6 fried tofu puffs, sliced paper-thin

400 grams (14 oz) bean sprouts, tails trimmed

400 grams (14 oz) garlic chives, sliced into 6 centimetre ($2\frac{1}{2}$ in) lengths

$1\frac{1}{2}$ tablespoons oil

Garnish:

3 eggs

salt and pepper, to taste

1 tablespoon oil

1 bunch (100 g / $3\frac{1}{2}$ oz) coriander (cilantro) leaves

2 cucumbers, skins only, julienned

4 kaffir lime leaves, well shredded

6 limes, quartered

sambal oelek, as a relish

Method:

Make the omelette for your garnish in advance. Lightly beat the eggs and add salt and pepper. Heat the oil in a frying pan and fry the eggs so that they form a thin omelette. Remove from the pan and allow the omelette to cool, then roll it up and slice thinly. Set aside.

Place the noodles in a large bowl, cover with hot water and leave to soak for 20 minutes. Pour off the hot water, blanch the noodles in cold water, then drain.

Make the gravy and the sauce.

When you have made the gravy and the sauce, place half the noodles and half of the sauce in a wok on a medium heat and cook until the noodles are heated through. Make a well in the centre of the wok by pushing the heated noodles to the edge. Pile the bean sprouts, garlic chives, and the remainder of the noodles and the sauce into the well, bring the first lot of noodles back to the centre of the wok and toss together. Cover the wok and cook for 2 minutes on a high heat.

Half-fill serving bowls with warm gravy, add the noodles and sprinkle garnish over the top. The limes are to be squeezed onto the noodles, to taste. Provide a separate dish of sambal oelek for those who like their noodles extra hot.

Gravy:

Wash the black beans to remove excess salt, then mash them thoroughly. Heat the oil in a small saucepan and saute the garlic and black beans until the garlic is golden and aromatic. Add the water, bring to the boil, then simmer for 5 minutes.

Sauce:

Blend the sambal oelek, tamarind puree, garlic and onion together in a food processor or mortar and pestle. Heat the oil in a wok and saute the blended mixture on a high heat until the mixture releases its aroma. Add the prawns (shrimp) and fry on a high heat until they change colour. Add the tofu and stir well.

Boiled Seafood Noodles
(Mee Rebus)

The name 'rebus', which simply means 'boiled stock', does not do justice to this flavoursome dish of thick, yellow wheat noodles and prawns (shrimp) served with a rich, peanutty sauce.

Ingredients:

2 litres (64 fl oz) chicken stock

1 medium carrot, julienned

2 Spanish (red) onions

3 centimetre (1 in) length of ginger

3 cloves garlic

2 tablespoons white vinegar

1 tablespoon sambal oelek

4 candlenuts, ground

1 tablespoon chilli black bean paste

2 tablespoons oil

600 grams ($1^{1}/_{3}$ lb) fresh prawns (shrimp), peeled and deveined

4 tablespoons crunchy peanut butter

2 tablespoons sugar

1 teaspoon salt

$^{1}/_{2}$ teaspoon pepper

1 tablespoon mixed Malaysian curry powder (see page 172)

$^{1}/_{4}$ cup (60 mL / 2 fl oz) water

2 large potatoes, mashed

500 grams (1 lb) fresh thick yellow noodles (mee) or cooked spaghetti

1 cucumber seeded then julienned

three pieces of fried tofu pillows (tofupok), sliced paper-thin

3 cos (romaine) lettuce leaves, shredded

3 eggs, hard-boiled and quartered

Garnish:

400 grams (14 oz) bean sprouts, tails trimmed

2 tablespoons ready fried onions (see note)

2 limes, cut into wedges

Method:

Bring the stock to boil in a large saucepan. Add the carrots and simmer for 30 minutes, to make stock robust (strong in flavour). Remove the carrots with a sieve. Top up with water if necessary to retain 2 litres (64 fl oz) of liquid.

Blend the onions, ginger, garlic and vinegar in a food processor or a mortar and pestle. Add the sambal oelek, candlenuts, chilli black bean paste and roasted shrimp and blend together.

Heat the oil in a large saucepan and saute the blended onion mixture for 10–12 minutes, until the onions are caramelised.

Add the stock and prawns (shrimp) and bring to the boil. Simmer until the prawns (shrimp) redden in colour.

Add the peanut butter, sugar, salt, pepper and curry powder, stir and simmer on a low heat for 10–12 minutes for flavour to develop.

Add the mashed potatoes and stir well. Leave the sauce on a very low heat to keep it warm until you are ready to serve the noodles.

Place the noodles into serving bowls with cucumber, tofu, lettuce and boiled eggs. Pour the sauce, with prawns (shrimp) over the noodles and garnish with bean sprouts, fried onions and lime wedges.

NOTE: Ready fried onions are a dry ingredient available from Asian food stores.

Variation:

You can substitute the prawns (shrimp) with the same amount of thinly sliced chicken, or thinly sliced beef. For the beef variation, you would substitute beef stock for chicken stock.

Handkerchief Bread
(Roti Chanai)

A true roti chanai man will twirl the bread high in the air, creating elliptical shapes to form a huge roti which he will then fold into a handkerchief shape to grill — this is why roti chanai is called handkerchief bread in some countries.

Ingredients:

2 small eggs
1 teaspoon sugar
1 teaspoon salt
³/₄ cup (180 mL/ 6 fl oz) warm water
450 grams (14¹/₂ oz) plain (all purpose) flour
¹/₂ cup (150 g / 5 oz) ghee plus extra for baking and brushing
3 tablespoons oil
iced water

Method:

Lightly beat the eggs, sugar and salt then add water and mix well.

Sieve the flour directly onto a table. Make a well in centre and pour the egg mixture into it.

Combine the flour into the egg mixture, gradually mixing them together with your fingers until a soft dough is formed.

Have a bowl of iced water close by, to dip your fingers in while you knead the dough. Knead for approximately 5 minutes, until the dough bounces back when pressed.

Cover the inside of a large bowl and all sides of the dough thoroughly with the oil. Place the dough into the bowl, cover with a wet tea towel (dish towel) and leave to sit for at least 4 hours, preferably overnight.

Divide the dough into 7 equal parts and form them into balls. On a lightly floured surface, roll out each ball to a thickness of 1 cm (½ in) with a rolling pin. Spread ghee thinly over each flat round sheet.

Roll up each flat round sheet like a swiss roll, then stretch the roll by pulling at both ends. The aim is to create as many surface areas on the dough as possible, as this will help the rotis become puffy, like puff pastry. Suspend one roll at a time above the table so that the roll hangs vertically and make a knot at the uppermost end. Turn the roll so that the unknotted end is uppermost, and knot that end. Twirl the dough so that one knot sits on top of the other. Brush the knotted dough with oil. When you have done this to all the rotis, cover them with a wet tea towel (dish towel). Allow to rise for another 2 hours.

Roll the rotis out on an oiled board, stopping occasionally to stretch the dough and pull it on all sides. Roll each roti to a diameter of 30 cm (12 in) then fold the corners into the middle, like an envelope. Bake on a hot griddle or hot plate with ghee. Keep turning each roti until it has browned and give it a final crisping with a brushing of half a teaspoon of ghee over the top.

Clap the bread sharply together between your palms to break it up. Serve with curry or a kurmah.

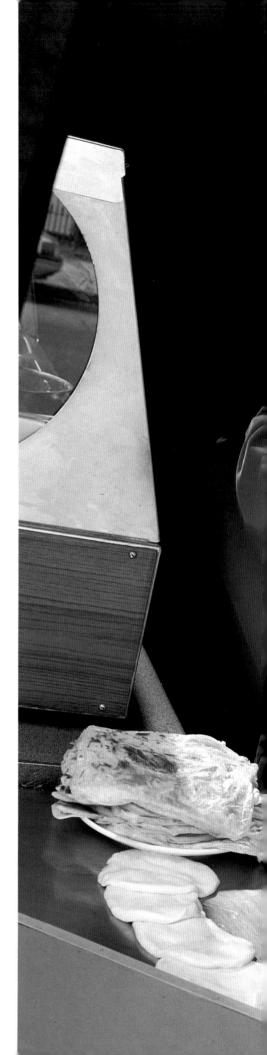

Making Handkerchief Bread (Roti Chanai)

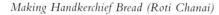

Vegetarian Beehoon

In Malaysia, meat is not eaten by Buddhists on feast days nor by Hindus on Friday, which is temple day, so Malaysian cooks have developed some very tasty and satisfying ways to serve vegetarian meals.

Sauce:

2 tablespoons Chinese red or black vinegar

1 tablespoon rice wine

1 tablespoon dark soy sauce

½ teaspoon sugar and ½ teaspoon salt to balance flavours

Ingredients:

1 packet (200 g / 7 oz) dried, thin Chinese rice noodles (beehoon)

80 grams (3 oz) tempe (fermented bean curd), finely cubed

¼ cup (60 mL/ 2 fl oz) oil, for frying tempe

2 tablespoons oil, for frying other ingredients

6 dried shitake mushrooms

4 dried cloudear fungus

3 cloves garlic, finely chopped

2 centimetre (³/₄ in) length of ginger, finely grated

80 grams (3 oz) Chinese brined cabbage (kiamchye), finely chopped

4 oyster mushrooms, halved

150 grams (5 oz) Chinese cabbage (wong ah pak), finely shredded, or 150—200 grams (5—7 oz) choy sum (stems included), finely shredded

6 tofupok or fried tofu puffs, shredded

1 small carrot, finely julienned

Sauce:

Mix together the vinegar, rice wine, dark soy sauce, sugar and salt in a small bowl and set aside for later.

Method:

Place the noodles in a large bowl and cover them with hot water. When they are soft and pliant, drain off the hot water, run cold water over to blanch them, then drain.

Heat ¼ cup (60 mL/ 2 fl oz) of oil in a saucepan. (To test whether the oil is sufficiently hot, insert a skewer; when bubbles appear around the skewer, the oil will be at the correct temperature.) Add the tempe and deep-fry until golden brown. Remove from the oil and drain on paper towel.

Place the shitake mushrooms in a medium-sized bowl and cover with warm water. Soak for 15 minutes, drain and squeeze out the excess water. Cut off and discard the stems. Thinly slice the caps of the mushrooms.

Place the cloudear fungus in a medium-sized saucepan and cover with warm water. Soak for 15 minutes. Place the saucepan on the heat, bring to the boil and cook for 4 minutes. Drain. Remove the hard and sandy parts of the mushrooms. Slice the rest of the mushrooms into strips.

Heat 2 tablespoons of oil in a wok on a high heat and fry the garlic and ginger until they release their aroma. Add the salted cabbage, carrot and tempe and stir-fry for several minutes.

Add the shitake mushrooms, cloudear fungus, oyster mushrooms, raw cabbage or choy sum, sauce mixture and lastly the noodles. Stir slowly until the noodles are evenly covered with sauce and are warm through. Serve immediately.

Rhio Chilli Beef Noodles with Coconut Milk

When making this dish you must remember to soak the instant noodles in cold water only, even though the packet may tell you to use hot water. To do so would make the noodles turn gluggy and stick to the wok. It may take longer to reconstitute the noodles in cold water but it's definitely worth the effort.

Ingredients:

2 packets (80 g / 2½ oz) instant noodles

3 pieces cloudear fungus

1 Spanish (red) onion, diced

2 cloves garlic

1 teaspoon shrimp paste, dry roasted

2 tablespoons sambal oelek

3 tablespoons vegetable oil

300 grams (10½ oz) round steak, cut into fine strips

2 green capsicums (bell peppers), seeded and thinly sliced

1 bunch asparagus, sliced, or one stick celery, sliced

½ green paw paw (papaya), peeled, seeded and thinly sliced

3 tablespoons lime or lemon juice

1 tablespoon fish sauce or 1 teaspoon salt

½ cup (125 mL / 4 fl oz) coconut cream

2 tablespoons sesame oil

Method:

Soak the noodles in cold water for 10–15 minutes. Drain.

Place the cloudear fungus in a medium-sized saucepan and cover with warm water. Soak for 20 minutes. Place the saucepan on the heat, bring to the boil and cook for 4 minutes. Drain. Remove the hard and sandy parts of the mushrooms. Slice the rest of the mushrooms into strips.

Put the onion, garlic, shrimp paste and sambal oelek and 1½ tablespoons of the oil into a food processor (or use a mortar and pestle) and blend until smooth.

Heat the remaining 1½ tablespoons of oil in a wok and fry the onion mixture on a medium heat for 10 minutes.

Add half of the beef and stir-fry for 3–5 minutes. Add the rest of the beef and stir-fry until all the beef is browned. Remove the beef from the wok.

Add the capsicums (bell peppers), asparagus or celery, paw paw (papaya) and the sliced mushrooms and stir-fry lightly on a medium heat for 3 minutes. Add the noodles, toss well and continue to fry for another 3 minutes, stirring continuously.

Add the lime or lemon juice, fish sauce or salt, coconut cream and sesame oil and return the beef to the wok. Toss well to combine all the ingredients and serve immediately.

Lacy Pancakes
(Roti Jala)

To make these you will need a roti jala sieve or a small, empty can with holes punched through the bottom with a nail. The holes should be quite large, but close together, as in a shower rose.

Ingredients:

2 cups (500 mL/ 16 fl oz) thick coconut milk

2 cups (500 mL/ 16 fl oz) water

250 grams (8 oz/ ½ lb) plain (all purpose) flour

3 large eggs, lightly beaten

1½ teaspoons salt

3 tablespoons oil

Method:

Mix the coconut milk and water together.

Place the flour in a bowl and gradually add the liquid, mixing well each time until all the liquid has been added. Run the mixture once through the sieve to eliminate all the lumps.

Add the eggs to the mixture and mix into a watery batter (do not beat the mixture into a froth). The batter should be just thin enough to flow through the holes of the sieve. If the batter is very thin, add a little more flour. Pass the batter through the sieve.

Add the salt, mix, and pass the batter through the sieve once more.

Heat the oil on a griddle or in a non-stick pancake frying pan.

Pour ½ cup (125 smL / 4 fl oz) of batter through the can and make concentric circles over the griddle or pan. Make circles within circles to create a lacy effect.

Cook for about 2 minutes then turn the pancake over and cook for 1 minute. Remove the pancake from the griddle or pan and fold into quarters.

These pancakes are best served with a Malay chicken curry.

Pictured on page 20.

Puri

Whenever I make puris it always seems like a miracle when the little discs of dough blister and puff up to form delicate, crisp bread. They are best eaten as soon as they leave the wok, with a curry.

Ingredients:

1 cup (155 g / 5 oz) plain (all purpose) wholemeal flour

¼ teaspoon salt

3 tablespoons plain yoghurt

1 tablespoon ghee, softened at room temperature

¼ cup (60 mL / 2 fl oz) iced water

2 cups (500 mL / 16 fl oz) vegetable oil

Method:

Combine the flour and salt in a large bowl. Create a well in the centre and place the yoghurt and ghee in the well. Rub the yoghurt and ghee into the flour with your fingertips until it resembles breadcrumbs.

Add the water and continue to mix with your fingers until the dough starts to come away from the sides of the bowl.

Place the dough onto a lightly floured surface such as a bench top. Using the heels of your palms and your knuckles, knead the dough well until it is soft and pliable. Cover it with a wet tea towel (dish towel) and put it into the refrigerator for 2 hours.

Divide the dough into 12 balls. Flatten the balls on a lightly floured surface and roll them out with a rolling pin into rounds with a diameter of approximately 9 cm (3½ in).

Heat the oil in a wok. The oil should be very hot but not smoking. Deep-fry the puris one at a time. Use a ladle to hold the puri in the oil for approximately 30 seconds until it rises to the surface as a blister puff. Remove from the oil and drain on paper towel.

Serve immediately with curry.

Saffron Rice
(Nasi Kunyit)

Valued for its unique flavour and orange colouring, saffron is hand-picked from the flower of the Crocus sativus, a plant which grows wild in the Middle East. It takes 70,000 to 80,000 plants to make 1 kilogram (2 pounds) of saffron. The combination of flavours in this dish creates a mind-blowing aromatic tapestry — a feast for both the mind and the eye.

Ingredients:

10 saffron threads

1 tablespoon warm milk

2 cups (440 g / 14 oz) Basmati or long-grained rice

¼ cup (60 mL / 2 fl oz) ghee or oil

¼ cup (80 g / 3½ oz) cashews

1 Spanish (red) onion, thinly sliced

5 cardamom pods, crushed then peeled

3⅓ cups (800 mL / 26 fl oz) coconut milk or 3⅓ cups of water

salt, to taste

Method:

Place the saffron threads in a small bowl and cover with warm milk. Allow the threads to soak for 10 minutes.

Put the rice in a saucepan, cover with water, stir several times, then drain off the water. Repeat this several times until the water runs clear. (This removes some of the starch from the rice.)

Heat the ghee or oil in a large frying pan and fry the cashews on a medium heat until they are golden. Remove the cashews, leaving the ghee or oil in the frying pan.

Add the onion and cardamom pods to the frying pan and fry on a medium heat until the onion has browned.

Add the rice and continue to cook for approximately 5 minutes, stirring continuously, until the rice grains become opaque. Transfer into a large saucepan. Add the coconut milk or water until it reaches 3.5 centimetres (1⅓ inches) above the level of the rice. Add the saffron threads and milk, and salt to taste.

Cook on a medium–high heat with the lid half covering the saucepan until the coconut milk or water has been absorbed by the rice, approximately 8–10 minutes (if the liquid has not absorbed, give the rice another 3 minutes). As soon as the liquid has been absorbed, reduce the heat to low and cover the pot tightly with the lid. Turn off the heat and allow the rice to steam for 10 minutes without removing the lid.

Run a fork through the rice before serving.

Variation:

For Ghee Rice (Nasi Minyak), use the above recipe but in addition to the cashews add ¼ cup (80 g / 2½ oz) toasted almonds and ¼ cup (40 g / 1½ oz) raisins.

Rainbow Fried Rice

This is a great recipe to experiment with. Use the vegetables outlined below, or make your own selection — the key is to create contrasting textures, flavours and colours. Though it's always best to use fresh produce, fried rice is also a delicious way to use up leftovers.

Ingredients:

200 grams (7 oz) bacon
1 tablespoon oil
1 Spanish (red) onion, diced
1 medium-sized carrot, finely diced
2 stalks celery (strings removed), diced
1 red capsicum (bell pepper), seeded and diced
1 green capsicum (bell pepper), seeded and diced
1 yellow capsicum (bell pepper), seeded and diced
3 cups cooked rice (cooled)
2 tablespoons light soy sauce
1 tablespoon sesame oil
salt and pepper, to taste
$^1/_3$ cup (40 g / $1^1/_3$ oz) pine nuts, or $^1/_3$ cup (40 g / $1^1/_3$ oz) toasted slivered almonds

Method:

Remove the rind from the bacon and discard it. Cut the fat from the bacon and keep it. Chop the bacon finely. Heat a wok and add the oil, bacon and bacon fat. Fry on a high heat until the bacon is crisp and the fat has melted. You should be left with about 2 tablespoons of melted fat. If there is more than this, discard some of it so that there is approximately 2 tablespoons of fat in the wok. Leave the fried bacon in the wok.

Return the wok to a very high heat and brown the onion. Then add the carrots, celery and capsicums (bell peppers) and stir fry until the vegetables begin to sweat. Be careful not to overcook them, they should be very crisp.

Toss a little water (approximately 60 mL / 2 fl oz) through the rice so that the grains do not stick together. Add the rice to the wok and stir well to combine. Pour soy sauce and sesame oil in from the edge of the wok, add salt and pepper to taste and continue to cook, stirring continuously. When the rice smells aromatic (in approximately 3 minutes), stir through some pine nuts and serve.

This rice can be stored and served the next day, so long as it is kept tightly covered in the refrigerator.

Pictured on page 20.

Lemon Rice
(Nasi Limau)

This subtle and refreshing rice dish is delicious served with pistachio nuts and diced cucumber.

Ingredients:

2 cups (440 g / 14 oz) rice
1 teaspoon ghee
a handful of curry leaves
juice of 2 lemons, plus rind of 1 lemon
water, enough to cover rice
$^1/_4$ teaspoon turmeric powder

Method:

Place the rice in a large bowl. Fill with water, stir several times and drain off the water. Repeat this several times until the water runs clear. (This removes some of the starch from the rice.)

Heat the ghee in a large saucepan and fry the curry leaves for a few seconds. Add the rice and lemon juice. Pour in enough water so that it rises to 3.5 centimetres ($1^1/_3$ inches) above the level of the rice. Add the turmeric and stir well.

Cook with the lid off, on a medium heat, until the rice has absorbed the water. Turn off the heat. Add the lemon rind to the saucepan, put the lid on and allow the rice to steam in its own heat for 5–10 minutes. Run a fork through the rice just before serving.

Coconut Rice
(Nasi Lemak)

Nasi Lemak was made especially for a Nonya event known as a 'runding', or meeting, when wedding guests would attend a ceremony on the twelfth day of a wedding and the matchmaker and the parents confirmed the virginity of the bride.

Ingredients:

2 cups (440 g / 14 oz) rice

1 cup (250 mL / 8 fl oz) thick coconut cream

2 aromatic screw pine leaves or pandan flavouring

1 onion, very finely diced

1 teaspoon salt

water, enough to cover rice

Method:

Put the rice in a heavy-based saucepan, cover with water, stir several times, then drain off the water. Repeat this several times until the water runs clear. (This removes some of the starch from the rice.)

Add the coconut cream, diced onions and salt. Add enough water so that it reaches 3.5 centimetres (1⅓ inches) above the level of the rice.

Drag the tines of a fork through the pandan leaf until it is shredded. Tie the leaf into a knot and place it on top of the rice.

Cook uncovered on a high heat for 8–10 minutes, until the liquid starts to bubble. Once it has begun to bubble, place the lid so that it half covers the saucepan, and cook on a low heat for approximately 8 minutes, until all the liquid has been absorbed by the rice. Remove the saucepan from the heat, cover tightly with the lid and allow the rice to cook in its own steam for 10 minutes.

Remove the pandan leaf and run a fork through the rice before serving. (If you put the leaf in a plastic bag in the refrigerator, it can be used again.)

Variation:

This dish can be cooked in a microwave oven. Place the rice, 2 cups (500 mL / 16 fl oz) of coconut cream, the onion, salt and the pandan leaf in a covered, microwave-proof container and cook on High for 20 minutes. Run a fork through the rice before serving, to separate the grains.

Back: Chinese Rice Porridge with Fish (Moi) (recipe, page 36)
Front: Coconut Rice (Nasi Lemak)

Makan-lah!

Chinese Rice Porridge with Fish
(Moi)

For me, the cooking of this dish evokes memories of being in bed with the measles or chickenpox, with a pile of comics and a bowl of steaming hot moi. This is Malaysian 'comfort food'.

Ingredients:

2 cups (440 g/ 14 oz) rice

5 cups (1.25 litres / 40 fl oz) water

1 tablespoon salted cabbage (kiam chye)

300 grams (10$\frac{1}{2}$ oz) fish fillets (perch or ling), cubed

1 tablespoon vegetable oil

2 cloves garlic, finely slivered

2 centimetre ($\frac{3}{4}$ in) length of ginger, finely julienned

1 teaspoon light soy sauce

$\frac{1}{2}$ teaspoon sesame oil

2 stalks spring onions, finely chopped

1 teaspoon salt

1 small bunch (100 g/ 3$\frac{1}{2}$ oz) Vietnamese mint, chopped finely

Method:

Place the rice and water in a large saucepan, bring to the boil and cook partly covered on a medium heat for 30–40 minutes. Stir occasionally and keep a close watch on the rice as you may need to occasionally top it up with a little boiling water. When the rice is soft and mushy, take the saucepan off the heat and leave the rice in it.

Wash the cabbage to remove the salt, drain it and chop finely.

Heat the oil in a large saucepan and fry the garlic over a medium heat until it is golden. Add the cooked rice and stir to combine. Add the fish, cabbage, ginger, soy sauce, sesame oil, spring onions and salt. Cook for 5 minutes. Finally, add the mint, stir to combine, take off the heat and serve.

Variations:

Instead of using fresh fish, you can use salted dried fish which has been very finely cubed and fried in oil until golden.

Alternatively, try using pork or chicken mince. The porridge can also be garnished with thinly sliced Eu Char Koay, a type of yeast-bread obtainable from Chinese grocery stores and bakeries.

Pictured on page 34.

Lontong

Lontong is an experience, not an individual recipe. It is a meal consisting of a series of sambals, sauces and vegetables cooked in a coconut sauce and accompanied by squares of compressed rice. Three Lontong dishes are provided here: Vegetable Gravy (Sayur Lodeh), Compressed Rice (Nasi Tinday) and Chilli Tempe Sambal.

Vegetable Gravy
(Sayur Lodeh)

This light gravy is traditionally served with Compressed Rice and sambals.

Ingredients:

150 grams (5 oz) cabbage leaves (not centre stem), roughly diced

2 small, long Asian eggplants (aubergines or brinjals), halved lengthways then quartered

100 grams (3$\frac{1}{2}$ oz) snake beans or french beans, thinly sliced

$\frac{1}{2}$ teaspoon turmeric powder

2 tablespoons oil

5 small Asian onions or 1 large Spanish (red) onion, finely sliced

2 tablespoons ground chilli

2 centimetre ($\frac{3}{4}$ in) length of galangal, sliced into 6 pieces or ground into a puree

$\frac{1}{2}$ teaspoon shrimp paste, dry roasted

3 cups (750 mL / 24 fl oz) coconut milk

400 grams (14 oz) medium-sized fresh prawns (shrimp), peeled and deveined (tails left on)

1 bean curd sheet (fuchuk), sliced in large chunks

100 grams (3$\frac{1}{2}$ oz) tempe (fermented bean curd), diced

$\frac{1}{2}$ cup (125 mL / 4 fl oz) coconut cream

juice of 1 lime

1 teaspoon salt

Method:

Place the vegetables in a large bowl and dust them with the turmeric. Stir the vegetables around so they get an even coating.

Heat the oil in a large saucepan and saute the onion and chilli for 4–5 minutes. Add the galangal and roasted shrimp paste and cook for a minute to allow the aromas to develop. Add the coconut milk. Cook on a low heat, gradually bringing up the heat to medium and cook for 2 minutes.

Add the prawns (shrimp), vegetables, tempe and tofu and keep simmering, stirring to prevent curdling. Do not cover the pan. Lower heat when the flavours have developed, after approximately 4 minutes.

Add the salt and coconut cream, stir once, then remove from the heat. Add the lime juice after doing so.

Compressed Rice
(Nasi Tinday)

This is an integral part of the Lontong meal, forming the basis for Vegetable Gravy (Sayur Lodeh).

Ingredients:
2 cups (440 g/ 14 oz) short-grained or broken rice
water
1 teaspoon salt

Method:
Place the rice in a medium-sized saucepan, cover with water and soak for 20 minutes. Drain off the water.

Pour 6 cups (1.5 litres / 48 fl oz) of water into the saucepan and bring to the boil. Continue to boil on a medium heat for approximately 30 minutes until about half the liquid has evaporated and the rice has softened.

Add the salt and simmer uncovered, stirring once every 6–7 minutes so that the rice does not stick to the pot. Keep a close watch on the rice as you may need to top it up with a little hot water from time to time. After about 20 minutes the rice should start to get mushy.

Mash the rice with a wooden spoon or hand-held electric mixer to break up the rice grains. Spoon the rice onto a greased, flat tray. The rice should be about 3 cm (1 in) thick. Smooth the top with a wooden spoon and cover with a piece of foil or cloth.

Chill until it has set. Remove the foil or cloth covering and cut the rice into diamond shapes about 3 cm (1 in) wide and about 6 cm (2½ in) long.

Serve the rice squares with Vegetable Gravy and Chill Tempe Sambal.

Chilli Tempe Sambal

This sambal is also part of the Lontong experience. Cut down on the number of curry dishes in a Lontong if you must, but not on this sambal which provides an important contrast in texture to the Compressed Rice and Vegetable Gravy. This sambal can be stored in a jar and used as a relish with other meals.

Ingredients:
2 centimetre length of fresh tamarind
¼ cup (60 mL / 2 fl oz) water
1½ cups (375 mL/ 12 fl oz) oil
100—160 grams (3½—5 oz) of hard tofu (bean curd), finely cubed
100 grams (3½ oz) tempe (fermented bean curd), finely cubed
8 red Asian onions or 2 Spanish (red) onions, thinly sliced
10 cloves garlic, thinly sliced
2 stalks lemon grass, thinly sliced
2 tablespoons chilli black bean garlic paste (chilli jam)
50 grams (1½ oz)dried prawns (shrimp), dry roasted
100 grams (3½ oz) medium prawns (shrimp), peeled and deveined
sugar, to taste
½ tablespoon salt
1 piece of peanut brittle, crushed
Juice of ½ a lime

Method:
Puree the tamarind with the water in a food processor or a mortar and pestle, drain off the dregs and keep the puree.

Heat the oil in a wok and fry the tofu until it develops a crisp crust. Remove the tofu from the oil with a slotted spoon and drain on paper towel. Fry and drain the tempe in the same way, using the same oil.

Soak the onions in some water (during soaking, liquid from the onions leaches out and this ensures that the onions will later turn crisp when fried).

Fry the garlic until it is golden, then remove it with a slotted spoon and drain on paper towel. Then fry the onions until they are crisp, remove and drain.

Pour out most of the oil, retaining 2 tablespoons, then fry the lemon grass and chilli black bean garlic paste until they release their aroma. Add the garlic, onions and dried prawns. Fry on a very high heat, stirring continuously. When the mixture loses its raw smell add the tamarind puree, the fresh prawns (shrimp), the tofu and the tempe. Cook, stirring continuously, until the sambal has been reduced to a dry mixture (about 10 minutes).

Season with sugar and salt. Sprinkle with the peanut brittle and squeeze the lemon over the top. Serve hot or cold with Vegetable Gravy and Compressed Rice.

Beef, Lamb and Pork

Clockwise from left: Mild Vinegared Lamb
(Kambing Kalia) (recipe, page 54), Beef Rendang (recipe, page 40)
and Balinese Roast Pork with Coconut
(Lawar Babi Guling Nangka) (recipe, page 62)

Beef Rendang

Lovers of Malaysian food are familiar with rendang, but few realise that this rich, spicy dish was originally a way of making old, overworked buffalo edible. It took hours of cooking to turn tired meat into tasty rendang, a problem you will thankfully not have to contend with today.

Ingredients:

2 stalks lemon grass
3 centimetres (1 in) length galangal
3 centimetres (1 in) length ginger
3 cloves garlic
5 dried chillies
2 tablespoons oil
500 grams (1 lb) chuck (blade) steak, cubed
10 red Asian onions, sliced
2 cups (500 mL / 16 fl oz) coconut milk
2 turmeric leaves
2 tablespoons Malaysian curry powder
(see page 172)
1 tablespoon thick soy sauce (kecap manis)
1 cup (250 mL / 8 fl oz) coconut cream
salt, to taste
sugar, to taste
½ cup (45 g / 1½ oz) desiccated coconut, dry roasted

Method:

Blend the lemon grass, galangal, ginger, garlic, chillies and 1 tablespoon of the oil to a paste in a food processor or mortar and pestle. Coat the meat well with the paste.

Heat the remaining oil in a wok and saute the onions until golden and aromatic. Add the meat and stir well. Lower the heat, cover the wok and cook for 10 minutes.

Add the coconut milk, turmeric leaves and curry powder and stir well. Cover and cook for 20 minutes, or until the beef is tender.

Add the thick soy sauce, coconut cream and salt and sugar to taste. Bring to the boil and cook uncovered for 5 minutes, stirring continuously. Lower the heat, add the desiccated coconut and stir for another 5 minutes. The curry should be quite dry by the time you've finished. Remove the turmeric leaves and serve with rice.

Pictured on page 38.

Mamak Stall-cooked Bifstik

The stalls run by Indian Muslim hawkers in Malaysia are portable and can be wheeled around to different sites. Bifstik (beef steak) is whipped up quickly in a wok and can be had any time of the day, for the hawkers often sleep on site.

Ingredients:

3 centimetre (1 inch) length ginger
1 cup (250 mL / 8 fl oz) oil
1 potato, cubed
3 cloves garlic, crushed
1 teaspoon ground black pepper
500 grams (1 lb) rump (sirloin) steak, thinly sliced
¼ cup (60 mL / 2 fl oz) oil
2 Spanish (red) onions, sliced in rings
¼ cup (60 mL / 2 fl oz) rice wine
¼ cup (60 mL / 2 fl oz) beef stock
2 tablespoons tomato paste
1 tablespoon thick soy sauce (kecap manis)
1 teaspoon chilli powder
juice of 1 lemon
1 tablespoon Worcestershire sauce
3 tomatoes, skinned, chopped and seeded

Garnish:

½ cup (60 g / 2 oz) cooked peas
30—50 grams (1—1½ oz) coriander (cilantro) leaves, chopped

Method:

Pound the ginger with a mortar and pestle or grate with a fine grater to produce 1 tablespoon of juice. Set aside.

Heat the oil in a wok or saucepan and deep-fry the potato until golden brown on the outside. Remove from the pan and drain on paper towels. Keep the oil in the wok.

Blend the garlic, pepper and ginger juice together and brush over the beef.

Heat the oil in the wok and sear the beef quickly at a high temperature. It is important to fry only a few pieces of the beef at a time because if you add too much to the wok at once the beef will stew rather than fry. Remove each batch of meat from the wok and cover the meat to keep it warm.

Lower the heat and fry the onions until they are golden, then remove them from the wok.

Deglaze the wok by swirling the rice wine around in it. Add the stock, tomato paste, soy sauce, chilli powder, lemon juice and Worcestershire sauce and cook on a medium heat to reduce. Add the fried onions and cook for 3 minutes, then add the tomatoes and stir well. Take off the heat.

Pour the sauce over the beef and serve hot with potatoes, warmed peas and coriander.

Rice

The soul of Asian cooking

Rice, the main sustenance for around half the world's population, has been cultivated since at least the 4th century BC. Although rice was originally grown in central Asia as a dry crop, it grows best in artificially irrigated fields. It is first planted in water-logged ground then ripened in drained soil.

Growing a good rice crop requires immense patience and back-breaking work. In most cases it is men who plough the fields, dig canals and raise bunds for water retention while women tend the crop, bending to plant the seeds in nurseries, replanting the shoots in muddy fields, then harvesting the rice stalk by stalk. The women also thresh and winnow the rice by hand.

Rice is so important to Malaysians that it forms part of the everyday greeting: 'Suda makan nasi?' ('Have you eaten rice?'). It is treated with respect and given a human persona: a woman with whims, fancies, appetites and a soul. It is believed that at budding time the rice spirit, just like a pregnant woman, needs to be offered food such as sour pickles to placate her cravings. When reaping time comes the plant is protected from knowing her fate by being harvested with a little knife known as a kuku kambing (goat's claws), which is hidden in the palm of the hand.

Superstitions and taboos about rice abound in Malaysia. As a young girl I learnt that if rice was spilt on the floor it was to be picked up grain by grain for to sweep it away or to step on it meant disrespect. One never played with rice grains for the same reason. When given a plate of rice, I finished every grain of it, for my Amah threatened that if I did not, my future husband's face would be pock-marked like the grains of rice left on the plate. Left-over rice is never thrown away but left in the cooking pot for the moon goddess Avial to collect, then fed to the birds the next day.

It is also traditional when moving house in Malaysia to carry some grains of rice and some salt from the old house to the new so that the cupboard will never lack salt or rice. When we were packing to leave Malaysia to live in Australia 20 years ago, we were so busy sorting and packing that the ritual completely slipped our minds but just before the doors of the container banged shut my Amah came running out and tucked a small newspaper packet into one of the boxes. I still have that packet, and replenish it with a few fresh grains of rice and salt every time I move house.

Bet's Beef Nonya Devil
(Nonya Diavolo)

*The Portuguese in Melaka have perfected the art of combining
Malaysian spices and herbs with the dishes their ancestors brought
with them to Asia. I got this wonderful recipe from Bet, a good
friend of my Portuguese sister-in-law. Bet has always cooked without
recipes, so her recipes read a little like this: 'A little onion, so much
garlic, only a small piece of lemon grass ...'*

Ingredients:

1 kilogram (2 lb) beef brisket

2 tablespoons dark soy sauce

4 cloves garlic, chopped

3 tomatoes, skinned and chopped

2 stalks lemon grass, pureed

¼ cup (60 mL / 2 fl oz) chilli garlic sauce

¼ cup (60 mL / 2 fl oz) tomato sauce (ketchup)

water to cover the meat

1 teaspoon sugar

juice of 1 lemon

1 tablespoon plum sauce

2 tablespoons oil

Method:

Put the beef into a large saucepan with
the soy sauce, garlic, tomatoes, lemon
grass, chilli garlic sauce and tomato
sauce (ketchup). Cover with water, put
the lid on and simmer slowly for 2–2½
hours, or until tender.

Remove the beef and cover with
foil to keep warm. Simmer the stock in
the saucepan for 10–15 minutes, until it
has reduced to about a quarter of its
volume.

Add the sugar, lemon juice and
plum sauce. Bring to the boil then
remove the saucepan from the heat.

Heat the oil in a wok and fry the
beef on a high heat for 2 minutes each
side, until all the sides are seared. Slice
it and serve with rice. Reheat the sauce
if necessary and pour it over the beef.

*Back: Bet's Beef Nonya Devil
(recipe, this page);
Front: Crispy Double-fried Szechwan
Chilli Beef (recipe, page 44)*

Crispy Double-fried Szechwan Chilli Beef

This recipe is Szechwanese in origin, but in Malaysia it is often cooked by Hainanese cooks in Cantonese restaurants — this is typical of Malaysia, a billion paradoxes of food and culture. It is important to marinate the beef and fry it in very hot oil, otherwise the double-frying may ruin it.

Ingredients:

400 grams (14 oz) round steak
1 tablespoon light soy sauce
2 teaspoons rice wine
1 teaspoon sesame oil
½ cup (60 g / 2 oz) cornflour (cornstarch)
1 tablespoon rice flour
2 cups (500 mL / 16 fl oz) oil

Sauce:

1 tablespoon cornflour (cornstarch)
1 cup (250 mL / 8 fl oz) water
1 tablespoon oil
3 cloves garlic, finely chopped
2 tablespoons chilli black bean paste
1 teaspoon sambal oelek
2 tablespoons sugar

Garnish:

1 tablespoon sesame seeds, dry roasted
½ Lebanese cucumber, thinly sliced
50 grams (1½ oz) basil leaves, whole

Method:

Freeze the beef for 1 hour or until firm. Trim the fat off and slice thinly. Place the light soy sauce, rice wine and sesame oil in a bowl, stirring well to combine. Add the beef, stirring so that it is evenly covered in marinade. Cover and refrigerate for 6–8 hours.

Combine the cornflour (cornstarch) and rice flour. Add half of the flour mixture to the bowl, mixing well. Save the rest for when you fry the beef for the second time.

Heat the oil in a wok until it is smoking. Remove the beef from the marinade and deep-fry it in four batches, removing each batch when it has browned. Drain the beef on paper towels. Set aside, cover and keep warm; leave the oil in the wok. Make the sauce, set aside and keep it warm.

Coat the beef with the remaining cornflour (cornstarch) and rice flour mixture. Heat the oil again and when it is smoking, fry the beef in four separate batches, removing from the oil and draining on absorbent kitchen paper when it is cooked.

Place the beef on a serving platter, pour over the sauce and garnish with roasted sesame seeds, cucumber and fresh basil.

Pictured on page 42.

Makan-lah!

Sauce:

Heat the oil in a saucepan and cook the garlic until it is golden. Add the chilli black bean paste, sambal oelek, sugar and the cornflour (cornstarch) mixed with water.

Bring the mixture to the boil and simmer, stirring until it has thickened. Set the sauce aside — but keep it warm — while you fry the beef for the second time.

Beef in Soy Sauce
(Daging Bifstik)

Daging means meat, and bifstik is a pidginised version of beef steak. Mutton steaks are sometimes called mutton bifstik — another of those paradoxes one finds in Malaysia. This is a typical Nonya dish from the northern mining town of Ipoh, where food styles and ingredients show a strong Chinese influence.

Ingredients:

7 peppercorns, crushed
7 Szechwan peppercorns, crushed
500 grams (1 lb) scotch fillet (rib eye) steak, thinly sliced
4 tablespoons oil
2 Spanish (red) onions, thinly sliced
2 tablespoons dark soy sauce
2 tablespoons rice wine
1 tablespoon oyster sauce
½ cup (125 mL / 4 fl oz) water or beef stock
1 small piece of cinnamon stick, whole
salt, to taste
50 grams (1½ oz) basil leaves

Method:

Rub the pepper into the meat. Heat 2 tablespoons of the oil in a wok on a high heat and fry the meat until it is browned. It is important to fry only a few pieces of the beef at a time because if you add too much to the wok at once the beef will stew rather than fry. Remove each batch of meat from the wok and drain on paper towels.

Return the wok to the heat and add the remaining oil. Fry the onions until golden, then add the soy sauce, rice wine and oyster sauce. Turn the heat down to low. Add the water or stock, cinnamon and meat. Simmer for approximately 30 minutes, until the meat is tender. If this takes longer than 30 minutes, top up with a little water.

Finally, add the basil leaves, and cook briefly on a high heat, stirring well.

This dish should not take more than 10 minutes to cook. It is best served immediately, with rice.

Malay Meat and Vegetable Casserole
(Bamiah)

Bamiah is a Malay dish which has its origins in Arab cooking. Like many dishes influenced by the Middle East it contains tomatoes and tomato paste.

Ingredients:

3 centimetre (1 in) length ginger

5 cloves garlic

1 tablespoon mixed Malaysian curry powder (see page 172)

1 tablespoon sambal oelek

1 teaspoon white pepper

750 grams (1½ lb) chuck or topside, cut into large cubes

2 tablespoons ghee

1 Spanish (red) onion, thinly sliced

1 cinnamon stick

5 cloves

2 tablespoons tomato paste

½ cup (125 mL / 4 fl oz) water

¼ cup (60 mL / 2 fl oz) oil

250 grams (½ lb) okra, stems trimmed

2 semi-ripe tomatoes, cubed

50 grams (1½ oz) mint leaves

Method:

Blend the ginger and garlic together in a food processor or mortar and pestle. Mix it with the curry powder, sambal oelek and pepper in a large bowl. Coat the beef thoroughly in the mixture, cover and marinate in the refrigerator for at least 2 hours.

Heat the ghee in a wok or saucepan on a medium–high heat and saute the onion, cinnamon, cloves and beef until the spices release their aromas and the meat is well browned. Add the tomato paste and water and cook on a medium–high heat for 20 minutes.

Heat the oil in another wok on a high heat and fry the okra until it is crisp. Remove the okra and drain on paper towel. (Don't discard the oil.)

Add the okra and tomatoes to the beef and cook for 5 minutes.

Heat the reserved oil on a very high heat and deep-fry the mint only until it is crisp (be quick — crisping occurs immediately).

Remove the beef from the heat and toss the deep-fried mint through it.

Beef, Chicken or Lamb Satay
(Satay lembu ayam dan kambing)

The name 'satay' is said to be a corruption of the English word 'steak'. In Malay, two consonants, such as 's' and 't', are never pronounced together; they are always separated by a vowel. Thus 'steak' became 'sa-tek', and eventually 'satay'. The dish is Middle Eastern in origin — a Malaysian version of the kebab.

Ingredients:

400 grams (13 oz) beef (rump or topside), lamb, or chicken thigh fillets

Marinade:

6 red Asian onions, pureed

2 cloves garlic, pureed

2 stalks lemon grass, processed or pounded in mortar and pestle

1 chilli, processed or pounded in mortar and pestle

1 teaspoon turmeric powder

1 teaspoon cumin, dry roasted and ground

1 teaspoon fennel, dry roasted and ground

2 teaspoons palm sugar

1 teaspoon thick soy sauce (kecap manis)

Baste:

⅓ cup (80 mL / 2½ fl oz) coconut cream

1 tablespoon oil

2 teaspoons brown sugar

Method:

Soak 20 bamboo skewers in water for 1 hour. (This will stop them from splintering when you thread the meat onto them.)

Slice the meat into long, flat pieces, about 3 centimetres (1 inch) wide and 1 centimetre (½ inch) thick. Slice the meat across the grain. Thread the meat onto the skewers. Trim off any straggly bits of the meat with a pair of scissors.

Combine all of the marinade ingredients. Coat the meat thoroughly with the marinade and allow to sit, in the refrigerator, for 30–60 minutes, or longer if time permits.

Mix together the coconut cream, oil and brown sugar.

Heat an open grill until it is very hot. Brush the grill lightly with some oil, then cook the skewers for 1–2 minutes on each side, brushing them with the coconut cream baste.

Serve on a bed of spiced rice accompanied with cucumber, or serve with Satay Peanut Sauce (recipe, page 145).

Murtabak Pastry Cabbage with Beef
(Murtabak kobis)

Murtabak is a type of layered pancake roti made by Indian Muslim hawkers. For this dish, the pastry is made in the shape of a cabbage and filled with meat.

Ingredients:

2 tablespoons oil

1 teaspoon mustard seeds

1 large Spanish (red) onion, finely diced

1 centimetre (¹/₂ in) length ginger, pureed

1 tablespoon Malaysian curry powder (see page 172)

¹/₄ teaspoon ground cloves

¹/₂ teaspoon cinnamon powder

200 grams (7 oz) beef mince

5 stems spring onion, thinly sliced or 50 grams (1¹/₂ oz) Vietnamese mint leaves

1 packet (500 g / 1 lb) ready-made filo pastry

¹/₄ cup (60 mL / 2 fl oz) melted butter

1 egg, lightly beaten

1 teaspoon sea salt (optional)

Method:

Heat the oil in a wok and saute the mustard seeds with the Spanish (red) onion until the onion is golden. Add the ginger, curry powder, cloves and cinnamon and fry on a medium heat until they release their aroma. Add the beef and fry, stirring continuously, until well browned. Remove from the heat, toss in the spring onions or Vietnamese mint and salt and allow to cool.

Assemble the pastry cabbage.

Brush the cabbage with egg white or milk and bake in a hot oven (200°C / 400°F) for 15 minutes or until the pastry is golden. Lower the heat to 180°C (350°F) and cook for a further 10 minutes.

Carefully remove the cabbage from the oven and allow it to rest about 10 minutes, for the pastry to relax. Slice a wedge in the same way that you would slice a Christmas pudding.

Serve the pastry cabbage with chopped lettuce and the 'wet' gravy with meat or vegetables.

Assembling:

Before beginning to assemble the pastry cabbage, you should first read through all the following instructions.

Separate the pastry sheets into two piles and place them on a table.

From one pile, cut a circle — cutting through all the sheets as if they were one — 13 centimetres (5 inches) in diameter (you will find it easier if you first cut a circle out of paper, and use that as a template). From the other pile, cut a circle 23 centimetres (9 inches) in diameter.

To start the cabbage, take 4 sheets of the small circle, brush with some butter, then spread 1¹/₂ tablespoons of mince in the centre. Spread water on the edges of the circle and draw up the edges of the circle into a bunch and squeeze to hold the bunched edges together.

Take another 4 sheets of the small circle, brush each with some butter, and place one on top of the other. Place the first parcel in the middle. Spread 1¹/₂ tablespoons of mince around the first parcel. Spread water on the edges of the circle and draw up the edges of the circle into a bunch and squeeze to hold the bunched edges together. Now the parcel is slightly larger. Repeat this process, using the small circles, two more times.

Now take 4 sheets of the big circle and continue the process, enclosing the same parcel. It will become increasingly hard to lift because of the bulk of meat, so work carefully so that the meat does not break through the pastry leaves.

Continue until the cabbage is quite large (20 cm / 8 in).

Murtabak Pastry Cabbage with Beef

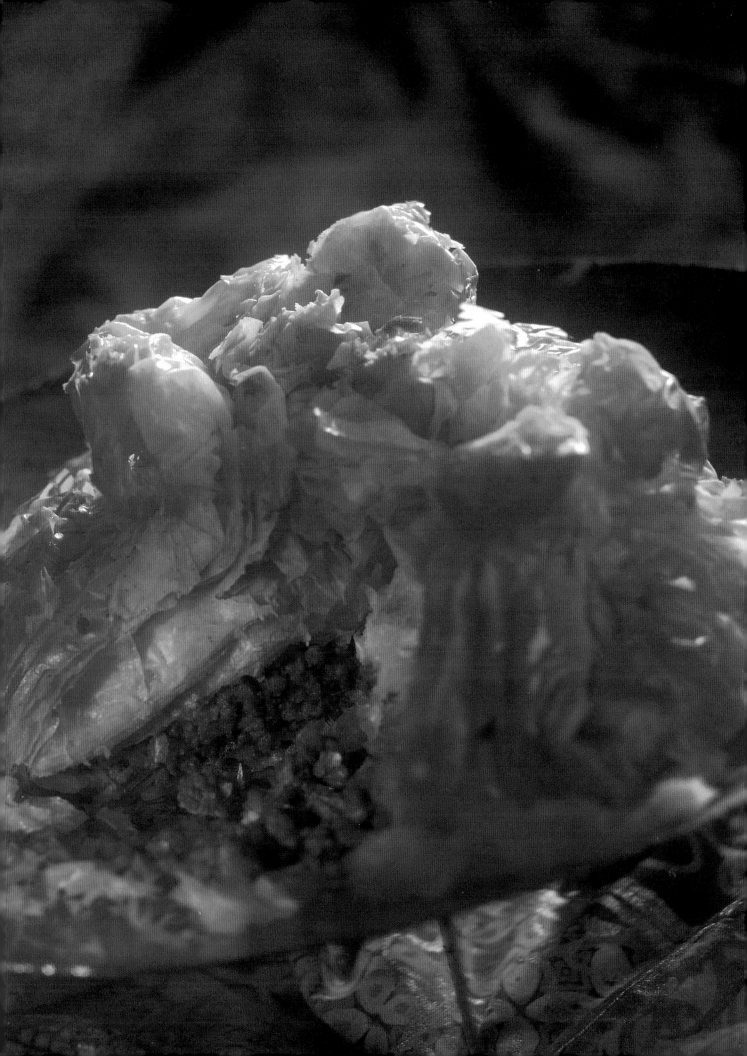

Serunding Beef

This is a dry Malay curry cooked with beef and coconut, similar to the Serunding Sambal. In Indonesia, this dish often used to be cooked with buffalo meat.

Ingredients:

500 grams (1 lb) scotch fillet (rib eye) steak, sliced in wide strips

2 centimetre (³/₄ in) length ginger

1 centimetre (¹/₂ in) length fresh turmeric or 1 teaspoon turmeric powder

3 stalks lemon grass

2 centimetre (³/₄ in) length galangal

2 dried chillies

¹/₂ cup (125 mL / 4 fl oz) oil

1 tablespoon coriander seeds, dry roasted

1 teaspoon cumin seeds, dry roasted

4 cm (1¹/₂ in) tamarind made into puree with 80 mL (2¹/₂ fl oz) of liquid from the cooked meat

2 tablespoons palm sugar

¹/₂ teaspoon salt, or to taste

1 pandan leaf, thinly shredded

500 grams (1 lb) desiccated coconut, dry roasted

Method:

Place the beef in a saucepan and add just enough water to cover it. Simmer on a low heat for 30 minutes, or until the beef is tender. Remove the beef from the saucepan and set aside. When it has cooled, shred it finely with your fingers. The water will have taken up the flavour of the beef, so save it and use it to make your tamarind puree.

Blend the ginger, turmeric, lemon grass, galangal and chilli together in a food processor or mortar and pestle. Heat 2 tablespoons of the oil in a wok or saucepan on a medium–high heat and fry the blended ingredients until they release their aroma. Add the meat, coriander, cumin, tamarind puree, sugar, salt and pandan leaf. Stirring continuously, cook on a medium heat for 20–30 minutes.

Add the coconut and continue stirring constantly for 10–15 minutes. You may feel that you should add more oil, but don't, as the coconut will release sufficient oil to stop the mixture from burning. The Serunding should be dry and dark brown in colour.

Pienang Curry

This curry is prepared by the Cape Malays who were transported to South Africa from Indonesia by the Dutch. Though the name may suggest Thai influences (the Thais have a Panaeng Curry made with spices similar to those used in Malaysia), this dish has more in common with a North Indian curry.

Ingredients:

6 cloves garlic

2 Spanish (red) onions, sliced thinly

4 bay leaves

1 cinnamon stick

6 whole cloves

piece (2 cm / ³/₄ in) of star anise

1 kilogram (2 lb) lamb, cubed

2 tablespoons oil

2 teaspoons garam masala

1 teaspoon turmeric powder

1 tablespoon tamarind puree

juice of 2 limes or lemons

1 tablespoon sugar

2 tablespoons almond meal

Method:

Blend the garlic, onion, bay leaves, cinnamon, cloves and star anise into a paste in a food processor or mortar and pestle. Divide the mixture in two and rub half into the lamb.

Heat the oil in a heavy-based saucepan and saute the other half of the paste on a medium–high heat for 3 minutes, until it releases its aroma. Add the lamb and fry on a high heat until browned.

Reduce to a low heat, cover the pan and allow the lamb to simmer in its own juices for 20 minutes.

Mix the garam masala, turmeric, tamarind puree, lime (or lemon) juice and sugar. Pour over the lamb and simmer on a low heat with the pan covered until the lamb is tender.

Toss the almond meal through the meat just before removing from the heat. Serve with rice or roti.

Serunding Beef

Lamb Buriyani
(Buriyani kambing)

Buriyani is a combination of rice and meat. This style of cooking was developed in the courts of the Muslim Sultans of India, which were influenced by exotic Persian cooking techniques, such as incorporating nuts and fruit into meat dishes.

Ingredients:

1 leg of lamb or mutton (500 g/ 1 lb)

Stock:

5 cups (1.2 litres / 40 fl oz) water

2 centimetre (³/₄ in) length of ginger, pounded in a mortar and pestle

2 teaspoons salt

1 teaspoon ground pepper

Rice:

2 cups (440 g/ 14 oz) Basmati rice

1¹/₂ tablespoons ghee

1 Spanish (red) onion, sliced

2¹/₂ cloves garlic, crushed

5 cardamom pods (seeds removed), crushed

2 cinnamon sticks, roughly broken

1 star anise

¹/₂ teaspoon ground pepper

Sauce:

1¹/₂ tablespoons ghee

2¹/₂ cloves garlic, crushed

1 Spanish (red) onion, sliced

¹/₄ nutmeg kernel, crushed or grated

3 pods cardamom, seeds removed, pounded

1 tablespoon curry powder

2¹/₂ cups (625 mL/ 20 fl oz) water

3 tablespoons plain yoghurt

¹/₄ teaspoon saffron or turmeric

Garnish:

¹/₂ cup (80 g / 2¹/₂ oz) ready fried onions

¹/₂ cup (100 g / 3¹/₂ oz) pistachio nuts

Stock:

Bone the leg of lamb or mutton. Place the bone in a large saucepan with the water, ginger, salt and pepper. Bring to the boil and simmer for 30 minutes.

While the stock is cooking, slice the meat into medallions about 3 cm (1 in) thick and 4 cm (1½ in) wide.

When the stock has simmered for 30 minutes, leave it to cool. Once the stock has cooled, skim off the fat and measure out 3 cups (750 mL / 24 fl oz) of stock for the rice and 2 cups (500 mL / 16 fl oz) for the soup. (Excess stock can be frozen and used in other recipes.)

Rice:

Put the rice in a large bowl, cover it with water, stir several times, then drain off the water. Repeat this several times until the water runs clear. (This removes some of the starch from the rice.)

Heat the ghee in a large saucepan and brown the onion. Add the rice, garlic, cardamom, cinnamon, star anise and pepper and fry for 3–4 minutes on a medium heat, stirring continuously, until the rice becomes opaque. Add the 3 cups of stock and cook the rice. Remove from the heat and cover to keep the rice warm.

Sauce:

Heat the ghee in a large saucepan and fry the garlic, onion, nutmeg and cardamom for 2 minutes. Add the curry powder and the meat and cook until the meat is browned. Add the water and simmer for approximately 20 minutes, or until tender. Take the saucepan off the heat. Remove the meat and set it aside. Mix the yoghurt and saffron together and add it to the saucepan, stirring to combine.

Soup:

Take half the sauce and pour it into a saucepan with 2 cups of the warm stock. This will make a thin soup to be served with the buriyani. Simmer gently while cooking the buriyani.

Cooking the buriyani:

Divide the rice into three portions, and the meat into two. Spread one portion of the rice in the bottom of a large greased casserole dish or rice cooker. Follow this with a layer of meat, then alternate layers of rice and meat, with a final layer of rice on top. Pour the remaining half of the sauce over and cover with foil. Cook in a medium oven for 20–30 minutes or in the rice cooker until the rice has absorbed the sauce.

Garnish with fried onions and pistachio nuts. Serve with bowls of the soup, accompanied by a crisp green salad.

Raffles

The man, the hotel
and the Singapore Sling

In 1819 Sir Thomas Stamford Raffles, lieutenant-governor of Benkulen in Sumatra, acquired the mosquito-infested island of Singapore for the British from the Temenggong (chieftain) of Johore. He instructed that Singapore was to remain a free port, as this was the only way the British could compete with the Dutch, who had the ports of Surabaya and Batavia.

In March 1819, the Calcutta Journal wrote enthusiastically of the new settlement, predicting that it would be the 'fulcrum for trade in the East' as it possessed a large, deep and natural harbour capable of servicing the whole of the area. Indeed, Singapore was to become the sea, rail and air centre of the East.

As an outpost of the East India Company, Singapore offered a 'convenient place of call to travellers of all description, all drawn by the potent lure of the East, from merchants, missionaries, to sailors and adventurers, explorers and writers'.

Of course, travellers who came to Singapore needed a place to stay. There were many rooming houses, 'public houses' and hotels in Singapore, some basic — others quite luxurious. It was the four Sarkies brothers who, in 1887, embarked on the task of providing Singapore with 'a really first-class hotel', which they named the Raffles Hotel in the same year that the statue of Sir Thomas was unveiled in the city.

The Raffles Hotel soon grew from a humble hostel to a grand temporary residence for visiting gentry, offering in their tiffin rooms 'cuisine of the highest character served at separate tables'. So popular was the new Raffles Hotel and its food that Rudyard Kipling, when travelling in Singapore in 1889, 'crept back to the hotel after dinner to eat six different chutneys with one curry'.

There are many legends connected with the hotel, among them the story of the tiger shot under the long bar and the creation of the Singapore Sling — this special cocktail was created for the thirsty colonial Raj by the Hainanese bar-tender Mr Ngiam Tong Boon.

Throughout the turbulent times Singapore and Malaysia went through during the Second World War, and during the formative years when both the countries were struggling for recognition and independence, the Raffles stood as a constant symbol of gracious hospitality and dignity.

Rich Malay Lamb Casserole
(Kuzi Lamb)

This dish was developed by Malaysian pilgrims on their way to Mecca. The use of canned tomato puree and evaporated milk made sense in the desert, where fresh ingredients were hard to find. When the pilgrims returned to Malaysia, they kept on using the canned ingredients which give this dish its characteristic flavour.

Ingredients:

2 Spanish (red) onions

4 cloves garlic

2 centimetre ($^3/_4$ in) length ginger

5 dried red chillies

1 kilogram (2 lb) leg of lamb, deboned and cubed

2 tablespoons ghee (clarified butter) or oil

$^1/_2$ cup (60 g / 2 oz) slivered almonds, toasted

1 tablespoon raisins

1 tablespoon coriander seeds, dry roasted and ground

2 teaspoons cumin seeds, dry roasted and ground

1 teaspoon fennel seeds, dry roasted and ground

10 cloves

$^1/_2$ nutmeg, ground

1 stick cinnamon

100 mL (2$^1/_2$ fl oz) tomato puree

2 cans (each 280 mL / 9 fl oz) evaporated milk

juice of 1 lime

1 teaspoon salt

1 tablespoon white pepper

2 eggs, hard-boiled and quartered

Method:

Blend the onions, garlic, ginger and chilli together in a food processor or mortar and pestle. Rub over the lamb and leave to sit for at least 15 minutes.

Heat the ghee (or oil) in a wok or saucepan on a medium–high heat and brown the almonds and raisins. When the almonds are golden, remove the almonds and raisins from the wok. Reserve for garnish.

Fry the coriander, cumin and fennel seeds, cloves, nutmeg and cinnamon in the wok for about 2 minutes, until they release their aroma (take care not to fry them for too long, as spices can burn and turn bitter).

Add the lamb and brown well. Add the tomato puree and milk and cook on a low heat for about 15 minutes, or until the lamb is tender. You must stir it well and make sure that it doesn't boil, otherwise the tomato puree and evaporated milk will curdle.

Add the lime juice, salt and pepper and remove from heat. Place the nuts and raisins on top and serve with the eggs on the side.

Back: Rich Malay Lamb Casserole (Kuzi Lamb) (recipe, this page); Front: Tikka-style Barbecued Lamb (recipe, page 54)

Makan-lah!

Tikka-style Barbecued Lamb
(Kambing Guling)

While their barbecuing equipment may not be as sophisticated as that used in western countries, Asians do have a barbecue tradition. Experiment with an Asian-style dish next time you barbecue, like this simple guling.

Ingredients:

500 grams (1 lb) lamb cut into flat, 4 centimetre (1½ in) squares

1 tablespoon butter or oil

¼ cup (60 mL / 2 fl oz) yoghurt

Marinade:

½ cup (125 mL / 4 fl oz) thick Greek-style yoghurt

2 cloves garlic, pureed

3 centimetre (1 in) length ginger, pureed

2 teaspoons chilli powder

½ teaspoon turmeric powder

1 tablespoon dried mango powder (amchur)

2 teaspoons ground cumin

juice of 2 limes

50 grams (1½ oz) mint leaves, shredded

½ teaspoon salt

½ teaspoon pepper

1 teaspoon paprika

Garnish:

2 bunches mint

2 limes, each cut into 8 wedges

Method:

Mix all of the marinade ingredients together and marinate the lamb in the refrigerator for at least 4 hours. Cover it well to prevent it from drying out.

Mix together the butter (or oil) and yoghurt. Set aside for basting.

Remove the lamb from the marinade. In two or three batches (thread meat onto metal skewers, if you wish), cook it on a hot grill or barbecue for 2 minutes on each side, brushing with the combined butter (or oil) and yoghurt. Remove from the heat and cover it to keep warm.

Pour the marinade into a saucepan along with any cooking juices from the lamb. Bring it to a simmer on a medium heat and stir for 5 minutes until it thickens. Season with salt and pepper to taste and pour over the lamb. Garnish with sprigs of mint and lime wedges.

Pictured on page 52.

Mild Vinegared Lamb
(Kambing Kalia)

It used to be that the only way to get a decent cut of mutton in Malaysia was to be on good terms with the local butcher, but air travel now means that high quality lamb is available all over the world.

Ingredients:

3 centimetre (1 in) length ginger

½ cup (100 g / 3 oz) thick Greek-style yoghurt

2 teaspoons vinegar

1 teaspoon salt

3 teaspoons chilli powder

2 teaspoons cumin powder, dry roasted

1 teaspoon turmeric powder

1 kilogram (2 lb) lamb from leg or chump, cubed

2 potatoes, cut into 2.5 cm (1 in) cubes

2 cups (500 mL / 16 fl oz) oil

½ teaspoon cumin seeds

3 centimetre (1 in) cinnamon stick

2 cardamom pods, split

4 cloves garlic, crushed

½ teaspoon sugar

4 Spanish (red) onions, sliced

2 bay leaves

1 tablespoon tomato puree

handful of coriander leaves, to garnish

Method:

Pound the ginger with a mortar and pestle or grate with a fine grater to produce 1 tablespoon of juice. Combine the yoghurt, vinegar, salt, ginger juice, chilli powder, cumin and ½ teaspoon of the turmeric powder. Marinate the lamb for at least 2 hours.

Coat the potato in the remaining ½ teaspoon of turmeric powder. Heat the oil in a wok or saucepan and deep-fry the potatoes until they are golden brown on the outside. Remove them from the oil and drain on paper towel. Let the oil cool a little and pour out all but 2 tablespoons of it.

Place the saucepan or wok back on a medium–high heat and fry the cumin seeds until they pop. Add the cinnamon, cardamom, garlic, sugar and onions and stir-fry until golden.

Add the meat (but not the marinade yet) to the saucepan or wok and fry on a medium–high heat until the meat is browned. Add the bay leaves, tomato puree and the marinade and lower the heat. Cover and simmer for 1 hour or until the lamb is tender. If the sauce is still a little thin when the lamb has finished cooking, simmer with the lid off until the sauce has thickened.

Toss the potatoes through, garnish with coriander and serve with rice, puri or Lebanese (lavash) bread.

Pictured on page 38.

Lentil Stew with Lamb and Vegetables
(Dalcha)

Lentils (also called dahl or pulses) provide the protein that keeps vegetarian Indians healthy. They are cooked in almost every South Indian home from London to Dubai to Sydney. Dalcha can be watery or thick, depending on whether it is to be eaten with rice or scooped up with roti.

Ingredients:

4 cups (1 litre / 32 fl oz) water
1 cup (200 g / 6½ oz) red lentils
2 centimetre (¾ in) length ginger
2 cloves garlic
2 Spanish onions
½ teaspoon salt
¼ teaspoon turmeric powder
2 tablespoons oil
10 lamb cutlets
1 teaspoon chilli powder
½ cup (125 mL / 4 fl oz) tamarind juice
2 tomatoes, quartered

Garnish:

1 tablespoon oil or ghee (clarified butter)
1 teaspoon mustard seeds
2 stalks curry leaves
2 cloves garlic, sliced
4 red Asian onions or 1 medium Spanish (red) onion, sliced

Method:

Boil 2 cups (500 mL / 16 fl oz) of the water in a saucepan and add the lentils. Boil for 10–15 minutes, until the lentils are soft and have doubled in size.

Blend the ginger, garlic, onions, salt and turmeric together in a food processor or mortar and pestle.

Heat the oil in a saucepan on a medium–high heat and saute the blended mixture until it releases its aroma. Add the lamb cutlets and brown well on both sides (about 2 minutes each side).

Add the remaining 2 cups of water and cover the pan. Simmer for 20 minutes.

Add the lentils, chilli powder, tamarind juice and tomatoes and simmer with the pan covered for another 20 minutes or until the lamb is tender.

Garnish:

Heat the oil in a wok on a high heat, add the mustard seeds and cook until they pop. Then add the curry leaves, garlic and onions and saute until golden. Pour over the Dalcha and serve immediately with rice.

Variation:

You can turn this recipe into a thick, full-bodied lentil soup by adding 1 litre (32 fl oz) of water when the lentils are added.

Eurasian Lime and Lamb Curry
(Daging Limau)

The chilli and lime juice in this dish not only tenderise the lamb but also cut its fat content. It can be served with rice, puri or even Lebanese (lavash) bread, which can be used as a scoop.

Ingredients:

500 grams (1 lb) lamb from leg or chump, cubed
2 tablespoons chilli powder
3 centimetre (1 in) length ginger
2 Spanish (red) onions
2 stalks lemon grass
3 tablespoons oil
2 bay leaves
1 tablespoon fennel, dry roasted
1 tablespoon cumin, dry roasted
½ teaspoon turmeric powder
1 tablespoon sambal oelek
juice and zest of 4 limes
⅓ cup (30 g / 3 oz) desiccated coconut, dry roasted
4 kaffir lime leaves, shredded

Method:

Coat the lamb with the chilli powder.

Blend the ginger, onions and lemon grass together in a food processor or mortar and pestle.

Heat the oil in a wok or saucepan on a medium–high heat and fry the bay leaves for approximately 30 seconds. Add the fennel, cumin, turmeric, sambal oelek and blended onion mixture and saute until golden and aromatic.

With the heat still on high, add the lamb. Brown and seal the lamb on all sides.

Add the lime juice and simmer, with the pot covered, for about 40 minutes, or until the lamb is tender. Add the coconut and simmer uncovered for 5 minutes on a medium heat until the sauce thickens.

Garnish with lime zest and shredded lime leaves.

Malaysian Markets

Colourful, noisy, exciting

I have the most endearing and exciting memories of a childhood spent with my Amah, who took me everywhere she went: to the butcher, to the crab and fish man, to chicken farms, to the tailor, to the Chinese herbalist, and to the market. Visiting the market was infinitely more inviting and exciting than doing my homework.

Markets would be open at dawn and shopping was done very early in the morning, before the heat of the sun wilted everything and before one went to work.

Malaysians still prefer to buy their meat and vegetables fresh, but today two-income families and the marvels of modern refrigeration translates into people in cities shopping for staples once a week, and fish and meat two or three times a week.

Malaysian markets are noisy, exciting places with the bustle of bargain shoppers, office workers hurrying to shop for fresh meat — carefully avoiding wet puddles — and people holding their skirts and sarongs close to avoid the spray of the hose that makes a regular sweep of every skerrick on the floor. The fish stalls, full of fish, prawns, clams and crab, are hosed hourly to keep the fish moist; the vegetable stalls are piled high with fresh greens, orange and red tomatoes, squat yellow cakes of tofu, scarlet chillies, black and grey salted eggs and huge vats of creamy tofu 'milk'. As markets are frequented by all races and religions, the pork stall is often tucked away out of sight, pork being taboo to Muslims.

Of special interest to me as a child was the Indian spice man who wielded the grinding stone, pulverising orders for impatient customers: a fish mixture with fenugreek, seventeen spices for a rendang meat curry, pure chilli-boh (ground chilli) for the mee seller, and tamarind and turmeric, cumin and coriander, an expectant mother's special order. At the mechanical coconut grater nearby, a young man cracked hundreds of coconuts and offered half-spheres to the whirring metal teeth that spun the flesh into basins below.

Lamb Cutlets with Spiced Coconut Crusts
(Kambing Masak Panggang)

The Szechwan peppercorns in this dish add a new dimension to the flavour of lamb. Make sure you don't overcook the lamb or it may become tough; it should be a light pink colour.

Ingredients:

2 tablespoons coconut cream

6 lamb cutlets, trimmed of fat

1/2 tablespoon Szechwan peppers, dry roasted and ground

80 grams (2 1/2 oz) shredded coconut, fresh or dried

1 lime, cut into wedges

Method:

Brush the coconut cream onto both sides of the lamb cutlets. Sprinkle both sides with the pepper, then coat with coconut. Grill on a high heat until the coconut is crisp and golden, approximately 5–6 minutes.

Serve with lime wedges and Mint Chutney (recipe, page 59).

Lamb Chops with Plum and Dates

This recipe is very western in concept, but makes use of Malaysian ingredients and techniques. Chinese red vinegar has a wonderful flavour quite unlike any other and tenderises meat well. You may have to search for it in a Chinese supermarket, but it's well worth it.

Ingredients:

4 chillies

3 cloves garlic

2 tablespoons lime juice

500 grams (1 lb) lamb chops, trimmed of fat

1 tablespoon oil

3/4 cup (180 mL / 6 fl oz) Chinese red vinegar

1 cup (250 mL / 8 fl oz) plum sauce

2 tablespoons soy sauce

1/2 cup (60 g / 2 oz) button mushrooms, thinly sliced

1/2 cup (100g / 3 1/2 oz) dates, quartered

2 tablespoons toasted almond flakes

Method:

Blend the chillies and garlic together in a food processor or mortar and pestle, then mix with the lime juice in a bowl. Brush the lamb chops with the lime juice mixture and marinate for 1 hour. Drain the liquid off and set it aside for later.

Heat the oil on a high heat in a saucepan or wok. Brown the lamb chops on both sides.

Add the vinegar, plum sauce and soy sauce and reduce to a low heat. Cover the saucepan or wok and simmer for 40 minutes or until tender. Remove the lid and add the reserved lime juice mixture. Continue to simmer for 20–25 minutes, until the sauce has reduced and thoroughly glazes the meat.

Add the mushrooms and dates and stir a little for 5 minutes on a low heat. Garnish with toasted almond flakes and serve hot, with rice. This dish goes well with simple steamed broccoli.

Arabic Lamb Stew with Mint Chutney
(Shanaz Kambing)

This curried stew is Arabic in influence. Accompanying it with rotis or puris and a simple mint chutney makes for an irresistible blend of flavours and textures.

Ingredients:

10 baby (new) potatoes, peeled

1 teaspoon turmeric powder

2 cups (500 mL / 16 fl oz) oil, for deep-frying

1 teaspoon white peppercorns

1 teaspoon cumin seeds, dry roasted

5 cloves garlic

3 centimetre (1 inch) length ginger

2 teaspoons sugar

1½ teaspoons salt

1 teaspoon sesame oil

2 tablespoons tomato sauce (ketchup)

1 tablespoon light soy sauce

2 cups (500 mL / 16 fl oz) water

2 tablespoons oil

10 lamb chump chops

4 large tomatoes, cut into wedges

1 Spanish (red) onion, sliced

6 small (pickling) onions

Mint Chutney:

80—100 grams (2½—3½ oz) fresh mint leaves

½ cup (45 g / 1½ oz) desiccated coconut

8 red Asian onions

½ teaspoon salt

2 tablespoons vinegar

Method:

Roll the potatoes in the turmeric so they are evenly coated. Heat the oil in a saucepan on high until it is very hot (but not smoking) and deep-fry the potatoes until they are golden brown. Remove them from the oil and drain on paper towels. Grind the peppercorns and cumin in a mortar and pestle.

Blend the garlic, ginger, 1 teaspoon of the sugar and 1 teaspoon of the salt together in a food processor or mortar and pestle.

Combine the remaining 1 teaspoon of sugar, ½ teaspoon of salt, sesame oil, tomato sauce (ketchup), light soy sauce and water in a bowl.

Heat the oil in a wok or saucepan on a medium heat and saute the blended garlic mixture, peppercorns and cumin until aromatic and golden.

Add the lamb and, on a high heat, fry well on both sides to seal (3 minutes each side). Pour in the sauce mixture and add the tomatoes. Cover and simmer for 30 minutes.

Add the Spanish (red) and small (pickling) onions and potatoes. Simmer partially covered for a further 30 minutes or until the meat is tender.

If the sauce is too thin, remove the meat and vegetables, simmer the sauce until it thickens and then return the meat and vegetables.

Serve hot with Mint Chutney and roti or puri.

Mint Chutney:

Blend all of the ingredients together in a food processor or mortar and pestle until they form a paste.

Chinese Barbecue Pork
(Char Siew)

For many of us, Chinatown is epitomised by the glistening red-coated barbecued pork that, along with other delicacies, hangs suspended from butchers hooks in store windows. Well, eat your heart out, Chinatown — authentic barbecue pork can be produced easily in any kitchen.

Ingredients:

1 kilogram (2 lb) pork neck, tenderloin or belly pork with fat

1½ teaspoons salt

2 tablespoons thick soy sauce (kecap manis)

1 tablespoon light soy sauce

2 cloves garlic, finely crushed

3 tablespoons Chinese malt vinegar (optional)

1 tablespoon rice wine

2 tablespoons plum sauce

2 tablespoons cornflour (cornstarch)

Method:

Rub the pork with salt and allow to stand for 2 hours. Pat dry with paper towel. Combine the remaining ingredients in a bowl and marinate the pork for 1 hour. Push some of the marinade between the skin and fat of the pork, or stab the skin with a knife and work the marinade into the holes.

While the pork is marinating, preheat the oven to 200°C (400°F). Bake the pork on a rack for 10 minutes. Reduce the heat to 170°C (350°F) and cook on the rack for a further 45 minutes.

Pour the fat out of the pan and pat the pork dry with paper towel (the skin has to be dry to make pork crackling successfully).

To make crackling, rub ½ teaspoon of the salt onto the pork skin. Put the heat back up to 200°C (400°F) and cook the pork for a further 10 minutes. Remove the pork from the oven and place it under a hot grill for 5–10 minutes, or until the rind is crisp.

Allow the pork to rest for 30 minutes, then slice thinly and serve with chilli garlic sauce — or use it instead of bacon in Rainbow Fried Rice (recipe, page 33).

Pork in Soy Sauce
(Babi Tauyu)

I once invited an important client to dinner who was so impressed with my Babi Tauyu that he raved about it for months afterwards. The project I was trying to put together with him came through soon after the dinner — my friend Ben has called this my 'lethal weapon' ever since.

Ingredients:

500 grams (1 lb) pork belly

500 grams (1 lb) pork neck

½ teaspoon Szechwan pepper, dry roasted and ground

2 star anise, ground

1 cucumber

½ cup (125 mL / 4 fl oz) black or red Chinese vinegar

2 tablespoons sugar

2 tablespoons oil

6 cloves garlic, roughly crushed

1 stick cinnamon, roughly broken

2 tablespoons sambal oelek (optional)

2 tablespoons chilli black bean garlic sauce

⅓ cup (80 mL / 2½ fl oz) thick soy sauce (kecap manis)

2 cups (500 mL / 16 fl oz) water

1 teaspoon palm sugar or castor sugar

2 tablespoons Chinese vinegar or rice wine

2 hardboiled eggs, shells left on

Method:

Remove the skin from the pork belly, retaining some of the fat. Cut the pork belly and pork neck into cubes. For the recipe to work well, there should be a small proportion of fat compared to meat.

Rub the pepper and star anise onto the pork and allow to stand for 1 hour.

Remove the seeds from the cucumber, but leave the skin on. Dice it very finely. Mix the cucumber, red or black vinegar and sugar together in a bowl and set it aside for later. (The cucumber needs to marinate for at least 1 hour.)

Heat the oil in a large saucepan and fry the garlic for 1 minute on a medium heat. Add the pork and cinnamon and fry on a medium–high heat until the pork is browned.

Add the sambal oelek, chilli black bean garlic sauce and soy sauce and continue to cook the meat to brown off some of the fat (that is, to reduce the fat from the meat). Add the water, palm (or castor) sugar and Chinese vinegar (or rice wine) and bring to the boil.

Simmer, stirring well, until the pork is tender. This will take between 40 and 60 minutes. Keep a close watch on the pot as you may need to add a little more water as the sauce reduces.

When the pork is tender add the eggs, still in their shells, to the pot.

When the pork is soft and almost falling off the bone, remove the eggs from the pot and set them aside. Reduce the liquid quickly on a low–medium heat without burning the sauce. The sauce should be rich, dark and glistening.

When the eggs have cooled, peel and quarter them. Drain the diced cucumber. Serve the Babi Tauyu hot, with the cucumber and eggs as garnish.

Back: Pork in Soy Sauce (Babi Tauyu) (recipe, this page); Front: Spicy Pork Rolls (Loh Bak) (recipe, page 62)

Makan-lah!

Spicy Pork Rolls
(Loh Bak)

I consider bean curd sheets (fuchok) something of a miracle as they are nothing but the thin skin that forms when soybean milk is made. They can be used to wrap any filling, but are quite brittle so should be handled with care.

Ingredients:
  4 large bean curd sheets (fuchok) (see note)
  250 grams (½ lb) pork mince
  250 grams (8 oz) lean pork mince
  6 water chestnuts (fresh or canned), finely diced
  ½ teaspoon pepper
  1½ tablespoons sugar
  ½ tablespoon sambal oelek
  1 tablespoon dark soy sauce
  1 teaspoon hoisin sauce
  ⅓ cup (30 g / 1 oz) glutinous rice flour
  2 cups (500 mL / 16 fl oz) oil
  2 Lebanese cucumbers, roughly chopped
  4 pieces (50 g / 1½ oz) fried tofu, cut into 1 cm (½ in) cubes

Dipping Sauce:
  2 red chillies
  1 tablespoon sugar or 3 tablespoons sweet chilli sauce
  2 tablespoons thick soy sauce (kecap manis)
  1 tablespoon rice wine

Method:

Soak two tea-towels (dish towels) in water, squeeze fairly dry then place one bean curd sheet in between the wet towels for about 10 minutes to soften it and make it pliable. (Do one sheet at a time or else the sheets will become too soft.) Remove each sheet carefully and place it on a separate damp towel from which you can work.

Mix the pork mince, water chestnuts, pepper, sugar, sambal oelek, soy sauce, hoisin sauce and rice flour in a bowl.

With your hands, roll the mixture into long sausages approximately 2 centimetres (¾ inch) thick.

Lay one of these sausages on each halved bean curd sheet, and roll it as you would a Swiss roll, until a firm coating is formed. If the sheet breaks, continue rolling to form a thick wrapping over the meat. (If the sheet breaks, you may find that you need more than half a sheet.)

Fold over the ends and press firmly to seal the edge, using a little water if necessary. Place the rolls in a steamer (you may have to cut them to fit them in). Steam them for 10 minutes. If you don't wish to eat the rolls straight away, allow them to cool then wrap them in foil, but do not freeze them.

Pictured on page 60.

When you are ready to serve the rolls, heat the oil to a medium–high heat in a wok or saucepan. Deep-fry the rolls until they are golden, then drain on paper towel. Slice them into 3 centimetre (1 inch) lengths.

Mix the dipping sauce ingredients together and drizzle over the rolls. Serve the rolls with the cucumber and tofu.

Note: Large bean curd sheets (fuchok) are 50 cm (20 in) long and 40 cm (16 in) wide. Once a sheet is soft, it can be cut in half to make wrappings for two rolls.

Balinese Roast Pork with Coconut
(Lawar Babi Guling Nangka)

Roast suckling pig served with crackling is a Balinese favourite. When coconut is used with pork, the combination is called a 'lawar' or special dish.

Ingredients:
  1 small unripe jackfruit
  1 tablespoon oil
  300 grams (9½ oz) cooked roast pork, chopped
  ½ cup (45 g / 1½ oz) desiccated coconut, dry-roasted
  chives for garnish
  juice of 1 lime
  black pepper, to taste
  salt, to taste

Bumbu Bali Spice Mixture:
  2 dried chillies, soaked in water then ground
  2 centimetres (¾ in) ginger, peeled then chopped
  1 centimetre (½ in) fresh turmeric, pounded
  2 cloves garlic, chopped well
  1 Spanish (red) onion, thinly sliced
  4 cloves, pounded well
  2 kaffir lime leaves, shredded

Method:

Blend the spice mixture ingredients together using a mortar and pestle. Add lime juice, pepper and salt to taste. Set aside.

Coat the unripe jackfruit (and fingers or gloves) with the oil for ease of handling. Cut a quarter from the fruit. Allow it to sit until some of the sticky milk has drained off.

Peel the jackfruit quarter and discard the skin. Cut the piece of jackfruit into chunks, then boil till soft. Drain. Chop the jackfruit into tiny pieces.

Mix the jackfruit with coconut and pork and toss with the Bumbu Bali Spice Mixture. Garnish with chives.

Pictured on page 38.

Makan-lah!

Pickled Pork Curry
(Babi Chukar)

Babi Chukar is similar to a vindaloo; both are Portuguese exports from Goa. Pork and vinegar is an effective combination, as vinegar 'cuts' the fat and makes the dish tasty and tender. It is important to sauté the pork to brown it well for the flavour to develop, as it could be a very bland curry otherwise.

Ingredients:

4 cloves garlic

4 centimetre (1½ in) length ginger

3 centimetre (1 in) length galangal

4 tablespoons oil

12 red Asian onions, sliced

½ teaspoon turmeric powder

3 tablespoons sambal oelek

2 teaspoons mustard seeds, coarsely ground

1 kilogram (2 lb) pork, cubed

2 tablespoons cumin seeds, dry roasted and ground

1 tablespoon mixed Malaysian curry powder (see page 172)

2 tablespoons tomato puree

1 turmeric leaf (optional)

1 cup (250 mL / 8 fl oz) water

1 cup (250 mL / 8 fl oz) red wine vinegar

1 teaspoon salt

1 tablespoon palm sugar

Garnish:

1 tomato, diced

Method:

Blend the garlic, ginger and galangal together in a food processor or mortar and pestle.

Heat the oil in a wok or saucepan on a medium–high heat and fry the garlic mixture, onions, turmeric and sambal oelek until the onions are golden. Add the mustard seeds and brown a little more, for about 30 seconds. Add the pork, cumin seeds, curry powder and fry on a medium heat until the pork is browned.

Add the tomato puree, turmeric leaf and water. Reduce the heat to low, cover the pot and simmer for 40–60 minutes or until the pork is tender.

Remove the lid and increase the heat to moderate. Add the vinegar, salt and sugar. Simmer rapidly for about 10–15 minutes, until the curry is very dry. Serve garnished with tomato.

Steamed Asian Meatloaf

This simple dish is good with rice, in stir-fries, or as a sandwich filling. Virtually indestructible, this recipe can be adapted to fit most types of meat or seafood, so experiment!

Ingredients:

100 grams (3½ oz) bacon or pancetta

2 slices bread

¼ cup (60 mL / 2 fl oz) milk

300 grams (10½ oz) lean pork mince

300 grams (10½ oz) cooked, mashed pumpkin (squash)

2 tablespoons crispy fried onions

½ bunch (50 g / 1½ oz) chives, chopped

2 tablespoons pickled ginger, chopped

50 grams (2 oz) water chestnuts (fresh or canned), sliced

½ teaspoon salt

1 teaspoon pepper

½ tablespoon sambal oelek

1 egg, lightly beaten

Method:

Dry-fry the bacon or pancetta on a high heat until crisp. Chop roughly.

Put the bread in a small bowl and pour over the milk. Soak for 10 minutes. Remove the bread and squeeze it lightly to remove some of the milk.

In another bowl, combine the bread with the pork, the fried bacon or pancetta pieces, pumpkin (squash), onions, chives, pickled ginger, water chestnuts, salt, pepper and sambal oelek. Mix well. If the mixture seems dry, add a little of the milk.

Shape the meatloaf into a round, flat disc approximately 3 centimetres (1 inch) thick. Grease a bowl 15–18 centimetres in diameter (6–7 inches) and 6 centimetres (2½ inches) deep, and put the meatloaf into it. Brush with egg.

Place the bowl into a steamer and steam for 30–40 minutes or until well cooked. Serve the meatloaf hot or cold.

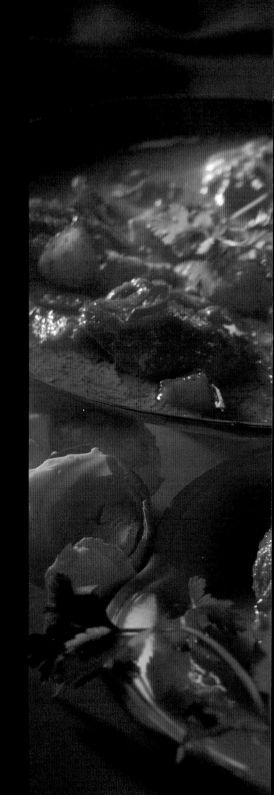

*Clockwise from left: Chicken Country Capitan (recipe, page 75),
Hainanese Chicken Rice (recipe, page 78)
and Szechwan Pepper Duck (recipe, page 79)*

Malaysian Roast Chicken with Coconut Sauce
(Ayam Panggang Bersantan)

This dish comes from the east coast of Malaysia, where the food more closely matches Thai flavours than it does the mix of Chinese/Indian flavours that flow through to Malay cooking elsewhere.

Ingredients:

1.5 kg (3 lb) chicken, skinned
1 teaspoon five spice powder
2 Spanish (red) onions, roughly chopped
10 small dried chillies, chopped
5 cloves garlic
3 cm (1 in) length ginger, chopped
2 cm (3/4 in) length galangal, chopped
2 stalks lemon grass, chopped
5 candlenuts
3 tablespoons coconut cream
1 teaspoon sugar
1 teaspoon tamarind puree
1 tablespoon oil
Vietnamese mint leaves

Method:

Cut the chicken in half along the breastbone using a pair of kitchen scissors or a heavy knife. Brush the five spice powder on the underside of the chicken.

Place the chicken with the powdered side down on a baking dish, then push firmly to flatten the chicken.

Blend the Spanish (red) onions, chillies, garlic, galangal, lemon grass and candlenuts together in a food processor or mortar and pestle to form a smooth paste.

Combine the coconut cream, sugar and tamarind puree with the paste in a bowl to form the sauce.

Heat the oil on medium heat in a saucepan or wok and cook the sauce for 5 minutes or until thick and aromatic.

Spread the sauce on the chicken. Char grill each side for 15–20 minutes under a moderately hot grill, so that some parts of the chicken are darkly coloured. Baste with any remaining sauce to keep the chicken moist.

Place on a serving dish and garnish with the mint. Carve at the table and serve with rice and Achar (recipe, page 132).

Chicken in Mild Curry Sauce
(Chicken Kurma)

Kurma is an elaborate dish, rich with yoghurt, cream and dry, blended almonds. It is very showy and is cooked by Malay families for weddings and other celebrations.

Ingredients:

2 tablespoons poppy seeds
2 tablespoons milk
8 almonds or 8 candlenuts
3 cloves garlic
2 cm (3/4 in) length ginger, chopped
4 cloves
4 cardamom pods, seeded
1/2 cup (125 g / 4 oz) yoghurt or fromage blanc
1 tablespoon oil
1 Spanish (red) onion, chopped
2 tablespoons coriander (cilantro) seeds, dry roasted
1 teaspoon cumin seeds, dry roasted
1 teaspoon fennel seeds
750 grams (1 1/2 lb) chicken thigh fillets, cubed
1 sprig curry leaves, stems removed
juice from 1 lime
salt, to taste

Method:

Soak the poppy seeds in the milk until they swell, approximately 15 minutes.

Purée the poppy seeds (with any milk that hasn't been soaked up), almonds, garlic, ginger, cloves and cardamom seeds in a food processor or mortar and pestle.

Beat the yoghurt well to prevent it breaking up.

Heat the oil in a wok until it is hot but not smoking and sauté the onion and purée until aromatic. Add the coriander, cumin and fennel and cook on medium heat for approximately 2 minutes.

Add the chicken to the pan and brown well on all sides to seal.

Add the curry leaves, yoghurt and lime juice, and stir well. Reduce the heat, cover and simmer for 40 minutes or until tender and the gravy has reduced and is quite thick.

Season and serve hot with buriyani rice (see page 50).

Chicken in Tamarind Curry

Tamarind, a fruit native to India, has distinctive feathery leaves and crescent-shaped green pods. As the pods ripen, they turn brittle and brown and fill up with a toffee-coloured flesh that tastes like sugared lime juice. Though the green pods are used to sour curries and soups in some other countries, the ripe fruit is used in Malaysia because of the mallic acid, which imparts a fascinating flavour when in combination with chilli and coconut. Never use aluminium when cooking with tamarind.

Ingredients:

500 grams (1 lb) chicken thigh fillets
2 stalks lemon grass, chopped
1 tablespoon shrimp paste, dry roasted (see page 172)
2 tablespoons oil
1 large onion, finely chopped
4 red chillies, seeded and chopped or 1 tablespoon sambal oelek
2 tablespoons pureed ginger
(using a 4 cm x 2 cm / $1^1/_2$ x $^3/_4$ in piece of ginger)
$^1/_3$ cup (80 mL / $2^1/_2$ fl oz) tamarind purée from 3 tablespoons tamarind paste
2 cups (500 mL / 16 fl oz) water
2 kaffir lime leaves, finely shredded
sugar, to taste
salt, to taste
orange slices

Method:

Slice the chicken fillets into 5 centimetre (2 in) pieces.

Blend the lemon grass and shrimp paste together in a blender or mortar and pestle.

Heat the oil on medium–high in a wok. Sauté the onion, lemon grass and shrimp paste purée, chillies and ginger until aromatic and the onion caramelises.

Add the tamarind purée and cook until aromatic.

Add the chicken pieces and cook on medium heat until golden brown.

Add the water, bring to the boil, reduce the heat and simmer for 5 minutes or until thickened.

Add the lime leaves, and sugar and salt to taste.

Place on a serving dish and garnish with orange slices. Serve with hot Ghee Rice (Nasi Minyak) (recipe, page 32) or Saffron Rice (recipe, page 32).

'Easy Enough for Andrew' Chicken

This Kuala Lumpur barbecued chicken is an alternative recipe for barbecued or baked chicken. Andrew is a friend who aspires to being a chef. He easily mastered this quick and simple recipe.

Ingredients:

1 kg (2 lb) chicken wings
1 cup (125 g / 4 oz) rice flour
2 tablespoons sweet chilli sauce
2 tablespoons plum sauce
2 tablespoons thick soy sauce (kecap manis)
2 tablespoons honey
2 tablespoons lime juice
$^1/_2$ teaspoon salt

Method:

Cut the chicken wings into two pieces, discarding the tips.

Combine the remaining ingredients in a bowl, and dip the chicken wings in. Roll the wings in the rice flour to coat. Bake at 170°C (340°F) for 30 minutes, or cook on a barbecue until tender.

Chicken in Tamarind
(Ayam Sioh)

This is a typical Nonya dish that shows how food preparation was taken to extremes, with many stages being followed before food was served at the table.

Ingredients:

500 grams (1 lb) chicken thigh fillets

4 tablespoons tamarind puree

1 large Spanish (red) onion, finely chopped

3 cloves garlic, crushed

2 teaspoons black pepper

1 tablespoon coriander (cilantro)

pinch 5 spice powder

$\frac{1}{4}$ cup (60 g / 2 oz) sugar

2 tablespoons soy sauce

2 tablespoons black Chinese vinegar

1 tablespoon cornflour (cornstarch)

$\frac{1}{2}$ cup (125 mL / 4 fl oz) oil

mint leaves

Method:

Cut the chicken thighs into large pieces. Prick all over with a fork so that the marinade can penetrate.

Mix all of the remaining ingredients except the oil and the mint in a bowl. Place the chicken into the bowl, ensuring it is completely immersed, and stand overnight or for at least 4 hours.

Remove the chicken from the marinade. Place the marinade in a saucepan, bring to the boil then reduce the heat and simmer for 10 minutes, covered.

Add the chicken and cook at medium heat for approximately 12 minutes or until it is only just cooked. Be careful not to overcook it.

Remove the chicken with a pair of tongs and drain on absorbent paper.

Continue cooking the remaining liquid at low heat until it reduces by half into a thick sauce. Toss through the mint leaves.

Heat the oil until it is very hot but not smoking in a heavy-based saucepan or wok and shallow fry the chicken a few pieces at a time until golden. Remove from the pan and drain.

Arrange the chicken pieces on a serving dish and drizzle with the sauce. Garnish with mint leaves.

Back: Chilli Chicken Wings (recipe, page 70); Front: Chicken in Tamarind (Ayam Sioh) (recipe, this page)

Chilli Chicken Wings

This dish, developed by my daughter Anu when she was ten, started with a simple barbecue/soy chicken. Left loose with a few sauce bottles and a hungry grandmother to feed, Anu quickly made this a staple.

Ingredients:

1 kg (2 lb) chicken wings
2 tablespoons sweet chilli sauce
2 tablespoons plum sauce
2 tablespoons thick soy sauce (kecap manis)
2 tablespoons honey
2 tablespoons lemon juice
1 cup glutinous rice flour
1 teaspooon salt
$\frac{1}{2}$ teaspoon pepper
$\frac{1}{4}$ teaspoon chilli powder
banana leaves (optional)
1 tablespoon sweet chilli sauce, extra
2 tablespoons plum sauce, extra

Method:

Cut the chicken wings into two pieces, discarding the tips. 'French' the chicken wings, that is, cut the muscle and push the flesh down the bones so that they look like miniature thigh bones.

Combine the sweet chilli sauce, plum sauce, soy sauce, honey and lemon juice in a bowl. Place the wings in the bowl and marinate overnight.

Combine the rice flour with the salt, pepper and chilli powder. Roll the wings in the flour, then place on the banana leaves on a baking dish. Bake for 30 minutes at 180°C (360°F).

Serve with the combined sweet chilli and plum sauces.

Pictured on page 68.

Kedah Curry

This curry comes from the north-west, an area where the Siamese ruled powerfully for much of its early turbulent history. In the days when there were no boundaries, food styles as well as cultural traits flowed naturally from one area to another.

Ingredients:

400 grams (13 oz) chicken with bone
1 teaspoon peppercorns, roughly pounded
2 tablespoons coriander (cilantro) seeds
2 cm square ($\frac{3}{4}$ in) length shrimp paste
2 stalks lemon grass, chopped
3 cm (1 in) piece galangal, chopped
1 cup red Asian onions, chopped
8—10 dried chillies, chopped or 2 tablespoons sambal oelek
8 cloves garlic
$1\frac{1}{2}$ cups (375 mL / 12 fl oz) coconut milk
5 kaffir lime leaves
1 teaspoon salt, or to taste
lime leaves

Method:

Cut the chicken into 4 cm (1½ in) square pieces.

Dry roast the peppercorns, coriander (cilantro) seeds and shrimp paste on medium–high heat for 2 minutes.

Purée the lemon grass, galangal, onions, chillies and garlic in a food processor or mortar and pestle.

Heat ½ cup (125 mL / 4 fl oz) of the coconut milk on medium heat in a wok, then add the peppercorns, coriander (cilantro) seeds, shrimp paste and purée and fry, stirring constantly, until aromatic.

Add the meat and cook on medium heat for 5 minutes, stirring constantly.

Add the remaining coconut milk, lime leaves and salt and simmer, covered, for 30 minutes or until the chicken is very tender.

Garnish with finely julienned lime leaves and serve with plain boiled rice.

Amah's Chicken Curry

My Cantonese Amah, who was nanny and second mother to me, was also housekeeper, manager of finances and a natural cook. (Mother had a busy career and wasn't interested in food anyway.) Amah had an uncanny ability to taste something and be able to reproduce it exactly. This curry was the result of a visit to an aunt who refused to teach her how to make my father's favourite chicken curry.

Ingredients:

650 grams chicken thigh fillets or on the bone
3 medium Spanish (red) onions
2 tablespoons vegetable oil or ghee
2 cloves garlic, crushed or chopped
2 cm ($^3/_4$ in) length ginger, shredded
4 curry leaf stems, chopped
2 cups (500 mL / 16 fl oz) coconut milk
1 teaspoon chilli powder
$1^1/_2$ tablespoons sambal oelek
1 teaspoon salt
$^1/_2$ cup (125 mL / 4 fl oz) coconut cream
$^1/_2$ teaspoon sugar
1 tablespoon ghee
4 onions, sliced into rings
juice of 1 lime

Amah's Malaysian curry powder:

1 tablespoon coriander (cilantro) powder (dry roasted)
$^3/_4$ tablespoon cumin seed (dry roasted and pounded)
$^3/_4$ tablespoon fennel seed (dry roasted and pounded)
ground cinnamon, nutmeg and cloves, to taste

Method:

Cut the chicken into 5 cm (2 in) pieces.

Finely chop two of the Spanish (red) onions, and slice the remaining one thinly.

Combine the curry powder ingredients, to make 3 tablespoons.

Heat the oil until it is hot but not smoking in a wok and sauté the garlic, Spanish (red) onions and ginger until browned. Add the curry leaf stems and fry until golden.

Add the chicken pieces and seal on all sides on medium high heat. Pour over $1^1/_2$ cups of the coconut milk, cover and simmer until tender, approximately 10–12 minutes.

Combine the remaining coconut milk with the curry powder, chilli powder, sambal oelek and salt. Add to the wok and cook on low heat, uncovered, until the sauce thickens, approximately 4–5 minutes.

Add the coconut cream and sugar to the wok.

Heat the ghee in a small pan on medium heat and fry the onion rings until golden. Toss through the curry mixture with the lime juice and salt to taste.

Twenty Chilli Curry

My mother-in-law brought this brilliant recipe from Jaffna (Sri Lanka) when she came to Malaysia as a bride. I once asked her if it had to have 20 chillies in it, and she was quite adamant — the flavour would be ruined if the amount varied. However, I have found it is possible to vary the amount with equally good results. Smoking the dried chillies beforehand adds an interesting flavour to the dish.

Ingredients:

20 medium dried chillies
750 grams ($1^1/_2$ lb) chicken thigh fillets
1 tablespoon fennel seeds, dry roasted
2 tablespoons oil
$^1/_4$ teaspoon fennel seeds, dry roasted, extra
6 cloves garlic, thinly sliced
2 cm ($^3/_4$ in) length ginger, thinly sliced
1 star anise
2 Spanish (red) onions, finely chopped
$1^1/_2$ cups (325 mL / 12 fl oz) very thin coconut milk
1 cup (250 mL / 8 fl oz) thick coconut cream
1 Spanish (red) onion, extra, cut into thin rings
salt, to taste
curry leaves, to taste
juice of one lime

Method:

Cover the chillies with water and soak for 20 minutes to soften.

Cut the chicken fillets into serving size pieces.

Grind or pound the chillies and fennel seeds to a fine paste. Use this mixture to coat the chicken pieces well.

Heat the oil on medium–high in a wok and saute the extra fennel seeds, garlic, ginger, star anise and onions until aromatic and the onions are caramelised.

Add the coated chicken to the wok and stir-fry on medium–high heat, browning the chicken all over. Add the coconut milk and cook on medium heat, stirring often, for 4–5 minutes.

Add the coconut cream, onion rings, salt and curry leaves. Simmer on a low heat until the liquid has almost disappeared, approximately 5–8 minutes. Turn off the heat and mix in the lime juice. Remove from the heat and serve.

This is a dry curry. Peeled potatoes quartered or cut into tiny chunks can be added with the coconut milk. If you intend to add more than two potatoes, add another 3 dried chillies to the paste.

Pictured on page 20.

M a k a n - l a h !

Nonya Aromatic Lime Chicken
(Ayam Masam)

It is unusual to use shrimp paste on chicken but in this case the shrimp paste is combined with lime to produce a perfumed and exotic dish.

Ingredients:

600 grams (1 lb 5 oz) chicken thigh fillets

8 red Asian onions or 2 Spanish (red) onions, roughly chopped

3 cloves garlic

2 stalks lemon grass, roughly chopped

2 tablespoons (more if preferred) sambal oelek

1 cm ($\frac{1}{2}$ in) piece fresh turmeric or 1 teaspoon turmeric powder

2 tablespoons oil

2 teaspoons shrimp paste, dry roasted (optional) (see page 271)

3 kaffir lime leaves, shredded

1$\frac{1}{2}$ cups (375 mL / 12 fl oz) coconut milk

4 pieces assam glugor or 4 pieces of tamarind fruit

1 cup (250 mL / 8 fl oz) coconut cream

spring onions (scallions), lime leaves or lime zest

Method:

Trim any fat from the chicken fillets and cut into 6 cm (2½ in) pieces.

Blend the onions, garlic, lemon grass, sambal oelek and turmeric together in a food processor or mortar and pestle to form a paste.

Heat the oil on medium heat in a wok and sauté the blended paste and the shrimp paste until aromatic.

Add the chicken and kaffir lime leaves and stir-fry until the chicken has browned.

Add the coconut milk and the assam glugor pieces, reduce the heat and simmer for 10 minutes or until the chicken is cooked.

Add the coconut cream and cook until the liquid has reduced and is thick and aromatic.

Pour onto a serving dish and garnish with spring onions (scallions), lime leaves or lime zest.

Nonya Aromatic Lime Chicken
(Ayam Masam)

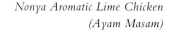

Indonesian-style Chicken with Wet Gravy
(Gulai Surabaya)

In this dish recipes and styles of cooking merge as many Malaysians have Indonesian origins, and many of the cooks in Malaysian homes are Indonesians.

Ingredients:

2 cups (500 mL / 16 fl oz) coconut milk

1 kg (2 lb) chicken wings with bone

10 dried chillies, roughly chopped

15 blanched almonds

¼ cup (60 g / 2 oz) poppy seeds

3 cloves garlic

3 cm (1 in) length galangal, roughly chopped

4 stalks lemon grass, roughly chopped

8 red Asian onions, roughly chopped

2 tablespoons oil

3 tablespoons Malaysian curry powder (see page 172)

½ cup (45 g / 1½ oz) grated fresh or desiccated coconut

3 small cassia or cinnamon sticks

5 ripe tomatoes, diced

1 cup (250 mL / 8 fl oz) coconut cream

Method:

Heat the coconut milk on medium heat in a saucepan then add the chicken and simmer, covered, for 30 minutes or until tender.

Blend the chillies, almonds, poppy seeds, garlic, galangal, lemon grass and onions together in a food processor or mortar and pestle.

Heat the oil on medium heat in a wok or saucepan and fry the blended spices and Malaysian curry powder until aromatic. Add the chicken and coconut milk mixture and simmer until the chicken is tender and the oil has begun to separate from the mixture, approximately 15 minutes.

Add the coconut, cinnamon sticks, tomatoes and coconut cream and simmer for 5 minutes. Remove the cinnamon sticks before serving.

Double-fried 'Enche Kabin' Chicken

A friend of Mother's, the wife of an American Methodist minister, had a brilliant Nonya cook. They lived alongside a row of paddy fields in Melaka, and when the fields flooded her cook used to produce the best Enche Kabin she had ever tasted . . . until she found out that the cook was using frogs' legs caught from the adjacent fields! It is interesting to note that Malaysians call frogs' legs 'padi chicken', 'padi' being Malay for rice paddy.

Ingredients:

3 tablespoons soy sauce

1 tablespoon sambal oelek

2 teaspoons thick soy sauce (kecap manis)

2 star anise, pounded

2 teaspoons salt

1 tablespoon sugar

¼ teaspoon pepper

1 cup (60 g / 2 oz) coriander leaves, chopped

½ bunch spring onions (scallions), cut into 3 cm (1 in) pieces

3 cm (1 in) length ginger, shredded

1 tablespoon Shao Hsing wine

1 cup (250 mL / 8 fl oz) Worcestershire sauce

1 tablespoon sweet red plum sauce (teemcheong)

1 teaspoon sugar

juice of one lime

1 kg (2 lb) chicken

2 cups (500 mL / 16 fl oz) oil

Method:

Combine all of the ingredients except the chicken and the oil together in a bowl.

Cut the chicken into 6 or 8 manageable pieces. Prick them all over with a fork then place in the bowl with the sauce. Marinate in the sauce in the refrigerator for at least 2 hours or overnight.

Remove the chicken from the sauce; reserve.

Heat the oil in a cast-iron wok until it is hot but not smoking. Deep-fry the chicken pieces until golden brown.

Drain the chicken on absorbent paper and cool, then place in the reserved sauce for another 30 minutes. Remove the chicken.

Reheat the oil until it almost hazes and deep-fry the chicken again in small batches. Drain on absorbent paper and serve warm with the reserved warm marinade.

Chicken Country Capitan

There are many stories connected with the name 'country capitan'. I've heard that the term 'capitan' is a pidginised version of the word 'capon' (fowl).

Ingredients:

$^1/_4$ teaspoon turmeric powder

2 medium potatoes, cubed

$^3/_4$ cup (180 mL / 6 fl oz) oil

7 candlenuts

2 star anise

5 fresh red chillies, seeded and chopped

4 cloves garlic

1 cm ($^1/_2$ in) length fresh turmeric, chopped or 1 teaspoon turmeric powder, extra

1 stalk lemon grass, chopped

500 kg (1 lb) chicken thigh pieces with the bone

2 tablespoons dried prawns (shrimp), dry roasted (optional)

3 large Spanish (red) onions, thinly sliced

2 cm ($^3/_4$ in) length cinnamon stick

$1^1/_2$ cups (375 mL / 12 fl oz) coconut milk

$^1/_4$ cup (60 mL / 2 fl oz) coconut cream

juice of 3 limes

2 tablespoons fried red Asian onions

1 tablespoon fried garlic slivers

2 tomatoes, peeled and diced

Method:

Rub the turmeric on to the potatoes. Heat the oil on medium high and fry the potatoes until crisp on the outside and tender on the inside. Reserve 3 tablespoons of the oil; discard the remainder.

Blend the candlenuts, star anise, chillies, garlic, turmeric and lemon grass together in a food processor or mortar and pestle. Brush half of this mixture on the chicken pieces and marinate for at least 2 hours.

Grind the dry-roasted prawns (shrimp) until the raw smell has vanished. This makes the sauce smell less strong while allowing the flavour to come through.

Heat the reserved oil on high and fry the Spanish (red) onions and the remaining blended spices until golden. Add the chicken and ground prawns (shrimp) and brown until aromatic.

Add the cinnamon stick and coconut milk, bring to the boil, then lower the heat and simmer, covered, until the chicken is tender, about 30 minutes. The curry can also be cooked by placing it in a covered casserole dish in a moderate oven (180°C / 360°F) for 1 hour.

Add the coconut cream and simmer, uncovered, allowing the liquid to reduce by half. Just before serving add the potatoes and lime juice, stirring carefully. Serve garnished with fried onions, garlic and tomatoes.

Pictured on page 64.

Nonya-style Chinese Roast Chicken

This chicken dish merges in my memory with the whiff of waxed batik and onions frying in the kitchen. Mother's friend in Melaka, who wore some beautiful sarongs and the daintiest of embroidered kebaya, used to cook in all her finery and produced the best Nonya-style roast chicken I've ever tasted. The chicken is so tender and the skin so crisp that this difficult recipe is well worth the trouble.

Ingredients:

$1^1/_2$ kg (3 lb) chicken with skin

1 teaspoon black pepper

2 star anise pounded well with $^1/_2$ teaspoon salt

1 cup (220 g / $7^3/_4$ oz) malt sugar or 1 cup (250 mL / 8 fl oz) corn syrup

$^1/_4$ cup (60 mL / 2 fl oz) Shao Hsing wine

2 tablespoons dark soy sauce

juice of 2 limes

4 cups (1 litre / 32 fl oz) peanut, vegetable or red palm oil

Dipping powder:

1 tablespoon salt, dry roasted

1 tablespoon Szechwan pepper, dry roasted

Method:

Wash and dry the chicken, and brush the insides with the pepper and star anise.

Half fill a stockpot large enough to immerse the chicken with water. Place on the stove and bring the water to the boil.

Add the malt sugar and, when the sugar melts, add the wine, dark soy sauce and lime juice to the water.

Tie the chicken legs together and, holding the chicken by the legs, immerse it in the boiling water for 10 minutes.

Remove the chicken and hang it in the sun or in a drafty corridor or in front of a fan (to create a wind-tunnel effect) for at least 3 hours. Place a pan under the chicken to catch any of the malt sugar mixture that drops, and use this and any remaining mixture to baste the chicken as it dries up. With this treatment some of the sweetness will be absorbed into the meat; it will also crisp the skin.

Heat the oil until it is very hot in a large wok. Suspend the chicken over the wok with a ladle, and spoon the hot oil over the chicken so that it slowly fries. After doing this a few times, immerse the whole chicken in the wok and cook on medium high, turning a few times, until it is golden brown in colour.

When cooked, remove the chicken and slice it into pieces with the bone and parts of the crispy skin attached. Serve warm with the dipping powder.

Dipping powder:

Grind the dry-roasted salt and pepper together.

Makan-lah!

Malaysian-style Roast Turkey
(Turkey Panggang)

The idea of cooking a naked turkey is abhorrent to the Asian cook,
who will dress anything with chilli, onions, garlic and ginger.
I tandooried and pangganged turkey, chicken or duck through desperation —
you would too if you had a fussy family to feed at Christmas.

Ingredients:

1 butterball turkey, approximately
4 kg (8 lb) in weight

1 teaspoon salt

1 teaspoon turmeric powder

2 teaspoons five spice powder

Ghee Rice (Nasi Minyak) for stuffing
(see Saffron Rice (Nasi Kunyit)
recipe on page 32)

Turkey Paste:

3 Spanish (red) onions, chopped

7 cloves garlic

4 cm (1½ in) length ginger

2 tablespoons sambal oelek

3 stalks lemon grass, chopped

1 cup (200 g / 6 oz) thick, Greek-style
yoghurt

3 tablespoons tomato paste

2 tablespoons almond meal

1 turmeric leaf, finely shredded

2 tablespoons cornflour (cornstarch)

Method:

Wash the turkey inside and out with the salt and turmeric. Wipe dry with kitchen paper.

Rub the five spice powder inside the turkey. Stuff with Ghee Rice.

Sew the flaps up for roasting or secure with satay skewers. Place on a baking tray.

Preheat the oven to 170°C (340°F).

Puree all of the paste ingredients except the cornflour (cornstarch) in a food processor or mortar and pestle. Gradually add the cornflour (cornstarch) until it forms a firm paste.

Brush the mixture on to the turkey, placing some on the underside if there is sufficient.

Cook the turkey for 3½ hours if it is 4 kg (8 lb) in weight, or for 4½ hours at 160°C (320°F) if it weighs 5–6 kg (10–12 lb). Baste continually throughout the cooking time with the liquid. Test to see if the turkey is cooked by inserting a metal skewer into one end of a leg—if the liquid runs out clear the turkey is ready.

Collect any basting mixture that has fallen into the baking tray and pat back on to the turkey. Cook under a medium grill for about 3 minutes. If you place a piece of bacon on the breast it will prevent the meat from overcooking.

Carve and serve with some of the stuffing. This dish is good with Nasi Kunyit and Achar, or with any vegetable pickle.

Malaysian-style Roast Turkey

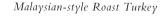

Hainanese Chicken Rice

This is an entire meal in itself — the rice is cooked in chicken fat then boiled in chicken stock, while the soup made from the stock is served with chicken pieces and chilli sauce. Although the preparation is lengthy, the result is worth the effort. This subtle and aromatic dish is my favourite way of preparing rice and, when served with all the condiments and peripherals, can make a memorable meal.

Ingredients:

2 cups (300 g / 10½ oz) long-grained rice

1½ kg (3 lb) chicken with skin

2 teaspoons sesame oil

2 star anise

3 cm (1 in) length ginger, chopped

6 cloves garlic

5 cups (1.25 litres / 40 fl oz) chicken stock

3 stalks spring onions (scallions), chopped

salt and pepper, to taste

2 teaspoons salted turnip (tung chye) or pickled radish (tangchai)

1 teaspoon sesame oil, extra

1 tablespoon dark soy sauce

salt, extra, to taste

2 tablespoons salted turnip (tung chye), extra or 2 tablespoons sliced tomatoes

1 cucumber, halved lengthwise and seeds removed

spring onions (scallions)

Sauce:

½ cup (125 mL / 4 fl oz) chilli garlic sauce or ¼ cup sambal oelek

2 tablespoons vinegar

2 cloves garlic

2 cm (¾ in) length ginger

Method:

Wash the rice in water until the water runs clear. Spread the rice on a tea towel (dish towel) in the sun and leave to dry.

Clean the chicken by removing the fat from under the skin and around the back. (You need about 50 grams / 2 oz of chicken fat.) Dice the fat and render (melt) in a wok on high heat until the oil is released.

Drain the fat into the dry rice. Heat the sesame oil on medium–high in a wok and fry the rice and fat until aromatic, about 4 minutes.

Blend the star anise, ginger and garlic together in a food processor or mortar and pestle. Rub the chicken inside and out with this mixture.

Place the chicken stock in a large saucepan and bring to the boil. Add the chicken to the saucepan with the spring onions (scallions), salt and pepper and salted turnip. Reduce the heat and simmer until the chicken is just cooked but not overcooked, approximately 3–4 minutes. The chicken meat should run red if pierced with a metal skewer. If preferred, the chicken can be coated with 2–3 tablespoons of soy sauce and lightly grilled on medium heat for 15 minutes until the skin turns dark and aromatic.

Remove the chicken from the stock. Skim off some of the 'scum' that will have formed on the stock — this is used for the sauce, to give a chicken aroma. Reserve the stock for soup and for cooking the rice.

Rub the extra sesame oil and dark soy sauce over the chicken and cool on a rack. Cut the warm chicken into serving-sized pieces just prior to serving.

Rice:

Cook the rice in a saucepan or rice cooker with 3 cups of the stock and salt to taste. The liquid should be about 3.5 centimetres (1¼ in) above the rice. Cook until the rice has absorbed all of the water, approximately 20 minutes. Turn off the heat and fork through any remaining sesame oil. Cover and keep the rice hot.

Soup:

Reboil the remaining stock with the extra salted turnip. Serve in small bowls with the rice.

Sauce:

Mix the chilli garlic sauce with the vinegar. Pound the garlic and ginger together. Gradually add to the soup scum. Place in bowls to be served on the side.

To serve:

Serve the pieces of chicken on the rice with the bowls of sauce and soup. Garnish with sliced cucumber and shredded spring onions (scallions).

Pictured on page 64.

Curry Devil
(Chicken Diavolo)

This recipe comes from the Portuguese Settlement where dark, Malay-looking Portuguese men fish the waters of the Straits. They live in a time warp — even the Christo (old style Portuguese) they speak dates to the time of the spice traders.

Ingredients:

10 red chillies, seeded
2 cm (³/₄ in) length shrimp paste (belacan), dry roasted
2 tablespoons sambal oelek (optional)
2 medium Spanish (red) onions, chopped
3 cm (1 in) length ginger, chopped
10 cloves garlic
3 stalks lemon grass, chopped
2 cm (³/₄ in) length galangal
10 candlenuts
1 kg (2 lb) chicken thigh fillets
1 cup (250 mL / 8 fl oz) vegetable oil
1 Spanish (red) onion, extra
¹/₂ tablespooon mustard seeds
3 cups (750 mL / 24 fl oz) chicken stock
3 medium potatoes, peeled and quartered
2 tablespoons tomato puree
3 ripe tomatoes, skinned and chopped
salt, to taste
¹/₄ cup (60 mL / 2 fl oz) wine vinegar or Chinese red vinegar
¹/₂ tablespoon palm sugar
coriander (cilantro), chopped

Method:

Blend the chillies, sambal oelek, onions, ginger, garlic, lemon grass, galangal and candlenuts together in a food processor or mortar and pestle. Brush some of this mixture on the chicken. Heat half of the oil on high heat in a wok or frying pan. Fry the chicken a few pieces at a time until golden brown. Drain on kitchen paper.

Halve the extra Spanish (red) onion and slice thinly. Heat the remaining oil in a wok on medium high and sauté the rest of the blended ingredients with the onion and mustard seeds until aromatic and the onion caramelises, approximately 5 minutes. Raise the temperature to high and cook until the mustard seeds pop, approximately 1 minute.

Add the chicken to the wok with just enough stock to cover the chicken. Add the potatoes, tomato purée, tomatoes and salt and simmer on medium heat until the chicken is cooked, about 20–40 minutes. Add the vinegar and sugar.

Serve garnished with coriander (cilantro) and with rice or bread. It improves with time, and can be made a day ahead.

Szechwan Pepper Duck

This is a good dinner-party dish as long as you remember that duck takes a bit longer to cook than chicken. The orange sauce is a combination of west and east, although the spice can be cut down to suit preferences.

Ingredients:

6 duck breast fillets
1 teaspoon dry roasted Szechwan pepper, pounded roughly
¹/₂ cup (60 g / 2 oz) plain (all purpose) flour
1 teaspoon turmeric powder
1 teaspoon salt
oil
1 red chilli, seeded and chopped
salt, to taste

Orange Sauce:

3 large oranges
1 Spanish (red) onion, roughly chopped
3 cloves garlic
2 cm (³/₄ in) length galangal, chopped
3 cm (1 in) length ginger, chopped
1 teaspoon turmeric powder
1 teaspoon coriander (cilantro) powder
1 tablespoon brown sugar
1 tablespoon sambal oelek
1 stalk lemon grass, roughly pounded
¹/₂ cup (125 mL / 4 fl oz) coconut milk

Method:

Pat the duck breast fillets dry with a paper towel. Coat in the combined pepper, flour, turmeric powder and salt.

Place under a grill and cook on medium heat for 4 minutes or until tender, turning the fillets regularly. The fillets can also be fried in ½ cup (125 mL / 4 fl oz) of oil until golden brown. Place on a serving dish and keep warm.

Orange Sauce:

The sauce can be made one day ahead and gently reheated.

Remove the zest from the oranges and reserve. Juice the oranges — you need 1 cup (250 mL / 8 fl oz) of juice.

Purée the onion, garlic, galangal and ginger together in a food processor or mortar and pestle.

Heat the oil on medium high in a wok and sauté the purée until golden and aromatic. Add the turmeric powder, coriander (cilantro) powder and brown sugar and sauté for 2 minutes.

Add the sambal oelek, lemon grass, coconut milk and orange juice. Bring to the boil, then reduce the heat and simmer, uncovered, for 20 minutes.

To serve, pour the sauce over the duck breasts. Garnish with the chopped orange zest and chilli and season with salt.

Pictured on page 64.

Makan-lah!

Seafood

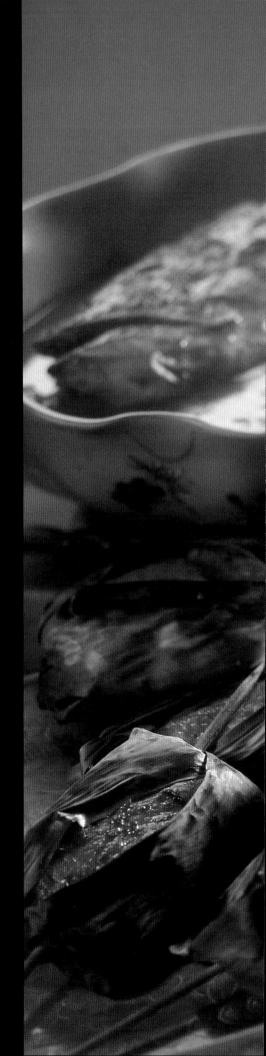

*Clockwise from left: Fish Head Curry (recipe, page 83),
Asparagus Prawn Rolls (recipe, page 91) and Prawns in Banana Leaves
(Pais Udang) (recipe, page 91)*

Fish in Hot Gravy
(Kuah Ladah)

This is a classic Nonya dish that always makes its appearance at lunch or dinner somewhere. The gravy is tart and tasty, especially when eaten with a mountain of rice and a sambal belacan.

Ingredients:

1 red chillies, seeded and finely diced
2 cloves garlic, chopped
4 small Spanish (red) onions, chopped
2 stalks lemon grass, chopped
2 cm ($^3/_4$ in) length galangal, chopped
2 cm ($^3/_4$ in) length turmeric, chopped
2 teaspoons shrimp paste, dry roasted
20 white peppercorns, roughly pounded
4 tablespoons oil
$^1/_4$ cup (30 g / 1 oz) diced eggplant (aubergine)
$^1/_2$ cup tamarind purée from 3 tablespoons tamarind
$4^3/_4$ cups (1.2 litres / 38 fl oz) water or fish stock
2 teaspoons sugar
1 teaspoon salt
500 grams (1 lb) ling or gemfish, cut into serving sized pieces

Method:

Blend the chillies, garlic, onions, lemon grass, galangal, turmeric, shrimp paste and peppercorns together in a food processor or mortar and pestle until well ground. Heat the oil on medium high in a wok and fry the ground ingredients until aromatic.

Add the eggplant (aubergine) and fry until soft. Pour in the tamarind purée, stock, sugar and salt. Reduce the heat and simmer, uncovered, until the gravy reduces, about 10 minutes.

Add the fish and simmer until just cooked and the fish looks opaque. This is a wet and watery sour curry best served with rice.

Fish Moolie

I remember talking to someone about a moolie and getting completely bewildered looks all round. I only learnt later that we were talking about two different things: a mouli is a food grinder, while what I meant was a mild curry dish.

Ingredients:

500 grams (1 lb) blue-eyed cod or snapper cutlets
$^1/_2$ teaspoon turmeric
$^1/_2$ teaspoon salt
2 tablespoons plain (all purpose) or besan flour
2 stalks lemon grass, chopped
2 cm ($^3/_4$ in) length galangal, chopped
3 cm (1 in) length ginger, chopped
1 cup (250 mL / 8 fl oz) vegetable oil
2 Spanish (red) onions, thinly sliced
3 cm (1 in) length fresh ginger, pounded or shredded, extra
1 tablespoon sambal oelek
2 cups (500 mL / 16 fl oz) coconut milk
1 tablespoon vinegar
1 tablespoon tamarind juice
1 tablespoon sugar
5 cloves garlic, cut into slivers and fried until golden
watercress leaves, stems removed

Method:

Cut the fish into 6 cm (2½ in) pieces. (If preferred, you can substitute chicken thigh fillets for the fish in this recipe — cut the fillets into similar-sized pieces as the fish.) Brush the combined turmeric and salt on the fish. Dust with the flour. Blend the lemon grass, galangal and ginger together in a food processor or mortar and pestle.

Heat the oil on high in a wok and fry the fish in batches until partly cooked (2 minutes for each batch). Remove the fish and drain on absorbent paper.

Pour off all but 2 tablespoons of the oil. Reheat the oil on high heat and fry the onions and extra ginger until golden. Add the blended ingredients and the sambal oelek and stir to mix well. Cook until aromatic.

Add the coconut milk, stirring it in well, and cook on medium heat. Simmer the mixture, uncovered, until it thickens, approximately 8 minutes. Add the vinegar, tamarind juice and sugar and simmer, uncovered, for a further 5 minutes.

Add the fish and stir gently until heated through. Serve garnished with the fried garlic slivers and watercress.

Chetty Fish Curry

This dish is Indian in origin, being developed by chetty moneylenders who do not eat other types of meat. It is a strong-tasting curry that needs the bold flavours of a fleshy fish to match its strength.

Ingredients:

1 tablespoon poppy seeds

2 tablespoons warm milk

600 grams (21 oz) fish steaks (trevally, snapper or red emperor)

1 tablespoon fennel seeds, dry roasted

3 Spanish (red) onions, chopped

5 cm (2 in) length ginger, ground or puréed

7 cloves garlic, puréed

grated flesh of ½ coconut or 1 cup (90 g / 3 oz) desiccated coconut

2 large ripe tomatoes, quartered

½ cup (125 mL / 4 fl oz) vegetable oil

1 tablespoon chilli powder or 2 tablespoons sambal oelek

1 tablespoon coriander (cilantro) seeds, dry roasted and ground

¼ cup (60 mL / 2 fl oz) boiling water

salt or lime juice, to taste

curry or lime leaves, stems removed

Method:

Soak the poppy seeds in the milk for 1 hour.

Dry roast the coconut until golden brown. This can be done by either stirring the coconut in a dry frypan on a low heat, or by cooking in a microwave oven for 3–4 minutes.

Purée the onions, then squeeze the juice from them. Reserve both the flesh and the juice.

Heat the oil on high heat in a wok until it hazes, then reduce the heat to medium and sauté the dry onion mixture, ginger and garlic, stirring well until the mixture caramelises, about 7 minutes.

Add the tomatoes, fennel seeds, chilli and coriander (cilantro) seeds. Stir until aromatic. Add the coconut and stir-fry until fragrant and the oil begins to separate from the spices, approximately 6–7 minutes.

Add the onion juice, poppy seeds (plus any milk that remains) and boiling water, bring to the boil then reduce the heat and simmer, uncovered, until the liquid reduces by two-thirds.

Add the fish pieces to the simmering mixture. Bring the mixture to a gentle boil then reduce the heat and simmer until the fish is cooked, no more than 5 minutes. Season with salt or lime juice. Place on a serving dish and garnish with curry or lime leaves.

Fish Head Curry

Fish heads are a delicacy in Malaysia as the flesh near the eyes and cheeks is particularly tasty. I've heard a story that kidnappers used to feed fish to a victim to determine if he was a millionaire, for only millionaires could afford to eat the head. If the victim ate the tail he was set free. This is a Nonya dish.

Ingredients:

1 large fish head (preferably snapper)

2 stalks lemon grass, chopped

2 cm (¾ in) length fresh turmeric, chopped or 2 teaspoons turmeric powder

2 cm (¾ in) length galangal, chopped

2 tablespoons oil

15 small red Asian onions or 2 Spanish (red) onions, thinly sliced

2 cloves garlic, finely chopped

2 tablespoons sambal oelek

2 cm (¾ in) length shrimp paste, dry roasted (optional) and crumbled

1 tablespoon tamarind purée (made from 3 cm / 1 in length tamarind and 3 pieces assam glugor or sour fruit, pounded together)

2 cups (500 mL / 16 fl oz) water

½ cup (50 g / 2 oz) Vietnamese mint leaves

salt, to taste

pepper, to taste

Method:

Cut the fish head in half and scale and clean thoroughly, especially around the cheeks and the eyes. Remove the gills and wash off any blood.

Blend the lemon grass, turmeric and galangal together in a food processor or mortar and pestle.

Heat the oil on high heat in a wok or earthenware pot. Add the onion and garlic and cook until golden. Add the lemon grass mixture and cook on a low heat until it caramelises, about 10 minutes.

Add the sambal oelek — use less than the stated amount if you don't want the dish to be 'hot'. Add the shrimp paste and cook for 1 minute. Add the tamarind purée, water, half of the Vietnamese mint, salt and pepper. Simmer on low heat for 3 minutes, or until the flavours mature. The curry needs to develop a flavour to your liking before the fish is placed in the pot, as the fish will cook very quickly.

Add the fish, raise the heat and bring the curry to the boil, then lower the heat and simmer for 3–5 minutes. Remove from the heat just as the curry begins to smell aromatic. Serve hot with rice and green vegetables, garnished with the remaining Vietnamese mint.

Pictured on page 80.

Makan-lah!

Grilled Fish
(Ikan Panggang)

Malaysia is a long, thin peninsula. The result? People live in close proximity to the water and fish is consumed more than any other meat. This recipe is a good way to cook fish, for I find that grilling, baking or frying leaves large sections of the skin on the grill or wok and dries the fish too early in the cooking process. Remember to soak the bamboo splints first.

Ingredients:

750 grams (1½ lb) whiting, snapper, bream or chub mackerel (ikan cencharu)

7 red chillies, seeded (optional)

3 stalks lemon grass bulbs, chopped

½ teaspoon turmeric powder or 1 cm (½ in) length fresh turmeric

2 medium Spanish (red) onions, roughly chopped

3 cm (1 in) length ginger, peeled and shredded

½ tablespoon tamarind purée

1½ cups (375 mL / 12 fl oz) thick coconut milk

10 fenugreek seeds, roughly pounded

salt, to taste

pepper, to taste

sugar, taste

½ cup desiccated coconut, dry roasted

¼ cup (60 mL / 2 fl oz) coconut cream

1 tablespoon oil

1 tablespoon water

lime wedges

Method:

Scale and gut the fish. Using a sharp knife, cut two pockets into the flesh on either side of the backbone. These are the pockets that the filling goes into.

Blend the chillies, lemon grass bulbs, turmeric powder, onions, ginger, tamarind purée, coconut milk, fenugreek seeds, salt, pepper and sugar together in a food processor or mortar and pestle. Reserve 2 tablespoons of this filling mixture and combine with the desiccated coconut.

Stuff the filling into the pockets along the backbone and into the gutted stomach area. Use skewers to secure the openings after stuffing. Brush the desiccated coconut mixture on the fish. Combine the coconut cream, oil and water in a bowl.

Make a bamboo splint by fastening two crossed pieces of bamboo or wood (that have been soaked in water to prevent them from burning) with a piece of wire at one end. The bamboo splints stop the skin from flaking off the fish.

You can also cook the fish by enclosing it in foil.

Grill or barbecue the fish over a moderate heat. Baste during the cooking process with the coconut cream mixture. The fish is ready when it is an opaque colour; this will take approximately 8 minutes. Serve with wedges of fresh lime, sambal belacan and plain boiled rice.

Grilled Fish (Ikan Panggang)

Curry with Fish or Eggs
(Venthiam Colombu)

The innocuous-looking tiny, toffee-coloured fenugreek seed, 'venthiam' (tamil), packs quite a flavour — sour verging on the edge of bitter. It is particularly good when curried in a gravy with small, sweet onions and fish. 'Columbu' refers to the consistency of the gravy.

Ingredients:

600 grams (21 oz) ling fillets or 6 hard-boiled eggs, peeled
1/2 teaspoon turmeric powder
1/2 teaspoon salt
oil, enough to half-fill saucepan
2 tablespoons oil, extra
1 tablespoon fenugreek, coarsely pounded
1 tablespoon whole mustard seeds
1 clove garlic, crushed
1 Spanish (red) onion, diced
1 teaspoon chilli powder
1/2 teaspoon cumin
1/2 teaspoon fennel
1 cup (250 mL / 8 fl oz) coconut milk
1 tablespoon tamarind purée
1 teaspoon tomato purée
curry leaves or chopped, fried onions

Method:

If using fish, coat with the combined turmeric and salt.

If using eggs, heat a small frying pan or saucepan half-filled with oil over high heat. Fry the eggs until the flesh starts to blister and is a golden colour. Remove and drain on absorbent paper.

Heat the extra 2 tablespoons of oil on high heat in a wok or saucepan. Cook the fenugreek and mustard seeds until they pop. Add the garlic and onion and cook until golden brown.

Add the chilli powder, cumin and fennel and fry for about 1 minute, until the spices are aromatic. Stir in the coconut milk and tamarind purée, then add the tomato purée.

If using fish, simmer the sauce on low heat for 5 minutes until it reduces by two-thirds. Add the fish and simmer further until the fish is opaque and flakes easily, approximately 5 minutes.

If using eggs, simmer the sauce on low heat for 8 minutes until thickened. Add the eggs and cook gently until heated through. Alternatively, the eggs can be halved and placed on a serving dish and the sauce poured over.

Serve the curry garnished with curry leaves or fried onions.

Fish Cakes in Banana Leaves
(Otak Otak)

The aroma of banana leaf blends into the fish in this recipe to create a beautiful mixture. Otak otak used to be served at street stalls as snacks; they make a very spectacular meal, especially when grilled slowly on coals.

Ingredients:

500 grams gem or ling fish fillets, minced
5 candlenuts or macadamia nuts, ground
2 stalks lemon grass, puréed
2 cm (3/4 in) length ginger, chopped
1 large green chilli, seeded and finely chopped
1 teaspoon salt
1/2 teaspoon turmeric powder
2 tablespoons sambal oelek
1 tablespoon cumin powder, dry roasted
2 tablespoons oil
1 tablespoon cornflour (cornstarch)
1 egg, beaten
3/4 cup (180 mL / 6 fl oz) coconut cream
1/2 cup (30 g / 1 oz) Vietnamese mint leaves, shredded
1 banana leaf
lime wedges

Method:

Combine all of the ingredients except the banana leaf and lime wedges and blend well to form a firm, sticky forcemeat. Cut the banana leaf into 12 x 15 cm (4½ x 6 in) rectangles.

Place 2 tablespoons of the mixture in the centre of each piece of banana leaf, fold both edges over the forcemeat and roll up. Secure with a skewer or toothpicks.

Grill or barbecue over a moderate heat for 8–10 minutes, turning the parcels halfway through the cooking time. Remove the parcels when they are an opaque colour.

Serve with cut lime wedges as an entrée or as part of a main meal.

There is a simpler method of preparing this dish — it won't taste exactly the same but it does closely replicate the flavours. Blend the minced fish with 1 cup (250 mL / 8 fl oz) of coconut cream and add half a beaten egg, 2 tablespoons of commercial curry paste such as green Thai curry paste or laksa curry paste, ½ cup (30 g / 1 oz) Vietnamese mint and some finely shredded kaffir lime leaves. Follow the directions for wrapping with the banana leaf pieces and grill as directed or place the parcels in a lightly greased dish and bake for 25 minutes at 180°C (360°F).

Cheong Liew's Prawn Sushi with Sushi Rice

My friend Cheong, one of the brilliant chefs responsible for shaping the food of Australia, often recounts his early life in Kuala Lumpur, and his stamping ground in the area around the Indian and Malay stalls near Jalan Masjid at the confluence of the two rivers. His food today reflects much of his past, his early experiences and a lively curiosity and creativity. He must have acquired his skills from both his father and from those early experiences.

Ingredients:

2 cups glutinous rice
1 teaspoon turmeric powder
1 teaspoon salt
6 large king prawns, shelled and deveined
zest $\frac{1}{2}$ lime
pinch salt, extra, to taste
pinch sugar, to taste
2 tablespoons peanut oil
2 tablespoons coconut cream
$1\frac{1}{2}$ tablespoons tamarind juice
1 tablespoon palm sugar
lime leaves, julienned

Paste:

2 cm ($\frac{3}{4}$ in) length galangal, finely grated
1 cm ($\frac{1}{2}$ in) length turmeric, finely grated
6 candlenuts, finely grated
1 red chilli, chopped
6—10 red Asian onions, chopped
3 garlic cloves, chopped
2 cm ($\frac{3}{4}$ in) length ginger, finely grated
1 teaspoon shrimp paste, dry roasted

Method:

Cover the rice with water and soak for 2 hours. Drain. Place the rice, turmeric and salt in a shallow pan and cover with water. Simmer, gently, until soft, topping up the water as necessary. Drain.

Cut the prawns in half lengthwise, sprinkle with the lime zest, salt and sugar and set aside. Blend all of the paste ingredients together in a food processor or mortar and pestle to form a smooth paste.

Heat the oil on medium high in a wok, add the paste mixture and coconut cream and stir-fry on a medium-low heat until the oil separates from the solid.

Add the prawns, tamarind juice and palm sugar and cook until the prawns change colour. Remove from the heat.

Place the prawn mixture on a bed of the sushi rice. Serve cold garnished with the lime leaves.

Prawn and Pineapple Curry
(Gulai Lemak)

The Nonya call a wet curry a 'gulai'; these are important in Malaysian cuisine as rice goes down well with a wet curry. The gravy takes on the flavour of the prawns and improves with keeping.

Ingredients:

500 grams (1 lb) prawns (shrimp)
2 tablespoons coriander (cilantro) seeds, dry roasted
1 tablespoon cumin seeds, dry roasted
8 red Asian onions or 1 large Spanish (red) onion, chopped
5 cloves garlic, chopped
2 stalks lemon grass, chopped
1 tablespoon sambal oelek
$\frac{1}{2}$ teaspoon shrimp paste, dry roasted
3 tablespoons oil
1 cm ($\frac{1}{2}$ in) fresh turmeric or 1 teaspoon turmeric powder
salt, to taste
pepper, to taste
$1\frac{1}{2}$ cups (375 mL / 12 fl oz) coconut milk
1 small, semi-ripe pineapple peeled, cored and sliced
$\frac{1}{2}$ cup (125 mL / 4 fl oz) coconut cream
mint leaves

Method:

Shell and devein the prawns, retaining the tails. Blend the coriander (cilantro) seeds, cumin, onion, garlic, lemon grass, sambal oelek and shrimp paste together in a food processor or mortar and pestle until a paste forms.

Heat the oil on medium high in a wok and saute the paste until golden and caramelised. Add the turmeric, salt and pepper to the mixture and cook until aromatic.

Add the coconut milk and, when it starts to simmer, add the prawns. Stir until they change colour, then add the pineapple and simmer, uncovered, on medium heat for 10 minutes. In this time the gulai should acquire the flavour of the pineapple.

Add the coconut cream and simmer until the sauce is quite thick, approximately 3–5 minutes. Stir and remove from the heat. Serve on a bed of rice, garnished with the mint.

Nonya-style Fishballs and Fishcakes

Making fishballs was regarded as a chore at home, but the temptation to sit in the kitchen and listen to the maids gossiping while preparing the ingredients was too great, so I often volunteered my services. I like to think that after all those hours in the kitchen I now make the best fishballs this side of Kuala Lumpur! This fish, prawn or squid forcemeat can be used to stuff vegetables (such as bittermelon, cucumber, eggplant and okra), or tofu squares and tofu puffs. Different seafoods should not be combined, however, as they will not hold together.

Ingredients:

300 grams (10½ oz) fresh ling or any other white fish fillets or 300 grams (10½ oz) green prawns, cleaned or small squid

1 teaspoon salt

2 teaspoons oil

2½ teaspoons cornflour (cornstarch)

pepper, to taste

salt, extra, to taste

a few chive stems, finely chopped (optional)

1 cup (250 mL / 8 fl oz) oil

Method:

Slice the seafood into small strips. Place the salt and oil into a small bowl of warm water. Pound a little of the fish meat at a time, adding a few drops of the warm water mix as you go, in a mortar and pestle until it amalgamates into a paste, approximately 15 minutes. The salty water and oil will crisp the fish paste and make it less rubbery.

Add the cornflour (cornstarch), pepper, salt and chives and sufficient water to give the paste a soft consistency for easy handling. Put a small amount of the forcemeat onto a spoon and, with another spoon, push it into the salted water. If the texture and shape hold well, then the forcemeat is of the right consistency and is ready to be used for stuffing or to make fishballs or fishcakes.

A food processor can be used, but the balls will never become firm nor will they be as tasty. However, if a food processor is used, double the amount of cornflour (cornstarch).

Fishballs:

Wet the palms of your hands with the salty water. Take a teaspoonful of the mixture and roll it into a ball. Place in the bowl of salty water for a few minutes to firm.

Bring a saucepan of water to the boil and drop in the fishballs. They are cooked when they rise to the surface. Spoon out and drain on several thicknesses of absorbent paper. The fishballs can also be steamed, or deep-fried and shredded.

Refrigerate and use as required in stir-fries, noodle dishes and soups.

Fishcakes:

Wet the palms of your hands with the salty water. Pat the mixture into cakes, about 4 cm (1½ in) long, 3 cm (1 in) wide and 2 cm (¾ in) thick. Place in the bowl of salty water for 1 hour, then drain on absorbent paper.

Heat the oil on high heat in a wok or heavy-based frying pan. When hot but not hazing or smoking, fry the cakes until golden brown. Drain and cool; refrigerate. Cut into thin slices and use in stir-fries and other dishes.

Blending ingredients in a mortar and pestle

Pasembor (Basembor) with Prawn Fritters

Pasembor is the salad most favoured by the many Indian Muslim stalls that trade on the streets of the larger cities of the west coast. The crispiness of the prawn fritters gives this salad a special crunch that adds to the texture and flavour, so much a part of the Malaysian food experience.

Salad:

1 Lebanese cucumber

1 medium-sized yam bean

200 grams (7 oz) bean sprouts

100 grams (3½ oz) water convolvulus (water spinach), kangkong or cos lettuce, chopped

100 grams (3½ oz) hard tofu

1½ cups (375 mL / 12 fl oz) oil

100 grams (3½ oz) squid

100 grams (3½ oz) unsalted peanuts

30 grams (1 oz) sesame seeds

Prawn Fritters:

1 cup (250 mL / 8 fl oz) water, approximately

1⅓ cups (200 g / 7 oz) wheat flour

¼ cup (30 g / 1 oz) rice flour

200 grams (7 oz) prawns (shrimp), shelled and minced

1 small onion, thinly sliced

pinch turmeric powder, to taste

salt, to taste

Sauce:

6 cloves garlic, diced

1 Spanish (red) onion, diced

1½ tablespoons sambal oelek

1¾ cups (430 mL / 14 fl oz) water

1 tablespoon tamarind purée

2 tablespoons sugar

salt, to taste or fish sauce, to taste

1 tablespoon cornflour (cornstarch)

3 tablespoons water, extra

pepper, to taste

Salad:

Cut the cucumber in half and scoop out the seeds. Shred, with the skin still on. Skin the yam bean, then wash and shred it.

Top and tail the bean sprouts. Cut both the stems and the leaves of the water convolvulus into 4 cm (1½ in) slices.

Fry the tofu on medium high in the oil until golden brown, drain and dice. Clean and score the squid, then dip it into boiling water for a few minutes to blanch. Slice into squares.

Dry roast the peanuts and sesame seeds until golden. Roughly chop the peanuts.

Prawn Fritters:

Add sufficient water to the wheat flour, rice flour and prawns (shrimp) to make a smooth batter. It should be rather thick and pour slowly.

Heat the oil on high heat in a wok until it is almost smoking. (If you place a spoon or metal skewer in the oil and bubbles appear around it, then the oil is ready for frying.) Pour a tablespoonful of batter into the wok and swirl around to make a flat, round shape. Remove the oil so that there is only about 1 teaspoon left so the batter cooks and crispiness develops slowly. Drain on absorbent paper and slice into pieces. Retain 2 tablespoons of the oil in the wok for the sauce.

Sauce:

Saute the garlic and onions on medium high in the retained oil and, when aromatic, add the sambal oelek and ¼ cup (60 mL / 2 fl oz) of the water. Stir for a few minutes then add the tamarind purée, sugar, salt and the remaining water.

Bring to the boil and cook, stirring constantly, until the sugar dissolves. Mix the cornflour (cornstarch) with the extra water and add it to the mixture. Season with the pepper and remove from the heat.

Assembling:

Decoratively arrange all of the prepared salad ingredients except the peanuts and the sesame seeds on a serving platter. Place the sliced prawn fritters on top and pour the sauce over. Sprinkle the peanuts and sesame seeds on top.

Asparagus Prawn Rolls

Formal Chinese dinners start with a mixed platter of exquisitely prepared cold dishes. Asparagus Prawn Rolls make a spectacular addition to the cold platter.

Ingredients:

200 grams (7 oz) thin and crisp asparagus

300 grams (10½ oz) prawn (shrimp) meat, minced

1 clove garlic, chopped

½ teaspoon pepper

¼ cup (30 g / 1 oz) chopped coriander (cilantro) leaves and some stems

3 cm (1 in) length ginger, peeled and chopped

rind and juice of ½ lemon

1 tablespoon cornflour (cornstarch)

4 shallots, sliced

1 tablespoon oil

Method:

Peel the skin off the thicker parts of the asparagus stem with a vegetable peeler, leaving the tender flesh.

Combine all of the ingredients except the asparagus, shallots and oil in a food processor. Blend until smooth, then remove the mixture and throw it on a flat surface a couple of times until it becomes firmer. Add the shallots and mix well.

Coat each asparagus stem with a thin film of oil so that it does not dry out in the cooking process. Use 2 tablespoons of the mixture to enclose each asparagus stem, pressing it well on to the vegetable (the ends will be sticking out).

Arrange the rolls in a bamboo steamer, cooking about 6 at a time, and steam for 6–8 minutes or until firm. Remove carefully, cool and serve either as an entrée or as a vegetable accompaniment to a main course. If served as an entrée you can include a mild plum and chilli sauce for dipping in.

Pictured on page 80.

Prawns in Banana Leaves
(Pais Udang)

Malaysians grow banana trees not only for the fruit but also for the leaves, which are used for countless cooking needs. The leaves should be washed well and softened in hot water to make them pliable.

Ingredients:

750 grams (1½ lb) medium prawns

juice of 1 lime

½ teaspoon turmeric powder

5 red Asian onions

2 cloves garlic

2 cm (¾ in) length galangal

4 candlenuts

2 red chillies, seeded

½ red capsicum (bell pepper)

1 teaspoon fish sauce

½ cup (125 mL / 4 fl oz) coconut cream

1 teaspoon palm sugar

1 teaspoon thick tamarind juice

2—3 banana leaves

tamarind juice, extra

chilli sauce

Method:

Soak about 6 satay skewers in water for 2 hours to prevent them from burning.

Shell, devein and clean the prawns. Butterfly the prawns by cutting lengthwise almost through the meat and flattening slightly. Brush with the lime juice and turmeric powder.

Blend all of the ingredients except the prawns and the banana leaf together in a food processor or mortar and pestle to form a smooth paste.

Cut the banana leaf into 10 x 15 cm (4 x 6 in) rectangles and soften for a few minutes in boiling water.

Place the paste in a saucepan and cook over a medium heat, allowing to simmer for 10 minutes or until aromatic. Remove from the heat and cool.

Place 1 teaspoon of mixture down the centre of a piece of banana leaf, place a prawn on top and cover with another teaspoon of the mixture. Fold the leaf over the prawn and secure with a satay skewer, threading it through both the banana leaf and the prawn. Grill under a medium heat until the prawns are cooked, approximately 4–5 minutes.

Serve the prawns in the banana leaf with the prawns partially uncovered, brushing with tamarind juice and chilli sauce. This dish makes an elegant entrée.

Pictured on page 80.

Chilli and Pepper Crabs

Crabs are a specialty in my family — we come from a town famous for its crabs and used to buy them fresh from the contractors when their sampans came filled to the brim from the outlying mangroves off Port Kelang. There is even an island called Pulau Ketam (Crab Island). The crabs may not be the largest but they certainly seem to be the tastiest in the world.

Ingredients:

2 medium-sized mud crabs

2 tablespoons oil

3 cloves garlic, chopped

3 cm (1 in) length ginger, grated

3 tablespoons garlic black bean sauce

1 tablespoon sambal oelek

1 tablespoon fresh black pepper, roughly ground

1/4 cup (60 mL / 2 fl oz) red wine

1 tablespoon sugar, or to taste

2 tablespoons light soy sauce

1 leek stalk, thinly sliced

1 tablespoon cornflour (cornstarch) mixed with 1/4 cup (60 mL / 2 fl oz) cold water

1/2 cup (50 g / 2 oz) garlic chives, cut into 3 cm (1 in) pieces

Method:

Clean the mud crabs and chop into pieces. (Blue swimmer crabs can also be used, but the result will not be as good.)

Heat the oil on medium high in a wok. Sauté the garlic and ginger until golden, then add the garlic black bean sauce and fry until aromatic. Increase the heat to high, then add the mud crab pieces and stir to mix well.

Add the sambal oelek, black pepper, wine, sugar and soy sauce. Cover and cook on high heat until the shells are brilliantly coloured, a good indication that they are cooked; this will take approximately 5–10 minutes.

Add half of the leek stalk slices. Remove the cover after 5 minutes and stir well. Add the cornflour (cornstarch) and stir to thicken. Toss in the garlic chives and stir well.

Cover and cook for 3 minutes. Place on a serving dish and garnish with the remaining leek slices.

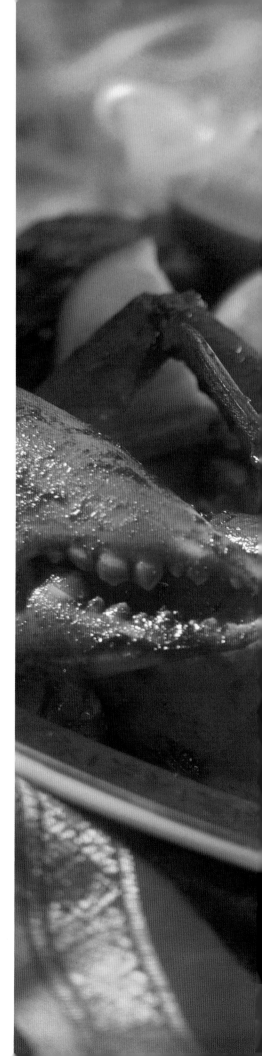

Chilli and Pepper Crabs

Prawn Mamak-style Sambal

The mamaks are Indian Muslim traders renowned for their cooking skills. While at university in Singapore, I often visited Wahab, an Indian Muslim hawker who slept next to his stall on wheels parked nearby. He was always on hand to make coffee, cook the odd plate of Mamak Mee, and proffer words of wisdom and comfort even at two o'clock in the morning.

Ingredients:

10 candlenuts or macadamia nuts
6 dried chillies, chopped or ½ tablespoon chilli powder
1 teaspoon shrimp paste, dry roasted
½ cup (80 g / 3 oz) small red Asian onions or 2 Spanish (red) onions, chopped
2 cm (¾ in) length tamarind
½ cup (125 mL / 4 fl oz) water
1 kg (2 lb) prawns (shrimp)
2 peeled, cooked potatoes cut into 8 pieces each
2 tablespoons mustard oil or gingelly oil
1 cup (250 mL / 8 fl oz) coconut cream
sugar, to taste
salt, to taste
1 tablespoon Malaysian curry powder (see page 172)
½ cup (50 g / 2 oz) desiccated coconut, toasted and finely pounded
3 curry leaf stalks, chopped

Method:

Blend the candlenuts, chillies, shrimp paste and onions together in a food processor or mortar and pestle until well ground. Grind the tamarind and combine with the water to form a juice (you need ½ cup / 125 mL / 4 fl oz of juice). Shell and devein the prawns, retaining the tails. Fry the potatoes until they are crisp.

Heat the oil on medium heat in a wok and fry the ground mixture until aromatic. Add the coconut cream, sugar, salt and tamarind juice. Bring to the boil and cook until the liquid reduces by two-thirds.

Add the prawns, curry powder and potato and cook on medium heat until the prawns are opaque in colour, approximately 4–5 minutes. Add the desiccated coconut and curry leaf stalks and cook on medium heat, adding oil only if the mixture becomes too dry (this is a dry curry dish).

Remove from the heat and serve with rice or roti or as a sandwich spread.

Mixed Vegetable Gravy with Prawns
(Chap Chye Lemak)

This dish has a flavour and bite all of its own ... a curry that is hot, aromatic and tangy all at the same time.

Ingredients:

6 fresh chillies, chopped
2 teaspoons shrimp paste
4 candlenuts
2 tablespoons salted black beans
2 Spanish (red) onions, chopped
2 sheets dried bean curd sticks
50 grams (2 oz) Chinese mushrooms
50 grams (2 oz) water lily buds (kim chiam)
50 grams (2 oz) cloud ear fungus
50 grams (2 oz) beanthread noodles
3 cakes (50 g / 2 oz) prefried tofu puffs, sliced
500 grams (1 lb) prawns (shrimp)
3 tablespoons oil
4 cups (1 litre / 32 fl oz) chicken stock
2 cups (500 mL / 16 fl oz) coconut milk
250 grams (8 oz) cabbage, cut into chunks
100 grams (3½ oz) bamboo shoots, sliced
salt, to taste

Method:

Blend the chillies, shrimp paste, candlenuts, black beans and onions together in a food processor or mortar and pestle until well ground. Cut the bean curd sticks into 10 cm (4 in) squares and steep in warm water for 10 minutes or until softened.

Wash the Chinese mushrooms and soak them in hot water for 10–15 minutes. Thinly slice the caps. Soak the water lily buds in hot water for 5 minutes then tie them in knots. Wash the cloud ear fungus, place them in a saucepan of warm water then bring them to the boil. Boil for 5 minutes, or until they expand, then remove from the heat. Cut off the hard bits.

Cut the noodles into 20 cm (8 in) lengths and soak them in warm water for 10 minutes. Shell and devein the prawns (shrimp).

Heat the oil on medium high in a wok and fry the ground ingredients until aromatic and the onions caramelise. Add the prawns, increase the heat to high and fry for 4 minutes or until they turn slightly pink.

Add the stock and bring to the boil. Add the remaining ingredients except the coconut milk and salt, bring back to the boil, lower the heat and simmer, for about 8 minutes or until the stock is flavoursome.

Add the coconut milk and season to taste. This all-purpose Malay vegetable curry is good eaten with Compressed Rice or Lontong (recipe, page 37).

Butter and Lemon Grass Prawns
(Udang Serai Mentega)

The tastes of Malaysia — lemon grass, chilli and coconut — are all present in this simple dish. Do not fry the coconut in anything but butter or the dish will not be as rich and flavoursome.

Ingredients:

500 grams (1 lb) green prawns (shrimp)

1 tablespoon light soy sauce

4 stalks lemon grass, chopped

2 cloves garlic, chopped

$1/4$ small onion, chopped

$1/2$ cup (125 g / 4 oz) butter

2 tablespoons chilli black bean paste or $1/2$ tablespoon chopped chillies and $1^1/2$ tablespoons black bean sauce

$1/2$ teaspoon sugar

$1/2$ cup (50 g / 2 oz) grated fresh or desiccated coconut

1 teaspoon chilli or paprika powder

Method:

Shell and devein the prawns, leaving the tails on. Brush the prawns with the soy sauce.

Blend the lemon grass, garlic and onion together in a food processor or mortar and pestle until it forms a smooth paste.

Heat 1 tablespoon of the butter on medium heat in a wok or saucepan and saute the paste until aromatic. Add the chilli black bean paste and sugar and cook for a few minutes more (be careful not to burn the butter).

Add the prawns and cook on high heat for 4–5 minutes or until they change colour. Remove the prawns from the wok and keep warm.

Add the remaining butter to the wok and, when hot, add the coconut and fry until aromatic, sprinkling the chilli powder over the frying coconut as it cooks.

Serve the prawns hot, garnished with the coconut mixture and with rice and vegetables.

Pictured on page 96.

Black Pepper Scampi, Lobster or Crab
(Ketam Lada Hitam)

Food trends keep changing, a testament to the ingenuity of chefs and creative cooks in Singapore and Malaysia. This dish is western in concept but has Asian spices and high-grade Sumatran black pepper added.

Ingredients:

2 kg (4 lb) mud or blue swimmer crabs, lobsters, scampi (large prawns/shrimp) or Balmain bugs

3 cups (750 mL / 24 fl oz) oil

Sauce:

120 grams ($4^1/2$ oz) butter or low-fat margarine

2 cm ($3/4$ in) length ginger, peeled and chopped

5 cloves garlic, diced or puréed

1 tablespoon sambal oelek

$2^1/2$ tablespoons oyster sauce

2 tablespoons light soy sauce

1 tablespoon dark soy sauce

1 tablespoon palm sugar

3 tablespoons strong Sumatran black pepper, pounded or milled

Method:

If using crab or lobster, clean and cut in half. If using scampi or Balmain bugs, clean and prepare.

Heat the oil on high heat in a wok and deep-fry the seafood in hot oil until the shells turn a bright red in colour. Drain and keep warm.

In a wok, melt the butter and saute the ginger, garlic and sambal oelek on high heat until aromatic. Add the oyster sauce, soy sauces, palm sugar and pepper, reduce the heat to medium and bring to a simmer. Add the seafood, stirring to coat it with the sauce, and cook until heated through.

Serve piping hot with rice and sauteed kangkong as a main meal.

Fresh Spring Rolls
(Poh Piah)

This recipe for spring rolls makes a wonderful dish for a party. Prepare the filling and the garnishes and have your guests make up their own rolls.

Ingredients:

1 packet fresh spring roll pastry or 1 packet dried Vietnamese spring roll sheets (riz galettes) (you need 20 sheets)

Filling:

2 tablespoons oil

4 cloves garlic, chopped

2 tablespoons black bean paste

250 grams (8 oz) prawn (shrimp) meat, diced into 1 cm ($^1/_2$ in) chunks

200 grams (7 oz) belly pork, cooked, sliced and shredded

1 x 400 gram (13 oz) can bamboo shoots, sliced and julienned

2 yam beans, peeled, sliced and julienned

4 fried tofu puffs, diced or shredded

2 teaspoons dark soy sauce, or to taste

salt, to taste

sugar, to taste

Garnish:

1 cos lettuce, washed and dried well

$^1/_4$ cup (60 mL / 2 fl oz) sweet red plum sauce (teemcheong) or thick soy sauce (kecap manis)

$^1/_4$ cup (60 mL / 2 fl oz) sambal oelek

200 grams (7 oz) prawns (shrimp), cleaned, deveined and cooked

1 cucumber, seeded and julienned

6 cloves garlic, slivered and deep-fried

5 eggs made into a thin omelette, then rolled up tightly and sliced into fine strips

200 grams (7 oz) crab meat, lightly cooked

coriander (cilantro) leaves, washed and chopped

chilli sauce

Filling:

Heat the oil on medium high in a wok and fry the garlic and black bean paste until aromatic. Increase the heat to high and add the prawn (shrimp) meat and belly pork. Fry briskly until cooked and the pork starts to darken in colour, about 4 minutes.

Add the bamboo shoots, yam beans, tofu puffs, soy sauce, salt and sugar and cook, stirring constantly, until the vegetables wilt and the sauce reduces so much that the mixture is almost dry, approximately 10–15 minutes. Place the mixture in a sieve to drain the liquid off.

Assembling the rolls:

Separate the lettuce leaves.

If using Vietnamese spring roll sheets, place them on a damp tea towel (dish towel) to keep them soft and pliable. If the sheets dry out too much they will tear.

Place one lettuce leaf on a spring roll sheet and brush with the sweet red plum sauce and sambal oelek. Place 2 tablespoons of the filling on the lettuce leaf and top with any mixture of the garnish ingredients, but finishing with the crab meat and coriander (cilantro).

Roll up by folding a piece of the spring roll sheet over the filling, then tucking both sides over the fold to secure the filling inside the sheet. Continue rolling. Place with the loose end down on plates and serve either cut into pieces or as a roll with chilli sauce for dipping.

Clockwise from back: Black Squid (Sotong Masak Hitam) (recipe, page 100), Butter and Lemon Grass Prawns (Udang Serai Mentega) (recipe, page 95) and Fresh Spring Rolls (Poh Piah) (recipe, this page)

Grilled Stingray Fins
(Ikan Panggang Pari)

The bones of stingray fins are gelatinous and almost melt in the mouth.
If stingray is unavailable, you can substitute a whole fish.

Ingredients:

2 tablespoons vegetable oil

10 Spanish (red) onions, chopped

1 tablespoon shrimp paste, dry roasted

1 tablespoon thick soy sauce (kecap manis)

2 cloves garlic, chopped

2 candlenuts

1 teaspoon sugar

3 tablespoons lime juice

500 gram (1 lb) stingray piece, or whole fish

1 large banana leaf

kaffir lime leaves or pandan leaf, finely shredded

Method:

Blend the oil, onions, shrimp paste, soy sauce, garlic, candlenuts, sugar and 2 tablespoons of the lime juice together in a food processor or mortar and pestle.

Coat the stingray or fish with the blended mixture and place on a banana leaf (the banana leaf prevents the stingray from burning).

Place the leaf on a barbecue plate or well-oiled flat saucepan and cook, turning the stingray on the leaf until cooked. Serve the stingray on pieces of the banana leaf with the remaining tablespoon of lime juice sprinkled over and garnished with the kaffir lime leaves.

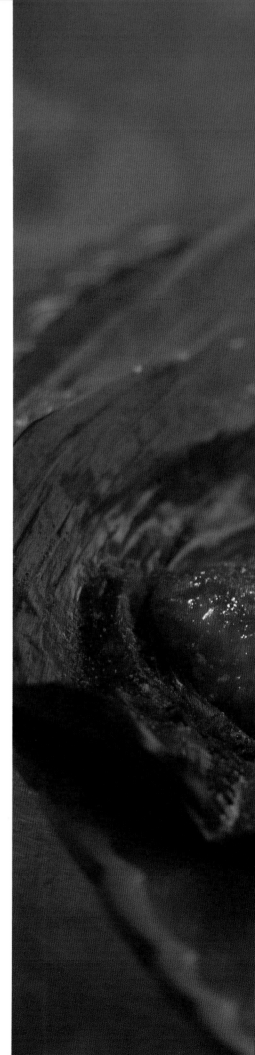

Grilled Stingray Fins
(Ikan Panggang Pari)

Tofupok in Yongtahu Soup or Taucheo Sauce

Tofupok is a Nonya dish of vegetables such as okra, chillies, cucumber and bittermelon stuffed with fish or prawn meat. Make the fishballs from cooked, deboned fish or shelled, deveined, cooked prawns (see recipe for Nonya-style Fishballs and Fishcakes, page 88). Cut a slit in the okra, chillies and cucumber, seed carefully, then stuff with the fishballs. Cut bittermelon cross-wise into thick slices, remove the seeds and pith and stuff with the fishballs.

Taucheo Sauce:

1 tablespoon oil

3 cloves garlic, chopped

2 tablespoons whole salted black beans

1 tablespoon sambal oelek

1 tablespoon thick mushroom soy sauce

1/4 cup (60 mL / 2 fl oz) water

1 tablespoon red or black sweet Chinese vinegar

salt, to taste

sugar, to taste

1 1/2 cups (375 mL / 12 fl oz) pork or chicken stock

Yongtahu Soup:

1 tablespoon vegetable oil

5 cloves garlic, chopped

4 cups (1 litre / 32 fl oz) pork or chicken stock, strained

fish sauce, to taste

pepper, to taste

1 tablespoon pickled radish (tangchai)

2 spring onion (scallion) stalks, chopped

100 grams (3 1/2 oz) beanthread noodles

1/2 cos lettuce, finely shredded

1/4 cup crispy fried onions (see page 172)

Taucheo Sauce:

Clean the black beans and mash with the back of a fork.

Heat the oil on medium high in a wok and saute the garlic until golden. Add the black beans and sambal oelek and cook until aromatic. Be careful that the mixture does not burn.

Add the mushroom soy sauce, water, vinegar, stock and a selection of the stuffed vegetables. Bring to the boil, then lower the heat and simmer for 3–4 minutes. Remove from the heat and serve hot.

Yongtahu Soup:

Heat the oil on high in a wok and brown the garlic. Add the stock, fish sauce and pepper and bring to the boil. When the stock is boiling, add the pickled radish, spring onions (scallions) and a selection of the stuffed vegetables.

Simmer on a low heat only to heat through. Add the beanthread noodles and stir until heated through.

To serve, place some of the shredded lettuce in bowls and pour the hot soup over. Garnish with crispy fried onions. This soup can be served as an entree or as a main course.

Pictured on page 16.

Black Squid
(Sotong Masak Hitam)

This dish is a northern specialty. Squid is best bought fresh and cleaned at home, before use. Pre-cleaned squid tubes, sliced from larger squid and calamari, toughen easily. I buy very small squid, no longer than 10 cm (4 in); these need to be cooked very quickly in a hot wok. The ink lends a fascinating flavour to the dish, which is quite unique.

Ingredients:

450 grams (14 oz) squid

3 tablespoons oil

3 cloves garlic, chopped

1 small Spanish (red) onion, puréed

3 tablespoons sambal oelek

fish sauce, to taste

3 tablespoons tamarind juice

2 cm (3/4 in) length palm sugar

juice of 1 lime

basil (kemangi)

Method:

Remove the body of the squid from the tentacles, making sure the ink sacs remain attached, and clean. Remove the skin and slice the tubes in half, across the tubes.

Heat the oil on high in a wok. Add the garlic and onion and stir-fry until golden.

Add the sambal oelek and cook until it loses its raw smell, approximately 3–4 minutes.

Add the squid, fish sauce, tamarind juice and palm sugar and stir-fry as the ink sacs spill out into the gravy. Continue stirring until the liquid reduces by half.

Add the lime juice. The squid ink may curdle when the lime juice is added but the flavour will not be marred by this reaction. Remove from the heat and toss through the basil.

Pictured on page 96.

Makan-lah!

The Baba Nonya

The people and their cuisine

During the fifteenth century the Chinese Ming court sent many diplomatic missions to Melaka. It was hoped that close ties would develop between the two States when the ruler of Melaka, Sultan Mansur Shah, married a young Chinese Princess, Hang Li Po, and brought her to her new home in Melaka.

The marriage opened the way for Chinese traders to settle in Melaka. The town soon became an important trading port rather than merely a temporary safe haven for sailors sheltering from the monsoons.

The Chinese traders soon adopted the local Malay customs, language and dress, and sometimes married local girls, and this integrated community became known as the Baba Nonya — from the Malay word Bapak *(Grandfather) and the Portuguese* Nona *(Grandmother). They spoke a language that was a mixture of Hokkien (from Southern China) and Malay, with a smattering of Indian and Portuguese.*

The Baba Nonya integrated culturally but did not convert to Islam. They remained Confucianists, Buddhists and Taoists, with ancestor worship and the family altar (and food for the altar) forming an integral part of family life.

Nonya is the name given to the cuisine of the Baba Nonya. The Chinese traders had brought with them their wok and stir-fry methods, and introduced tofu and soy sauce, which blended with indigenous Malay herbs and spices, with Portuguese food, and with traditional ingredients of the Indians (whose influence and cultural traditions were in place in the Southeast Asian region long before the Melaka Sultanate). From this fusion of tastes come such dishes as Laksa, Lantong and Mee Siam — Malay spices, Indian curries and Chinese noodles.

Nonya food rose to its heights in the 19th and early 20th centuries. The Baba Nonya were brilliant at taking simple Chinese fare and embellishing it, changing and adapting it to Malay tastes — with spices, coconut, turmeric leaf, pandan, lemon grass and the kaffir lime leaf — improving it to the extent that the original dish is completely transformed.

Clockwise from left: Fresh Fruit and Vegetable Kerabu (recipe, page 127),
Bean Sprouts with Salted Fish (recipe, page 108)
and Stuffed Banana Chilli Peppers in Sour Sauce (recipe, page 104)

Stuffed Banana Chilli Peppers in Sour Sauce

The green pawpaw (papaya) remains crunchy even when cooked ... a definite reason for including it in this stuffed pepper recipe, as most Asian food relies on contrast in texture. Here the crunch contrasts with the soft, smooth and silky tofu.

Ingredients:

6 medium banana chilli peppers
1/4 green paw paw (papaya)
6 kaffir lime leaves
150 grams (5½ oz) green prawn (shrimp) meat, finely chopped
50 grams (2 oz) fish fillet, pounded
1 tablespoon sambal oelek
2 cloves garlic, chopped
1/4 cup (30 g / 1 oz) coriander (cilantro) leaves, finely chopped
1 Spanish (red) onion, pureed or finely chopped

Sauce:

1 tablespoon sambal oelek
2 tablespoons tamarind purée from 3 cm (1 in) length tamarind block
1 tablespoon fish sauce
1 tablespoon palm sugar, or to taste
2 tablespoons water

Method:

Slit the banana chillies open and remove the pith and seeds. Peel and thinly grate the paw paw (papaya). Finely shred 4 of the kaffir lime leaves (reserve the other 2 for garnish; finely shred these as well).

Combine all of the ingredients except the sauce ingredients in a bowl and mash well with a fork. Stuff the mixture into the centre of the banana chillies so that it closes well without falling out of the chilli.

Place the sambal oelek, tamarind purée, fish sauce, sugar and water in a wok and bring to the boil. Place the banana chillies in the sauce, cover and steam or braise for 4–5 minutes, or until the chillies are cooked. Push the filling back into the chillies if it falls out.

Serve hot on a platter, pouring the sauce over, with the reserved kaffir lime leaves as garnish. This goes well as a main vegetable dish with rice.

Pictured on page 102.

Salad with Banana Flower or Jackfruit
(Jurut Urab Lawar)

The purple, cone-shaped banana bract (it is not really a flower) grows on the tip of a bunch of bananas. It can be removed while the bunch is green and the bunch actually benefits from this cut, with more nutrition being saved for the fruit. Jackfruit is an aromatic fruit often confused with the durian, as both have spiky skins. The jackfruit is much larger, hasn't got prickly thorns and has a thick, gummy secretion in the flesh that sticks to the fingers and everything else it comes in contact with.

Ingredients:

500 grams (1 lb) unripe young jackfruit or banana flower bract or banana flowers or heart of banana palm
100 grams (3½ oz) sweet potato (yam) leaves or kang kong leaves
2 tablespoons red beans
5 snake beans
2 red chillies, seeded and chopped
1 cm (½ in) length shrimp paste, dry roasted and crumbled
1 cup (60 g / 2 oz) freshly grated coconut
1 cup cooked chicken or roasted pork meat, shredded
juice of 1 lime or ½ cup (125 mL / 4 fl oz) coconut milk
salt, to taste
curry leaves or pandan leaves, finely shredded

Method:

If using jackfruit, oil your hands with vegetable oil, then cut the peel off. Chop, seeds and all. If using banana flower bract, remove the dark purple leaves from the banana flower or bract until the paler pink leaves are reached. Soak these paler leaves overnight in a bowl of water with 1 tablespoon of salt, then boil until soft. Chop into small pieces.

Steam the sweet potato (yam) leaves in a bamboo basket or steamer for 3 minutes. Soak the red beans overnight in water, then boil for 20 minutes. Drain. Steam the snake beans for 3 minutes then slice into 5 cm (2 in) lengths. Combine the chillies and shrimp paste.

Toss all of the ingredients together, using lime juice if the lawar is to be tart or coconut milk if it is to taste creamy. The lawar with lime juice is an ideal weight watchers' dish. Serve garnished with curry leaves or pandan leaves.

Hearts of Banana-palm Salad
(Jantung Pisang Kerabu)

Large, cone-shaped banana flowers are only tender on the inside, and their 'hearts' may only constitute one-fifth of their weight. It is sometimes better to buy a can of banana hearts to get the right quantities for a large salad.

Ingredients:

250 grams (8 oz) banana flower hearts

$1/4$ cup (30 g /1 oz) freshly grated coconut or desiccated coconut

200 grams fresh prawns (shrimp) shelled, deveined and chopped

juice of 2 limes or lemons

1 tablespoon sambal oelek

1 tablespoon white sugar

salt, to taste

2 tablespoons crème de menthe (optional)

mint leaves

Method:

Peel and discard the dark purple outer leaves from the banana flower until the paler pink leaves are reached. Cover with salty water and soak for 1 hour to remove the pith. Drain.

Cover the banana flower with fresh water in a saucepan, bring to the boil and cook for 15–20 minutes or until soft. Keep topping up with more water if necessary. Drain and slice into juliennes.

Dry roast the coconut until golden (if using fresh coconut, cook for about 8 minutes on high in the microwave or 4 minutes in a hot frying pan; halve the time for desiccated coconut). Pound in a mortar and pestle until fine and oily.

Toss the prawns in the lime juice, sambal oelek and sugar, seasoning to taste. Add the banana hearts, coconut and liqueur, tossing well, just prior to serving. Serve cold, garnished with the mint leaves.

Bean Sprout and Crab Salad
(Kerabu Ketam)

This salad forms the perfect balance for hot and pungent salads and rice dishes. It is better to use canned crabmeat, as preparing fresh crabmeat is rather time consuming.

Ingredients:

100 grams ($3^1/2$ oz) bean sprouts, topped and tailed

1 medium Spanish (red) onion, sliced into thin juliennes

1 small ginger flower (bunga kentan) (optional) or 2 red chillies, chopped

1 tablespoon sambal oelek

3 tablespoons desiccated coconut, dry roasted and finely pounded

1 bunch (100 g / $3^1/2$ oz) Vietnamese mint leaves, chopped

150 grams ($5^1/2$ oz) cooked crabmeat

3 tablespoons coconut cream

salt, to taste

juice and rind of 1 lime

cos lettuce leaves or some betel leaves, well washed

Method:

Top and tail the bean sprouts (all that will remain is the white stems).

Combine the bean sprouts, onion, ginger flower, sambal oelek and coconut in a large bowl. Toss well. Add the Vietnamese mint (saving about 3 tablespoons for garnish) and crabmeat, then moisten with the coconut cream.

Combine the salt, lime juice and rind and toss into the salad just prior to wrapping in the cos lettuce leaves. If left for too long the coconut milk and lime juice will curdle; however the salad can be kept up to that stage in the refrigerator.

Garnish with Vietnamese mint.

Bittermelon in Coconut Milk

The bittergourd or melon is a vegetable that many people outside of Asia find difficult to accept. The five taste sensations — sweet, sour, salty, bitter and pungent — are all present in food, so how can one know sweet if one has not tasted bitter?

Ingredients:

1 large bittermelon

2 squares (80 g / 3 oz) hard tofu

1 tablespoon oil

1 Spanish (red) onion, puréed

1 teaspoon sambal oelek

½ cup (125 mL / 4 fl oz) coconut cream

salt, to taste

100 grams (3½ oz) scallops, sliced in half

kaffir lime leaves, shredded

Method:

Slice the bittermelon in half, scrape the seeds out with a spoon, slice into 2 cm (¾ in) half circles then soak in salted water for 10 minutes to reduce the bitterness. Cut the tofu into cubes and fry in a little oil until crisp. Drain.

Heat the oil on high in a wok and brown the onion until it is aromatic. Add the sambal oelek and the tofu, stirring carefully so that the tofu doesn't break up.

Add the bittermelon and fry for 1 minute, then add the coconut cream and salt and cook until the melon is soft. Add the scallops and cook for 5 minutes, or until the sauce reduces a little.

Serve garnished with shredded lime leaves.

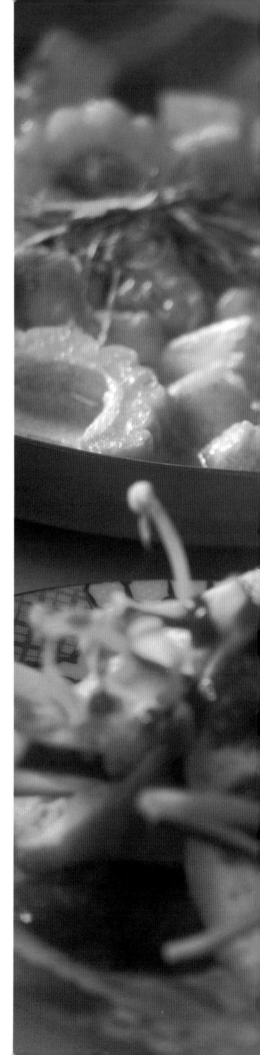

Clockwise from back: Bittermelon in Coconut Milk (recipe, this page), Tamarind Chilli Potatoes (recipe, page 122), and Stuffed Tofu (Tofu Sumbat) (recipe, page 122)

Bean Sprouts with Salted Fish

This dish is a special inclusion as it was my husband's favourite recipe and one he cooked as often as he was allowed in the kitchen. The dried fish should be crisply fried and then kept crisp until serving time for best results.

Ingredients:

50 grams (1 lb) salted threadfin (kurau) or pike
400 grams (13 oz) fresh bean sprouts
¼ cup (60 mL / 2 fl oz) oil
1 clove garlic, chopped
4 dried chillies, roughly chopped
2 teaspoons light soy sauce

Method:

Dice the fish into 2 cm (¾ in) pieces. Tail the bean sprouts and wash in several changes of water.

Heat the oil on high heat in a wok and fry the fish until crisp. Drain on absorbent paper and keep warm.

Pour off all but 1 tablespoon of the oil, reheat in the wok on high heat and sauté the garlic and chillies until smoking. Add the bean sprouts and quickly sauté, tossing.

Add the fish, turn off the heat then add the soy sauce. If the soy sauce is added while the dish is still cooking the bean sprouts will wilt. Toss and serve immediately.

Pictured on page 102.

Sautéed Cabbage with Egg
(Kobis Goreng)

Cabbage is used in many ways, but none so interesting as this stir-fry. Water should not be added to the cabbage, but if the wok is covered for a few minutes during the cooking process then the cabbage juices will add sweetness to the dish.

Ingredients:

1 tablespoon oil
1 teaspoon whole mustard seeds
2 cloves garlic, chopped
1 large Spanish (red) onion, halved and finely sliced
½ medium-sized savoy cabbage, thinly shredded
pinch of turmeric powder
2 eggs, beaten
dash of salt and pepper
1 stalk curry leaves, chopped

Method:

Heat the oil on medium high in a wok and cook the mustard seeds until they pop. Add the garlic and onion and sauté until golden.

Add the cabbage and turmeric, stir and toss well, then cover and allow to cook in the cabbage's own liquids on medium high heat for 5 minutes. Stir occasionally. Remove the cover and toss once more.

Make a well in the centre and pour in the eggs. Allow the eggs to set, then toss and scramble gently to mix with the cabbage. Season with salt, pepper and curry leaves. Serve immediately.

Curried Cauli Stir-fry

Cauliflower is used a great deal in Indian and Chinese cooking, though in Malaysia it was always considered an expensive vegetable. This recipe can be used with cabbage, broccoli or sliced up Brussels sprouts.

Ingredients:

300 grams (10^1/$_2$ oz) cauliflower

1 teaspoon salt

2 tablespoons oil

1 teaspoon whole mustard seeds

1 small Spanish (red) onion, halved and finely sliced

2 cloves garlic, thinly sliced

2 cm (^{3}/$_4$ in) length ginger, peeled and chopped

2 sprigs (30 g / 1 oz) curry leaves

1 teaspoon chilli powder

1 teaspoon ground cumin

1 teaspoon turmeric powder

^{1}/$_2$ cup (125 mL / 4 fl oz) water

1 tablespoon tamarind puree made from 2 cm (^{3}/$_4$ in) block tamarind

1 cup (250 mL / 8 fl oz) coconut milk

^{1}/$_4$ cup (60 mL / 2 fl oz) coconut cream

juice of ^{1}/$_2$ lime

Method:

Cut the cauliflower into small florets and soak in a small basin of water with 1 teaspoon of salt for 10 minutes.

Heat the oil on high in a wok and cook the mustard seeds until they brown and pop. Add the onion, garlic and ginger to the wok and cook until golden brown.

Add the curry leaves, chilli powder, cumin and turmeric powder and stir into the onion mixture. Cook for 1 minute to heighten the flavours. Add the water and tamarind purée and simmer for 3 minutes.

Add the cauliflower and coconut milk and cook until the cauliflower is tender but not mushy and still retain some crunch. Add the coconut cream, stir through and remove from the heat, finally adding the lime juice. Serve hot with Puri (recipe, page 32) or rice.

Malaysian Choko Kerabu

This is a simple salad dish, one that started off as a cucumber salad. This is the answer to that perennial question: 'What does one do with choko?' If shrimp paste and dried prawns do not appeal, omit them.

Ingredients:

2 chokos, peeled and thinly sliced

^{1}/$_4$ cup (60 mL / 2 fl oz) white vinegar

2 tablespoons sugar

1 tablespoon desiccated coconut

2 tablespoons shrimp paste

1 teaspoon dried prawns (shrimp)

3 red chillies

2 tablespoons chopped shallots

1 tablespoon ginger purée

juice of 1 lime

salt, to taste

6 red Asian onions, thinly sliced

Method:

Soak the chokos overnight in the combined vinegar and sugar. Discard the liquid.

Dry roast the coconut, shrimp paste and dried prawns (shrimp) (see page 172). Pound the shrimp paste and dried prawns (shrimp) into a powder using a mortar and pestle.

Toss all of the salad ingredients together except the onions. Allow to stand at room temperature for 30 minutes before serving to allow the flavours to develop.

Fry the red Asian onions in hot oil until golden. Garnish the salad with the fried onions just before serving.

Steamed Mushrooms with Mustard Greens

This is a simple and delicate dish that has to be eaten as soon as it is cooked. It is wonderful when served with steaming hot rice and a steamed pork or chicken platter. I learnt to cook this by the agak, or estimation, method, whereby one relies on the eyes and nose for the correct amounts to be used.

Ingredients:

12 flat, golden or honey mushrooms

1 teaspoon green tea

800 grams (26 oz) mustard greens (choy sum)

2 cloves garlic, sliced

¼ cup (60 mL / 2 fl oz) oil

1 teaspoon oyster sauce

1 teaspoon sesame oil

Method:

Steam the mushrooms, leaving them whole, for 5 minutes. Sprinkle the green tea in the steaming water. Chop both the stems and leaves of the mustard greens into 6 cm (2 in) lengths and steam separately. Be careful that the greens don't overcook.

Fry the garlic slices in the oil. Drain.

Place the vegetables on a platter and drizzle with the oyster sauce and sesame oil. Garnish with the garlic. This dish is best served piping hot with rice.

Back: Watermelon Rind Kerabu (recipe, page 127); Front: Steamed Mushrooms with Mustard Greens (recipe, this page)

Corn Curry

In Malaysia, corn is eaten as a teatime snack; stall vendors steam large ears with husks twisted around each cob. In this curry a tiny piece of asafoetida, a resin, is used to combat the 'wind' that corn sometimes causes.

Ingredients:

$^1/_4$ cup (50 g / 2 oz) peanuts

2 cm ($^3/_4$ in) length ginger, chopped

2 green chillies, seeded and chopped

2 tablespoons besan (chick pea) flour

$1^1/_2$ cups (375 g / 13 oz) yoghurt

1 tablespoon oil

1 teaspoon mustard seeds

1 teaspoon cumin seeds

$^1/_4$ teaspoon asafoetida

1 onion, finely chopped

500 grams (1 lb) corn on the cob or corn kernels

1 teaspoon salt

lime juice, to taste

Method:

Roast the peanuts and grind or purée roughly with the ginger and chillies. Combine the besan (chick pea) flour and yoghurt and mix well, eliminating any lumps. Set aside.

Heat the oil on high heat in a wok and fry the mustard and cumin seeds until they pop. Add the asafoetida, onion and puréed mixture and sauté until aromatic.

Add the combined flour and yoghurt mixture and simmer for 1 minute. Add the corn and salt and cook for 8 minutes or until the corn is tender.

Season with the lime juice and serve hot with rice or Puri (recipe, page 32).

Cucumber Kerabu

A Kerabu is a tossed salad. In Malaysia, a meal often consists of salads and relishes served with rice. The more sambals, salads and sauces the more varied each mouthful tastes.

Ingredients:

2 cucumbers, roughly chopped

50 grams (2 oz) dry roasted prawns (shrimp)

3 cm (1 in) length shrimp paste, dry roasted (optional)

6 fresh chillies, chopped

1 ginger bud (bunga kentan), thinly sliced (optional)

$^1/_4$ cup (30 g / 1 oz) coconut flakes, dry roasted

sugar, to taste

salt, to taste

juice of 2 limes

Method:

Slice the cucumber into two lengthwise and scoop out the seeds with a spoon held at right angles to the sliced edge. Cut into thin juliennes.

Pound or grind the prawns (shrimp), shrimp paste, chillies, ginger bud and coconut flakes until the coconut oil is released.

Combine the cucumber and prawn mixture with the sugar and salt. Add the lime juice just before serving.

Festivals

Ramadan, Deepavali, Thaipusam, Chinese New Year and Chingay

Foremost among the holidays celebrated in Malaysia is the Muslim festival of Ramadan, celebrated after a month-long fast, when people visit each other and feast on Rendang and the compressed rice dish called Ketupat.

Deepavali, the Festival of Lights, is celebrated by Indians. Special on the island of Penang is Thaipusam, a spring festival that culminates in the carrying of altars to the favourite deity. During these spectacular processions, men and women pierce themselves with needles, spears and hooks to atone for favours granted during the year.

All over Malaysia, the lunar festival of Chinese New Year is the most welcomed event. Traditionally, for the agricultural people of China, this was an important time to give thanks for the harvest and to pray for the coming one, to review plans, to consolidate family ties and to make way for the new.

The family reunion dinner held on New Year's Eve is very important to Malaysian Chinese, and family members journey for miles to be in attendance. Traditionally, even if someone was absent, a seat was reserved for them at the table.

During this dinner the Chinese eat foods with names connected to wealth, health, happiness and longevity, in the hope that the family will eventually attain these qualities. Prawns, for example, will give laughter and happiness, as their name, ha, is a diminutive of the sound of laughter.

On the day before the New Year the house is swept (no one sweeps on the first day of the New Year, as to do so would sweep away good luck). All debts are settled before New Year; on New Year's Day, red packets containing money are distributed — red being the colour of prosperity, and of life.

New Year is the time when all Chinese take holidays for a week or two, and businesses, shops, restaurants and hawker-stalls are closed.

The Chingay (the fifteenth day after the spring festival) is celebrated in Melaka by maidens throwing oranges, symbols of the moon, into the river in the hope that this will ensure the catch of a good husband during the year.

Eggplant Tofu

The eggplant, Indian in origin, is a versatile vegetable that lends itself to many different preparations — but this Nonya recipe is my favourite.

Ingredients:

300 grams (10½ oz) eggplant (aubergine)

6 spring onion (scallion) stalks

⅓ cup (80 mL / 2½ fl oz) vegetable oil

3 cloves garlic, chopped

200 grams (7 oz) silken tofu

2 tablespoons oyster sauce

dash plum sauce, to taste

2 red chillies, slit and seeded

Method:

If possible, use the long, thin Asian variety of eggplant (aubergine). Cut diagonally into 2 cm (¾ in) slices. Cut the spring onion (scallion) stalks vertically halfway down and place in a bowl of cold water until they open up like flowers.

Heat the oil on high heat in a wok and fry the eggplant (aubergine) in batches until golden and crisp at the edges. Drain on absorbent paper and keep warm while cooking the rest of the dish. Fry the garlic until golden, remove and drain.

Drain off all but 1 tablespoon of oil from the wok. Place the tofu in the palm of your hand and gently cut off 2 cm (¾ in) slices, lowering each slice into the oil. Gently fry the tofu for 3–5 minutes or until it has a crisp outer skin, then remove.

Place the eggplant and garlic back in the wok and toss well. Gently add the tofu. Add the oyster sauce, plum sauce, spring onion (scallion) stalks (reserving a few for garnish) and chillies and stir to heat through.

Unripe Jackfruit Curry or Heart of Banana Palm Curry
(Gulai Nangka)

The jackfruit is said to resemble 'poor man's meat' as it tastes like meat, especially when cooked in a curry. The banana heart can be used the same way. Always make sure to rub oil on your hands or to wear gloves before cutting into the fruit, as it contains a sticky white sap that is difficult to remove.

Ingredients:

500 grams (1 lb) unripe jackfruit or 500 grams (1 lb) banana flower pickled in brine, drained

1 cm (½ in) length fresh turmeric, or 1 teaspoon turmeric powder

100 grams (3½ oz) fresh prawns (shrimp)

10 red Asian onions or 2 medium Spanish (red) onions, chopped

1 tablespoon sambal oelek

2 stalks lemon grass, chopped

2 tablespoons vegetable oil

2 cm (¾ in) length shrimp paste, dry roasted and crumbled (see page 172)

2 cups (500 mL / 16 fl oz) thin coconut milk

1 cup (250 mL / 8 fl oz) coconut cream

salt, to taste

juice of 1 lime

Method:

Peel off the thick outer skin of the jackfruit and cut into chunks. Wait 10 minutes for the sap to ooze out, wipe the outside of the fruit then boil in water until semi-soft. Chop the fruit into tiny pieces.

If using fresh banana flowers rather than jackfruit, remove all of the thick purple petals until you get to the soft pink bud or heart inside. Soak the heart overnight in salt water then boil until soft then chop.

Rub the turmeric powder over the prawns (shrimp).

Blend the onions, sambal oelek and lemon grass together in a food processor or mortar and pestle until well ground.

Heat the oil on high heat in a wok and sauté the ground ingredients until aromatic. Add the shrimp paste and prawns (shrimp) and cook for 3 minutes.

Add the coconut milk and simmer, uncovered, for a further 20 minutes. Add the coconut cream, salt and lime juice and stir until heated through.

Long Beans with Egg Fuyung

Long beans (also known as snake beans) came to Malaysia from China where the farmers grow them to maturity, using the dried peas for stews. There are two varieties, one thick, fleshy and light green and the other crisp, thin and dark green. The thin variety is best for Malaysian cooking as it retains its flavour and crunch.

Ingredients:

4 eggs
salt, to taste
pepper, to taste
2 tablespoons oil
1 large Spanish (red) onion, chopped
2 cloves garlic, chopped
500 grams (1 lb) long beans or snake beans, cut into 4 cm (1^1/$_2$ in) slices
5 mushrooms caps, thinly sliced
3 spring onions (scallions), chopped
1 teaspoon sambal oelek
^{1}/$_2$ bunch (80—100 g / 3—3^1/$_2$ oz) coriander (cilantro) leaves, chopped

Method:

Beat the eggs and add the salt and pepper to taste.

Heat the oil on high heat in a wok and sauté the onion until golden. Add the garlic and cook until golden. Add the long beans, mushroom caps and spring onions (scallions) and toss lightly.

Make a well in the centre of the wok. Add the beaten egg and allow it to sit in the wok over medium heat for 2 minutes, or until slightly firm. Add the sambal oelek and coriander (cilantro) to the centre of the egg and scramble, keeping the vegetables to the outside.

Bring the vegetables into the middle of the wok and toss with the scrambled egg. This is a simple and nutritious dish that goes well with rice and soup.

Green Mango Kerabu

Kerabus, raw salads, are popular on the east coast of Malaysia. Dried prawns (shrimp) can be very strong in taste if fried, but when flossed or blended they are quite refreshing.

Ingredients:

2 green mangoes or ^{1}/$_2$ green paw paw (papaya)
^{1}/$_2$ teaspoon salt
1 tablespoon oil
2 cloves garlic, flaked then crisply fried
2 tablespoons dried prawns (shrimp)
200 grams (7 oz) cooked pork, finely chopped

Dressing:

1 tablespoon fish sauce
2 tablespoons lime juice
1 teaspoon palm sugar
1 tablespoon plum sauce
1 teaspoon chilli powder
2 tablespoons crushed roasted peanuts
^{1}/$_2$ teaspoon thick soy sauce (kecap manis)

Method:

The mango should be hard and green. Cut, unpeeled, into large chunks; discard the seed. (If using paw paw, skin then finely grate.) Soak the prawns in hot water for 5–10 minutes, squeeze dry and then pound them finely.

Toss all of the salad ingredients together in a large bowl. Mix all of the dressing ingredients well and combine with the salad just before serving.

Orange Pumpkin Curry

This Colonial curry sauce goes well with fish or boiled eggs.

Ingredients:

1 tablespoon oil

1 tablespoon shrimp paste, dry-roasted then crumbled (optional)

2 cups (500 mL / 16 fl oz) chicken stock

1 teaspoon tamarind

2 cups pumpkin, cubed

1 carrot, cubed or grated

1 yellow capsicum, cubed

2 tablespoons fish sauce

sugar, to taste

juice of 2 limes

1/3 cup (80 mL / 2 1/2 fl oz) orange juice

salt and pepper, to taste

Paste:

3 tablespoons sambal oelek

2 cloves garlic, chopped

1/2 cm (1/4 in) fresh turmeric or 1/2 teaspoon turmeric powder

3 Spanish (red) onions, dark-red outer layers only, chopped

1 tablespoon shrimp paste, dry roasted then crumbled (see page 172)

1 tablespoon rice vinegar

Garnish:

orange rind, sliced finely

nasturtium flowers

Method:

Prepare the paste. Pound all the paste ingredients well and blend into a paste. Use half of the paste for the curry; the other half can be refrigerated for use another time.

Fry the paste and the dry-roasted shrimp paste in the oil until smooth and aromatic.

Add the stock and simmer with tamarind. Add the pumpkin and carrot and cook slowly for about 15 minutes.

When the pumpkin and carrot are cooked, add the capsicum, fish sauce, sugar, lime and orange juice. Simmer to combine all the flavours. Season with salt and pepper.

Garnish with orange rind and nasturtium flowers. Serve with rice.

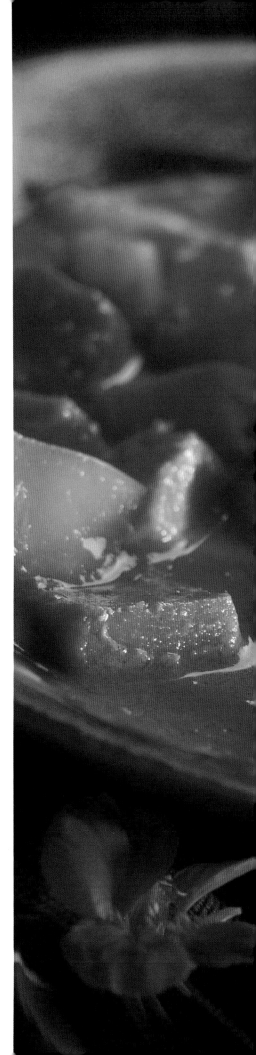

Orange Pumpkin Curry

Mushroom and Cashew Pengat

This curry uses milk and cream to blend with the mushrooms — this gives a better result than coconut milk. Cashews, which grow in Asia, are used in curries because they can be treated like meat.

Ingredients:

3 tablespoons ghee or vegetable oil

2 cloves garlic, thinly sliced

2 cm (³/₄ in) length ginger, thinly shredded

1 Spanish (red) onion, halved and thinly sliced

1 tablespoon chilli powder

¹/₂ tablespoon cumin powder

1 kg (2 lb) mushrooms, thinly sliced

2 green chillies, slit and seeded

salt, to taste

1 cup (250 mL / 8 fl oz) milk

¹/₂ teaspoon sugar

1 cup (155 g / 5¹/₂ oz) unsalted roasted cashews

mint leaves, chopped

¹/₂ cup (125 mL / 4 fl oz) cream

Method:

Use medium-sized button mushrooms if possible.

Heat the ghee on medium high and sauté the garlic, ginger and onion until golden and caramelised. Add the chilli powder and cumin powder and stir-fry well until aromatic.

Add the mushrooms, chillies and salt and sauté for 2–3 minutes. Add the milk and sugar and bring to the boil, stirring, then lower the heat and simmer for 5 minutes or until the gravy reduces a little.

Add the cashews and cook for 3 minutes or until the gravy has thickened. Stir well, season with mint leaves, then add the cream and heat through. Stir once more and remove from the heat.

This pengat can be served as a meal on its own, as a vegetarian stew or thick curried sauce, or it can be used as a base for a meat rissole-type curry. Cooked meatballs can be popped in after the curry has thickened and before the cream is added.

Stuffed Okra

Okra should be washed before slicing to minimise the stickiness. Malaysians also blanch small, whole okra and dip them into a light sambal belacan before eating with rice. To check if okra is tender, snap off the tip — it should snap off crisply.

Ingredients:

300 grams (10¹/₂ oz) medium okra

2 tablespoons dried prawns (shrimp), dry roasted then finely ground

1 tablespoon dried mango (amchur) powder

2 cm (³/₄ in) length ginger, ground to a purée

1 tablespoon sambal oelek or chilli sauce

salt, to taste

¹/₄ cup (30 g / 1 oz) cornflour (cornstarch)

¹/₂ teaspoon turmeric powder

1 cup (250 mL / 8 fl oz) vegetable oil

¹/₂ cup (125 g / 4 oz) thick yoghurt, beaten

chilli powder

Method:

Wash the okra then wipe dry. Cut an opening in the side of each okra with a sharp fruit knife, making sure that the slit does not extend to the thin bottom. Carefully remove some of the seeds and pith.

Combine the prawns (shrimp), mango powder, ginger, sambal oelek and salt.

Open up the aperture and stuff with the filling, using a chopstick to press the mixture in.

Combine the cornflour (cornstarch) and turmeric. Roll each okra in this mixture. Heat the oil on high in a wok and shallow pan-fry a few okra at a time for crispy results. Each batch will take about 3 minutes. Drain on kitchen paper.

Serve hot, arranged on a platter and garnished with the yoghurt and chilli powder.

Sweet—Sour Pineapple Gravy
(Gulai Nenas)

This curry goes well with fish or prawns. Cooking with fruit in Malaysia is quite popular, but only in earthenware pots. The pots should be seasoned before cooking by soaking in water overnight.

Ingredients:
3 large Spanish (red) onions, chopped
4 cloves garlic, chopped
3 cm (1 in) length ginger, chopped
1 tablespoon coriander (cilantro) powder
$^3/_4$ tablespoon cumin powder
$^3/_4$ tablespoon fennel powder
cinnamon, nutmeg and cloves, to taste
2 tablespoons oil
2 lemon grass bulbs, thinly sliced
2 tablespoons sambal oelek (less if preferred)
2 cups (500 mL / 16 fl oz) water or vegetable stock
sugar, to taste
salt, to taste
$^1/_2$ pineapple, thinly sliced

Method:
Blend the onions, garlic and ginger together in a food processor or mortar and pestle. Combine the coriander (cilantro) powder, cumin powder, fennel powder, cinnamon, nutmeg and cloves (you need 2 tablespoons of this curry powder).

Heat the oil on medium high in a frying pan and add the blended ingredients. Stir-fry until browned and aromatic.

Add the lemon grass, sambal oelek and curry powder and stir well. Add the stock, sugar and salt, bring to the boil, reduce the heat and simmer for 3 minutes to reduce slightly.

Just before removing from the heat add the pineapple slices. Boil again to reduce the liquid if the curry is too watery and not to your liking. It is meant to be a thin gravy. This dish goes well with lentils or with meat added.

Masala Mashed Potatoes

This dish is a glamorised version of the mashed potato. Try this one on the kids (but omit the chilli) and see if they refuse spuds ever again!

Ingredients:
5 cooked potatoes, peeled and roughly cut
1 green tomato, peeled and finely diced
2 teaspoons dried mango powder (amchur)
1 teaspoon black pepper
salt, to taste
1 fresh red chilli, chopped (seeded if preferred)
1 bunch (125 g / 4 oz) fresh mint, washed and shredded

Method:
Mash the potatoes. Add the tomato (with its juices) and mango powder and mash well.

Add the pepper, salt and chilli. Mix well, then toss in the mint. Chill and serve. You can also use this dish as a garnish for meatloaf.

Red Onion Kerabu

*This is a spectacular salad especially if you soak the onions
in a little bit of red cochineal before the salad is made up. Spanish
red onions are favoured by Asian cooks because they are sweeter, aren't
as strong as the white or brown varieties and are closer in flavour
to the little red onions used in Asia.*

Ingredients:

2 medium Spanish (red) onions,
halved and thinly sliced

1 teaspoon salt

1 teaspoon chilli powder

1/4 teaspoon paprika powder

1 tablespoon dried mango powder
(amchur)

1/2 teaspoon cochineal

1/4 bunch (80—100 g / 3—3 1/2 oz)
coriander (cilantro), chopped

1/4 bunch (50 g / 2 oz) mint leaves,
finely shredded

2 green chillies, seeded and chopped

juice of 1 lime

1 firm red tomato, skinned, seeded
and chopped

Method:

Crush the onion between your fingers
to break up the fibres and release the
juices.

Combine all of the ingredients in a
bowl. Toss with forks. Chill before
serving.

Serve with Tikka-style Barbequed
Lamb (recipe, page 52) or a tandoori or
as a relish with Mamak-style Prawn
Sambal (recipe, page 94). It also goes
well with Coconut Rice (Nasi Lemak)
(recipe, page 34).

Chinese Rojak Mixed Salad

*This Chinese salad has an unusual dark, sweet sauce made with a type
of shrimp paste known as Rojak (or haekoe).*

Ingredients:

1 cucumber, unpeeled

1 medium yam bean

1/2 pineapple

1 teaspoon salt

1 firm green mango

2 starfruit

2 firm kiwifruit

2 pieces (150 g / 5 oz) squid

100 g (3 1/2 oz) hard tofu

2 tablespoons oil

Sauce:

2 tablespoons rojak paste (haekoe)

2 tablespoons oyster sauce

1 1/2 tablespoons palm sugar

1 tablespoon sambal oelek

1 tablespoon sesame seeds,
dry roasted

Method:

Chop the unpeeled cucumber. Skin the
yam bean and chop it into bite-sized
pieces. Core the pineapple, brush it
with the salt, rinse off and chop.

Chop the unpeeled mango and
discard the seed. Cut the starfruit into
thick slices. Chop the unpeeled
kiwifruit.

Blanch the squid for a few seconds
in boiling water, chill then thinly slice.
Lightly fry the tofu in the oil until it
crisps, then cut into cubes.

Combine all of the sauce ingredients
together except the sesame seeds just
before serving. Pour over the combined
salad ingredients and garnish with the
sesame seeds.

Red Onion Kerabu

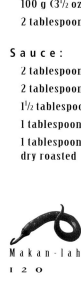

Tamarind Chilli Potatoes

The flavour of tamarind, lemony and sugary, takes on an extra dimension with potatoes. This is my Irish friend Harvey's favourite recipe. A beautiful Galway crystal potato sits on my desk, constantly reminding me of the debt we all owe to Columbus for his voyage to the New World.

Ingredients:

400 grams (13 oz) small new potatoes
1 tablespoon cumin seeds, dry roasted
1 teaspoon fennel seeds, dry roasted
2 tablespoons sambal oelek
5 cloves garlic, chopped and ground
$^1/_2$ teaspoon mustard seeds
pinch asafoetida powder
3 tablespoons tomato paste
$^1/_4$ cup (125 mL / 4 fl oz) tamarind purée from 4 cm (1$^1/_2$ in) tamarind block
6 sprigs curry leaves
$^1/_2$ cup (30 g / 1 oz) sun-dried tomatoes, chopped

Method:

Boil the unpeeled potatoes until they are almost fully cooked (a fork goes in easily but the potato doesn't break up).

Pound the cumin and fennel seeds in a mortar and pestle until smooth, then add the sambal oelek and garlic.

Dry heat the mustard seeds in a wok or frying pan until they pop, then add the ground mixture and sauté until aromatic. Add the asafoetida, tomato paste and tamarind purée and cook on medium heat for 3–4 minutes, adding 5 of the curry leaves as the curry matures.

When the oil seeps from the curry, add the sun-dried tomatoes and potatoes. Cover and cook for about 3 minutes to mix the flavours.

Remove and serve hot, garnished with the remaining sprig of curry leaves. An easy alternative for this recipe is to use scalloped, cooked potatoes and layer them with the sauce when completed. This can also be a good potato pasta mixture.

Pictured on page 106.

Stuffed Tofu
(Tofu Sumbat)

At school I was perpetually in disgrace because of the red chilli stains on the pockets of my uniform. This never deterred me from eating my favourite snack: spongy tofu pillow sandwiches crammed full of crunchy cucumber and sweet chilli sauce.

Ingredients:

8 square, deep-fried tofu puffs (about 80—100 g / 3—3$^1/_2$ oz)
2 cucumbers
1 cup (60 g / 2 oz) bean sprouts

Sauce:

$^1/_3$ cup (80 mL / 2$^1/_2$ fl oz) boiling water
$^1/_2$ tablespoon palm sugar
2 red chillies, chopped
1 clove garlic, chopped
1 tablespoon thick soy sauce (kecap manis)
1 tablespoon vinegar
3 tablespoons roasted peanuts, roughly pounded

Method:

Cut the tofu puffs into half triangles, then slit them open to form a pocket.

Shred the unpeeled cucumbers and tail the bean sprouts. Combine the cucumber and sprouts and stuff into the pockets of the tofu. Pour the sauce over the puffs and serve.

Sauce:

Put the palm sugar a bowl with the boiling water and stir until the sugar has dissolved. Combine with the remaining sauce ingredients. The consistency should be smooth, except for the peanuts.

This dish can be served as an entrée or as a second dish in a vegetarian meal.

Pictured on page 106.

Crisp-fried Tofu with Peanut Sauce
(Tauhu Belado)

I have tasted this when the dried squid and tofu are crisply grilled then doused with a sauce or a gutsy sambal. Malaysians eat a lot of rice with little morsels of meat, held together with sambals.

Ingredients:

1 cup (250 mL / 8 fl oz) oil

3 pieces (120 g / 4 oz) hard tofu, cubed

1 piece (50 g / 2 oz) tempe (fermented bean curd) (optional)

1 Spanish (red) onion, chopped

6 red chillies, seeded and chopped

3 cloves garlic, chopped

2 stalks lemon grass, thinly sliced

$^1/_2$ teaspoon shrimp paste, dry roasted

juice of 2 limes

2 spring onion (scallion) stalks, shredded

thick soy sauce (kecap manis)

Peanut Sauce:

1 cup (125 g / 4 oz) peanuts or 3 tablespoons crunchy peanut butter

10 large red serrano chillies, seeded

3 cloves garlic, chopped

2 cm ($^3/_4$ in) length ginger, chopped

1 Spanish (red) onion, chopped

1 tablespoon oil

1 cup (250 mL / 8 fl oz) water

$^1/_4$ cup (60 g / 2 oz) palm sugar

1 tablespoon tamarind from 2 cm ($^3/_4$ in) length tamarind pulp

salt, to taste

lemon grass bulb, shredded

Method:

Blend the onion, chillies, garlic, lemon grass and shrimp paste together in a food processor or mortar and pestle until puréed.

Heat the oil on high in a wok. Deep-fry the tofu until crisp and golden, remove from the oil and drain. Deep-fry the tempe in the same hot oil, drain.

Discard all but 2 tablespoons of the oil and fry the purée on medium heat until aromatic and caramelised. Using kitchen paper, dab at the oil and remove as much as possible without disturbing the ingredients — by this stage the oil should have separated from the mixture.

Add the lime juice to the wok, stir well and toss in the tofu and tempe. Remove from the heat and cool. Serve hot or at room temperature with the peanut sauce and rice. Garnish with the spring onion (scallion) stalks and dot with a few drops of the soy sauce.

Peanut Sauce:

Dry roast the peanuts until golden, then pound them roughly so that chunky pieces remain in the mixture. Blend the chillies, garlic, ginger and onion in a food processor or mortar and pestle until puréed.

Heat the oil on medium heat in a saucepan and sauté the purée for 3 minutes, until the onion caramelises. Add $^1/_2$ cup (125 mL / 4 fl oz) of the water and the sugar. Bring to the boil, reduce the heat to medium and simmer until the sugar has melted.

Add the peanuts or peanut butter and stir well; this will cause the sauce to thicken.

Add the remaining water, tamarind purée and salt and stir well. Once the oil has separated from the sauce it is ready; this will take approximately 10–12 minutes. Season and serve garnished with the lemon grass bulb.

As well as being served with the Tauhu Belado, this sauce can also be used for steamed or raw vegetables, lettuce salads, or with Tofu Omelette (recipe, page 126).

Tofu and Carrot Balls

This dish presents another simple method of giving children a vegetable meal they can easily eat.

Ingredients:

2 hard tofu squares (80 g / 3 oz)

1 slice bread

$^1/_4$ cup (60 mL / 2 fl oz) milk

2 spring onions (scallions)

1 carrot, well grated

1 stick celery or $^1/_4$ capsicum (bell pepper), seeded and finely diced

2 lemon grass bulbs, finely chopped

$^1/_2$ teaspoon chilli powder

mint leaves, chopped

1 egg, separated

salt, to taste

pepper, to taste

$^1/_2$ cup (60 g / 2 oz) rice flour

2 cups (500 mL / 16 fl oz) oil

Method:

Mash the tofu well. Remove the rind from the bread and soak in the milk for 5 minutes. Remove and squeeze out as much milk as possible. Chop the spring onions (scallions), including some of the green stem.

Combine the tofu with the carrot, celery, spring onions (scallion), lemon grass bulbs, chilli powder and mint. Add the bread, egg yolk, salt and pepper and mash well with a fork.

Lightly beat the egg white. Shape teaspoonfuls of the mixture into balls, dip into the beaten egg white then roll in the flour.

Heat the oil on high in a wok and deep-fry the balls until golden. Serve hot.

Six Friends Salad
(Enam Sekawan)

This salad has a hot and spicy, tamarind-flavoured dressing and is from the east coast of Malaysia. It is for my six friends whom I'm thanking with this book.

Ingredients:

6 puffy pieces (80 g / 3 oz) of deep-fried tofu, quartered

150 grams (5¹/₂ oz) green prawns (shrimp), cooked and peeled

4 hard-boiled eggs, quartered

1 tin (¹/₂—²/₃ cup / 125—140 mL / 4—5 fl oz) petai bean seeds
or 10 snowpeas, 6 pickled baby onions or 1 zucchini, roughly chopped

100 grams (3¹/₂ oz) baby green cauli-brocco or cauliflower

2 carrots, julienned in thin strips or 50 grams (2 oz) rocket

1 tablespoon sesame seeds, dry roasted

Dressing:

2 tablespoons oil

2 Spanish (red) onions, chopped and puréed

4 cloves garlic, puréed

1 tablespoon chilli bean paste

2 tablespoons tamarind concentrate from 3 cm (1 in) tamarind block

1 tablespoon palm sugar

salt or fish sauce, to taste

juice of 1 lime

Dressing:

Heat the oil on medium hot and sauté the onions and garlic until aromatic and caramelised. Add the chilli bean paste, tamarind and palm sugar and cook on medium heat. As the sugar melts, turn the heat down so it doesn't burn.

Add the salt and lime juice and taste, adding more sugar or salt as needed.

Salad:

Drain the petai bean seeds. Steam the baby green cauli-brocco or cauliflower until partially cooked, al dente.

Toss all of the salad ingredients except the sesame seeds in a large salad bowl, adding the dressing as you go. Serve garnished with sesame seeds. If using rocket, it can be warmed before adding.

Preparing Six Friends Salad
(Enam Sekawan)

Steamed Tofu

Tofu contains more protein than any other food and, because of its blandness, adopts the flavours of anything it is cooked with. It can even be substituted for meat. Tofu was supposed to have been developed by an impoverished and overworked Chinese official who didn't earn enough and couldn't afford meat. Men like him were called 'tofu officials'.

Ingredients:

250 grams (8 oz) silken or soft tofu

1 spring onion (scallion), finely sliced

60 grams (2 oz) minced pork

100 grams green prawn (shrimp) meat, minced

2 teaspoons light soy sauce

salt, to taste

pepper, to taste

1 egg white

2 red chillies, seeded and finely chopped or two spring onion (scallion) bulbs, chopped, extra

few drops sesame oil

Method:

Push the tofu through a sieve. Combine with the spring onion (scallion), pork, prawn (shrimp) meat, soy sauce, salt and pepper.

Beat the egg white until stiff but not dry. Fold through the tofu. Pour into a greased pie plate and cover with the chillies and sesame oil. Brush with some more of the sesame oil and steam for 10 minutes. The tofu will set like a meatloaf; it can be sliced or cut into pieces. Serve hot with rice.

Tofu in Tamarind Sauce
(Assam Tofu)

The tofu in this case absorbs and reflects the taste of the chilli and tamarind, marrying flavours and techniques from one end of Asia to another.

Ingredients:

2 packets (150—200 g / 5—7 oz) silken tofu or smooth tofu

$^1/_2$ cup (125 mL / 4 fl oz) vegetable oil

5 cloves garlic, finely sliced

5 small onions, finely sliced

1 teaspoon sweet chilli sauce

1 tablespoon tamarind purée from 2 cm ($^3/_4$ in) length tamarind block

$^1/_2$ cup (125 mL / 4 fl oz) water

2 tablespoons palm sugar

3 spring onion stalks, chopped

$^1/_4$ cup (30 g / 1 oz) crispy fried onions

Method:

Cut the tofu gently from the rolls into slices 3 cm (1 in) thick.

Heat the oil on medium in a wok and gently fry the tofu slices until lightly browned. Lift out carefully and drain on absorbent paper.

Drain off all but 2 tablespoons of the oil. Fry the garlic and onions on medium heat until golden and crisp. Add the chilli sauce, tamarind purée and water. Bring to the boil and add the palm sugar, reduce the heat and simmer for 2–3 minutes.

Remove from the heat. Place the tofu slices on a serving dish, pour the sauce over and serve with rice. Garnish with spring onion (scallion) stalks and crispy fried onions.

Tofu Omelette

This is a good vegetarian dish even if tofu does not especially appeal to you, for tofu takes on the flavours of whatever it is cooked with.

Ingredients:

2 square packs (about 250 grams / 8 oz) firm white tofu

6 eggs

$^1/_2$ teaspoon salt

1 tablespoon light soy sauce

2 tablespoons vegetable oil or butter

1 Spanish (red) onion, finely chopped

4 stalks garlic chives, washed and finely chopped

2 chillies, seeded and shredded

1 teaspoon rice flour

salt, to taste, extra

pepper, to taste

Method:

Mash the tofu well. Lightly beat the eggs with the salt and soy sauce.

Heat the oil or butter on medium high in a wok and sauté the onion until golden. Add half of the chives and cook for 1 minute.

Add half of the chillies and half of the egg mixture and swirl in the wok, keeping the heat on medium until the egg sets.

Add the tofu and the remaining chives and chillies to the centre of the omelette and cook for 3–4 minutes.

Stir the rice flour through the remaining egg mixture with the salt and pepper and add it to the wok. Lift some of the set egg so that the runny mixture gets under it and cooks also. This will set like a frittata or Spanish omelette. The tofu will absorb the flavours of the other ingredients while the rice flour in the second lot of egg mixture will create a crispy collar around the omelette.

Lift carefully out of the wok with a flat fish slice. This omelette is substantial enough to be served as a meal on its own, or can form part of a meal with rice.

Fresh Fruit and Vegetable Kerabu

This salad comes from Northern Malaysia. Asian markets present a treasure trove of colour, flavour and aroma: rambutan, mangosteens, mangoes, durians, jambu, duku and langsat. Malaysian fruits are not overly sweet, but tend to have subtle and refreshing flavours.

Ingredients:

100 grams (3½ oz) green paw paw (papaya)

50 grams (2 oz) snake beans

1 Lebanese cucumber

50 grams (2 oz) tender heart of tientsin cabbage

2 dried red chillies

3 red Asian onions, peeled and chopped

2 cloves garlic

1 egg

1 mandarin

2 tablespoons palm sugar

juice of 3 limes

½ teaspoon salt

6 Tom Thumb tomatoes, halved

1 bunch (125 g / 4 oz) tender sweet potato leaves and tendrils

2 tablespoons fish sauce

salt, to taste, extra

pepper, to taste

Garnish:

½ bunch (60 g / 2 oz) coriander (cilantro) or mint leaves, finely shredded

1 tablespoon sesame seeds, dry roasted

½ packet (80 g / 3 oz) prefried noodles, broken up

Method:

Peel and finely shred the paw paw (papaya). Blanch the snake beans then finely slice lengthwise. Peel and seed the Lebanese cucumber then slice. Shred the cabbage heart.

Roast the chillies over a flame then blend in a food processor or mortar and pestle with the onions. Finely slice the garlic and fry it until crisp and golden brown.

Make the egg into an omelette, roll up and finely slice. Peel the mandarin, divide into segments and remove the membranes. Blend the palm sugar with the lime juice.

Place the paw paw (papaya), snake beans, cabbage heart and Lebanese cucumber in a bowl. Add the salt and, after 10 minutes, gently squeeze the fruit and vegetables to remove any liquid that has disgorged. Pour off the salty liquid. Add the chilli and onion mixture and garlic to the bowl. Toss.

Shake the fish sauce, extra salt and pepper together with the combined sugar and lime juice in a bottle. Taste the dressing to make sure that sweet and sour are balanced. Adjust as necessary and toss through the salad with the tomatoes and potato leaves.

Gently mix in the mandarin segments and shredded omelette. Garnish with the coriander (cilantro), sesame seeds and noodles. This salad is often eaten with crispy barbecued pork and rice.

If you wish, you can include tiny pieces of cooked barbecued pork (char siew) or cooked prawns (shrimp) with the vegetables. *Pictured on page 102.*

Watermelon Rind Kerabu

This is an unusual and very tasty salad containing freshly cooked fished.

Ingredients:

¼ (1 kg / 2 lb) watermelon

½ cup (125 mL / 4 fl oz) vegetable oil

2—3 (100—125 g / 3½—4 oz each) small sand whiting or yellowtail, cleaned and scaled

6 chillies, seeded and finely chopped

1 Spanish (red) onion, halved and finely sliced

salt, to taste

pepper, to taste

juice of 1 lime

Method:

Slice the red part of the watermelon away from the green rind. The rind is the part used for this salad — keep the red part for dessert.

Scrape as much of the green base as possible into shaved curls using a vegetable peeler, or cut into thin juliennes.

Heat the oil on high heat and fry the fish as crisply as possible. Flake the flesh and put into a serving bowl. Place the remaining ingredients in the bowl with the fish and toss well.

This salad is good eaten on its own or with a meat curry. It goes very well with mild kurma (curry). The textures and flavour are exceptional.

Pictured on page 110.

Thick Vegetable Pengat

This is an upmarket vegetable stew that can be dressed up with more herbs, or dressed down by using parsnips or sweet potato and carrots. Microwaving the pumpkin eliminates much of the hard work of peeling. Pengat can be eaten with the fingers, lifting a portion of bread or roti and scooping the thick, flavoursome stew into the mouth, so the gravy shouldn't be watery.

Ingredients:

1 kilogram (2 lb) butternut pumpkin

2 tablespoons sambal oelek

2 Spanish (red) onions, chopped

4 cloves garlic, chopped

2 stalks lemon grass, chopped

1 tablespoon coriander (cilantro) seeds, dry roasted

4 cardamom pods

3 tablespoons oil

1 cup (250 mL / 8 fl oz) thick coconut cream

1 cup (250 mL / 8 fl oz) chicken stock

3 cm (1 in) length ginger, finely shredded

$^1/_2$ teaspoon nutmeg

salt, to taste

$^1/_2$ teaspoon turmeric

2 red chillies, slit open

1 tablespoon fish sauce

juice of 2 limes

3 kaffir lime leaves, shredded

1 tablespoon palm sugar

2 cm ($^3/_4$ in) length ginger, extra, shredded

Method:

Pierce the skin of the pumpkin with a fork and boil or steam for 10 minutes. Peel and roughly chop. Combine the sambal oelek, onions, garlic, lemon grass and coriander (cilantro) together in a food processor or mortar and pestle until puréed. Remove the seeds from the cardamom and roughly pound.

Heat the oil on medium heat in a wok and sauté the purée until aromatic, about 7–8 minutes, making sure that the mixture does not stick to the bottom of the wok. Add the coconut cream, chicken stock, ginger, pounded cardamom seeds, nutmeg, salt, turmeric and chillies and cook on medium heat for 8–10 minutes.

Add the pumpkin and cook on low heat for about 30 minutes. Add the fish sauce, lime juice, 2 of the kaffir lime leaves and sugar. Stir well, being careful once again that the mixture does not stick to the bottom of the wok.

Remove from the heat and serve garnished with the remaining lime leaf and extra ginger.

Vegetables in Black Bean Paste
(Taucheo Tumis)

Taucheo, or salted black beans, have such an exciting aroma, especially when added to chilli, that one can taste the food long before it hits the palate. We savour with our eyes, ears and noses long before we eat anything.

Ingredients:

$^1/_4$ cup (60 mL / 2 fl oz) oil

1 square (80—100 g / 3—$3^1/_2$ oz) silk tofu, carefully cubed (optional)

400 grams (13 oz) any fresh vegetables or a combination of French beans, okra and bittermelon, sliced on the diagonal

1 tablespoon black beans

200 grams (7 oz) green prawns (shrimp), cleaned or 200 grams (7 oz) pork

3 cloves garlic, thinly diced

2 Spanish (red) onions, halved and thinly sliced or 8 red Asian onions, chopped

1 tablespoon sambal oelek (or to taste)

dash of fish sauce

Method:

Heat the oil on medium in a wok and gently fry the cubes of tofu until pale golden on the outside. Drain on several thicknesses of absorbent paper. Drain off all but 2 tablespoons of the oil.

If you do not like the flavour of bittermelon, soak the vegetable in salted water for about 30 minutes. Bittermelon comes in the same form as cucumber, with seeds and pith at the centre, so slice it lengthwise in half and scoop the seeds out by running a spoon down the centre at right angles to the vegetable.

Black beans are usually very highly salted; wash some of the salt off in water, then pound or mash the beans with the back of a spoon. If the prawns are large, slice right through the length to create two halves.

Reheat the remaining oil on medium high in a wok and sauté the garlic until golden. Add the onions and stir-fry until aromatic. Then add the black beans and sambal oelek and continue to cook on medium or low heat until the aroma is released without burning the mixture.

Add the prawns and stir-fry briskly for 2 minutes. Add the vegetables of your choice, stir-fry to combine the ingredients, cover the pan and cook for 2 minutes on high to allow the ingredients to sweat. Remove the lid, stir once more, add the fish sauce and remove from the heat before the vegetables wilt.

Serve garnished with the tofu on top. The vegetables should be crisp and firm, which is how they will turn out if you use a heavy, cast-iron wok.

This method of vegetable stir-fry can be adapted to any vegetable such as green capsicum (bell pepper) with beef or lamb.

Vegetables Stuffed with Fish or Prawn Meat in Taucheo Sauce

Vegetables suitable for stuffing in this dish include bittermelon, chilli, cucumber, eggplant and okra.

Ingredients:
vegetables of your choice
fish or prawn forcemeat (see Fishballs and Fishcakes, page 88)

Taucheo Sauce:
2 tablespoons salted whole black beans
1 tablespoon oil
3 cloves garlic, chopped
1 tablespoon sambal oelek
1 tablespoon thick mushroom soy sauce
$1/4$ cup (60 mL / 2 fl oz) water
1 tablespoon red or black Chinese vinegar
$1^1/_2$ cups (375 mL / 12 fl oz) pork or chicken stock
salt, to taste
sugar, to taste

Method:
Prepare the vegetables for stuffing. For bittermelons, cut off the ends, remove the seeds and pith and cut the flesh into thick slices. For chilli and okra, make a slit along the length of the vegetable and carefully remove the seeds.

Place the forcemeat in the centre of each vegetable and steam.

Taucheo Sauce:
Rinse the black beans in water to remove excess salt. Mash with the back of a fork and set aside.

Heat the oil on medium heat in a wok and sauté the garlic until golden. Add the black beans and sambal oelek and cook until aromatic, being careful that the mixture doesn't burn.

Add the mushroom soy sauce, water, vinegar and stock, increase the heat and bring to the boil.

Add the stuffed vegetables, season to taste, bring back to the boil then lower the heat and simmer in the sauce for 3–4 minutes. Remove from heat and serve hot.

Beanthread Vermicelli Salad

The Nonya use a great deal of beanthread noodles, which is called suhoon in Malaysia. The smooth and silky textured beanthreads look and taste interesting in salads.

Ingredients:
2 cups (500 mL / 16 fl oz) water
100 grams ($3^1/_2$ oz) beanthread noodles
100 grams ($3^1/_2$ oz) squid tubes
100 grams ($3^1/_2$ oz) prawns (shrimp)
1 tablespoon dried shrimp
juice of 2 limes
1 red chilli, seeded and chopped
2 teaspoons fish sauce or salt
$1/2$ Spanish (red) onion, thinly sliced
2 spring onion (scallion) stems, sliced
1 tablespoon palm sugar
6 cos lettuce leaves, washed and wiped dry or 200 grams (7 oz) watercress leaves
$1/4$ cup (30 g / 1 oz) mint leaves, chopped

Method:
Bring the water to boil in a saucepan and immerse the beanthread noodles for 5–8 minutes to soften. Strain and cut into 5–6 cm (2–2½ in) pieces.

Slice the squid tubes open, score the insides with a fork, then blanch in boiling water for a few seconds. Blanch the prawns (shrimp) in hot water for 1 minute or until they just change colour. Combine the squid and prawns (shrimp) in a mixing bowl.

Deep-fry the dried shrimp until golden and crisp, then roughly pound.

Combine the lime juice, chilli and fish sauce together in a jar. Shake, add to the squid and prawns (shrimp) and toss. Combine all of the salad ingredients except the dried shrimp, lettuce (or watercress) leaves and mint leaves.

Arrange the lettuce (or watercress) leaves on a platter large enough to hold the salad. Serve the salad on the bed of lettuce garnished with the dried shrimp and mint.

Sambals,
Sauces, Pickles
and Relishes

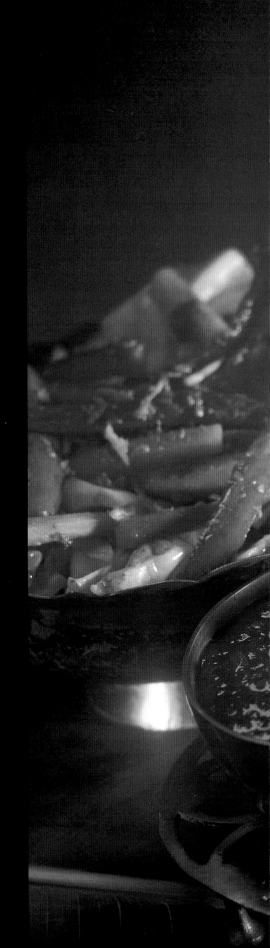

Clockwise from left: Achar (recipe, page 132), Date Chutney (recipe, page 133), Coconut Serunding Sambal (recipe, page 132), Pickled Limes (recipe, page 140), and Home-made Sambal Oelek (recipe, page 148)

Makan-lah!

Achar

Achar is a typical Nonya pickle, the making of which is done in three stages: the first is grinding the spice and herb mixture, the second is preparing the vegetables, and the third is blanching the vegetables and combining the ingredients. Achar is so time consuming to make that Malaysians make it only for festivals such as the Chinese New Year or for the feast of Ramadan, Hari Raya.

Ingredients:

2 cm (³/₄ in) length fresh turmeric

8 cups (2 L / 64 fl oz) vinegar

salt, to taste

1 cup (250 mL / 8 fl oz) vegetable oil

2 cups (250 g / 8 oz) white sugar

salt, extra, to taste

1 cup (125 g / 4 oz) sesame seeds, toasted

Vegetables:

400 grams (13 oz) long beans

3 carrots, peeled

4 Spanish (red) onions

300 grams (10¹/₂ oz) cabbage

300 grams (10¹/₂ oz) cauliflower

400 grams (13 oz) green paw paw (papaya)

100 grams (3¹/₂ oz) dried shrimp, dry roasted (optional)

2 long, broad chillies (optional)

³/₄ cup (180 mL / 6 fl oz) sambal oelek

¹/₄ cup (60 mL / 2 fl oz) chilli black bean paste or 1 teaspoon chopped chilli and 1 tablespoon black bean paste

15 cloves garlic, chopped

3 Spanish (red) onions, chopped

4 lemon grass bulbs, chopped

5 cm (2 in) length ginger, chopped

Method:

Lightly pound the turmeric in one piece in a mortar and pestle.

Cut the long beans into 4 cm (1½ in) lengths. Finely julienne the carrots. Roughly chop the onions and cabbage, discarding the centre of the cabbage. Cut the cauliflower into florets. Peel and julienne the paw paw (papaya).

If using the dried shrimp and chillies, pound the dried shrimp until it looks like floss then stuff into the chillies.

Blend the sambal oelek, chilli black bean paste, garlic, onions, lemon grass and ginger together in a food processor or mortar and pestle until puréed.

In a saucepan, heat the vinegar and salt on high heat and blanch each of the vegetables separately for 1 minute. Drain each vegetable as it is cooked and place in a porcelain or glass bowl with the stuffed chillies.

Pictured on previous page.

Makan-lah!

132

Heat the oil on medium high in a wok and fry the turmeric until aromatic. Discard the turmeric. In the remaining oil, sauté the puréed mixture on medium high until aromatic then reduce the heat to low and cook for 10 minutes, or until the onions are caramelised.

Add the sugar to the wok and stir until dissolved. Be careful not to allow the mixture to stick to the wok; however, it should caramelise. Season to taste with the salt and stir well. The mixture should be a reddish yellow in colour.

Place the sambal mixture into the bowl with the vegetables and mix, using a clean, dry spoon or spatula to toss well. Add the sesame seeds and set aside to cool.

Decant into sterile jars and leave for at least 2 days. Serve with rice or Ghee rice (Nasi Minyak) (See recipe for Saffron Rice (Nasi Kunyit) on page 32). This achar will keep well in the refrigerator for at least 2 weeks.

Coconut Serunding Sambal

Serunding comes from the word 'runding', meaning 'meeting'. This particular sambal, which uses dried coconut, is served with Coconut Rice (Nasi Lemak) (recipe, page 34) which is served traditionally on the twelfth day after a Nonya wedding.

Ingredients:

2 tablespoons vegetable oil

10 small onions, finely sliced

3 stalks lemon grass, finely sliced

2 tablespoons sambal oelek

2 tablespoons dried shrimp, dry roasted until crisp, then pounded

2 cups (185 g / 6 oz) coconut, grated and dry roasted until golden

1 red chilli, seeded and finely sliced

salt, to taste

sugar, to taste

2 tablespoons chilli oil

Method:

Roughly pound the dried shrimp.

Heat the oil on medium high and fry the onions, lemon grass, sambal oelek and dried shrimp for 5 minutes. Add the coconut, chilli, salt and sugar and fry on low heat, stirring all the time, until golden. Add the chilli oil around the edges of the wok if needed and adjust the seasoning if necessary. Continue frying until crisp. Remove from the heat and cool.

Stored in sterilised jars and serve cold sprinkled on salads, as a topping or as a sandwich spread.

Pictured on previous page

Cucumber and Pineapple Pachidi

Malaysians eat rice in copious amounts; a typical plate would have a spoonful of Achar (recipe, previous page), and a sambal and pickle with meat or vegetables on the side. These would be eaten with the rice, so that each mouthful is a different combination of flavours and textures.

Ingredients:

2 cucumbers, unpeeled

$1/2$ pineapple, peeled, cored and roughly chopped

2 Spanish (red) onions, sliced

2 chillies, seeded and chopped

$1/2$ cup (125 mL / 4 fl oz) vinegar

2 tablespoons sugar

1 cup (250 mL / 8 fl oz) lime or lemon juice

1 tablespoon fish sauce

$1/2$ teaspoon salt

$1/2$ cup dried shrimp, dry roasted then pounded

Method:

Cut the cucumbers in half lengthwise and remove the seeds by running a spoon at right angles down the halves. Cut into diagonal slices. Place in a bowl with the pineapple, onions and chillies.

Combine the vinegar, sugar, lime juice, fish sauce and salt and mix well. Pour over the pineapple mixture.

Sprinkle the dried shrimp over the salad and serve cold. This salad is best prepared just before eating.

Vinegared Cucumber Pickle
(Sambal Chukar)

This is a simple pickle that can be made in a hurry. Sliced choko can take the place of cucumber with satisfying results.

Ingredients:

1 cucumber sliced in half along its length

1 cup Chinese vinegar

2 tablespoons sugar

1 chilli, seeded then chopped

ginger, sliced

Method:

Remove the cucumber seeds by scooping them out with a spoon held at right angles to the cucumber. Slice each half in diagonal slices. Soak the cucumber pieces in vinegar, sugar, chilli and ginger for a few hours. Pour off the vinegar before serving.

Date Chutney

This chutney comes from South Africa and from the Cape Malays. It is reminiscent of the date pickles of the Ceylon Malays and of Indian Muslims in Malaysia. Food represents comfort in any chaotic new environment, so it is not surprising that food styles and recipes remain with people generations after they have forgotten language and even culture.

Ingredients:

450 grams (14 oz) pitted dates

5 cloves garlic, chopped

3 cm (1 in) length young ginger, chopped

1 cup (250 mL / 8 fl oz) vinegar

$1/2$ cup (90 grams / 3 oz) brown sugar

10 cloves

1 cinnamon stick

2 tablespoons chilli powder

salt, to taste

6 pickled limes, quartered or slivered (see recipe, page 140)

2 tablespoons slivered almonds, toasted until golden

Method:

Chop the dates reasonably finely with a knife, leaving some dates in chunky pieces. Blend the garlic, ginger and vinegar together in a food processor or mortar and pestle until puréed.

Place the puréed mixture in a saucepan with the dates, sugar, cloves, cinnamon stick and chilli powder and cook on medium heat, stirring well, until the sugar has dissolved. Add the salt and continue to cook on medium heat for 10 minutes or until it reduces to a thick consistency.

Add the limes (with a small amount of the jelly they were pickled in) and almonds, stir through and remove from the heat. Bottle when cool in sterilised jars.

Pictured on page 130.

Cincaluk Sambal

Cincaluk are small pink krill that look like microscopic prawns; they can be purchased pickled in bottles. They are a Nonya specialty from Melaka. My mother used to survive on this sambal with some rice and fried kang kong (water convolvulus) as an orphan in a boarding school in Penang. She remembers the combination of flavours as a highlight in her life.

Ingredients:

3 tablespoons cincaluk (or small pink krill or prawns pickled in brine)

6 large red chillies, seeded and chopped

1 cm (½ in) length shrimp paste, dry roasted then crumbled

3 red Asian onions, chopped or ½ medium Spanish (red) onion, peeled and thinly sliced

juice of ½ a lime (retain some of the zest, to taste)

salt, to taste

Method:

Soak the cincaluk for 1–2 minutes in enough water to cover then drain to remove the salt. When drained it will clump together in a wet mass; this will not affect the taste.

Pound the chillies with the shrimp paste. Add the onions, pounding until the mixture is semi-smooth.

Add the lime juice, zest and salt. The mixture should be somewhat lumpy. Add the cincaluk and stir well. Refrigerate. Serve with ulams (leafy salad herbs) or with rice and sautéed vegetables.

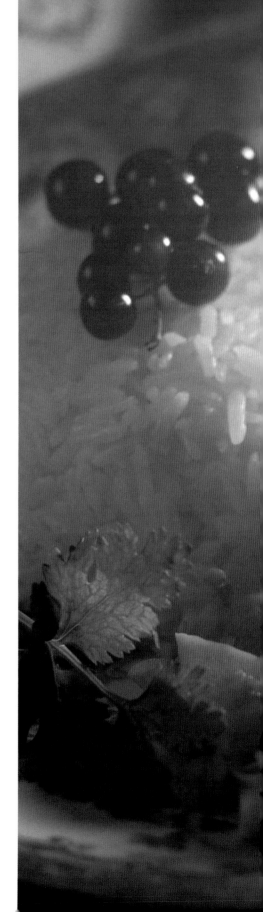

Clockwise from back: Green Paw Paw Pickle (recipe, page 144), Cincaluk Sambal (recipe, this page) and Mango Sambal (recipe, page 141)

Eggplant Relish
(Brinjal Pachidi)

This is my mother-in-law's recipe, one that she cooked with finesse. The preparation is very similar to the way Lebanese prepare eggplant, perhaps a reminder that Persian and middle Eastern influences were very strong in the Mogul period of India's and Asia's history.

Ingredients:

2 medium-sized eggplants (aubergine)

$^1/_2$ teaspoon turmeric powder

juice of 1 lime

3 green chillies, seeded and finely chopped

1 Spanish (red) onion, halved and finely diced

salt, to taste

2 tablespoons thick coconut cream

Method:

Slice the eggplants (aubergine) in half and brush with the turmeric powder.

Place the eggplants (aubergine) under a gas flame or a grill and roast on medium heat. Remove after about 6–10 minutes or when they smell roasted and the flesh becomes opaque.

Scoop out the pulp into a bowl with a spoon. Mash the pulp with the lime juice, chillies, onion and salt. Add the coconut cream, mix and mash well.

Chill and serve. This dish is good as a pachidi (relish); it can also double as a dip for crackers.

Eggplant Sambal
(Brinjal Pahi)

Pahi is a Malay–Indian term meaning a sambal, relish or pickle. This is a recipe my grandmother used for making a large quantity of brinjal pickle. The rempah (spice mix) has to be fried carefully so that the gravy will be clear and bright. My old machik (grandmother) relied on her sense of sight, sound and smell to tell whether the rempah was ready for the other ingredients.

Ingredients:

2 large eggplants (aubergine) or 400 grams (13 oz) small, thin eggplant

2 teaspoons salt

1 teaspoon turmeric powder

1 cup (250 mL / 8 fl oz) oil

3 cm (1 in) length ginger, shredded

4 cloves garlic, finely chopped

2 Spanish (red) onions, halved and thinly sliced

$2^1/_2$ tablespoons cumin seeds, dry roasted then ground

1 tablespoon fennel seeds, dry roasted then ground

2 tablespoons black mustard seeds, roughly ground

1 tablespoon chilli powder

1 cup (250 mL / 8 fl oz) vinegar

1 tablespoon sugar

$^1/_4$ cup (50 g / 2 oz) sultanas (optional)

$^1/_4$ cup (50 g / 2 oz) cashews, toasted

Method:

Cut the eggplant (aubergine) into 2 cm (¾ in) thick slices and brush with the combined salt and turmeric. Leave for 10 minutes then drain away any juice that has formed.

Heat the oil on high heat in a frying pan and cook the eggplant (aubergine) slices in small batches until golden. Drain on absorbent paper.

Drain off all but 3 tablespoons of the oil. Reheat the oil on high heat in a wok and sauté the ginger, garlic and onions until aromatic. Add the cumin seeds and fennel seeds and sauté until aromatic. Add the mustard seeds and cook for 2 minutes.

Add the chilli powder, vinegar and sugar and stir to combine. Turn the heat down to medium as the food begins to boil. Add the sultanas and cashews, then gently add the eggplant (aubergine) slices and stir.

Remove from the heat and cool. When cold, bottle in sterile jars and refrigerate. This sambal can be served either hot or cold as a chutney; it also goes well with baked ham.

Ginger Achar

A balanced Malaysian meal relies on a variety of dishes: one meat or fish, a couple of vegetables, maybe soup and lots of side serves of achar, sambal or chutney.

Ingredients:

4 young, tender carrots, peeled

6 cm (2 in) length tender ginger

2 green chillies, seeded and chopped

1/4 cup (60 mL / 2 fl oz) coconut cream or 1/4 cup (60 mL / 2 fl oz) vinegar

salt, to taste

sugar, to taste

Method:

Grate the carrots and ginger. Combine the chillies, coconut cream, salt and sugar. Place all of the ingredients in a bowl and toss well.

If using vinegar instead of coconut cream, allow the vegetables to steep in it for at least 1 hour, then mix and toss as directed.

Chilli Grapefruit Marmalade

I like the taste of grapefruit and feel that the bite of chilli heightens the flavours rather than masks them. This is very good as a relish on roast lamb or beef, or with turkey breasts.

Ingredients:

4 grapefruit

4 oranges

6 cups (1 1/2 L / 48 fl oz) water

1 1/4 cups (200 g / 7 oz) ginger, finely shredded

6—8 chillies, seeded and finely shredded in thin long strips

8 cups (2 kg / 4 lb) sugar

few strands of saffron

Method:

Remove the zest from 1 of the grapefruit and from 2 of the oranges, shred finely and set aside. Cut the rind and white pith from the fruit and discard. Cut the fruit into pieces, removing and saving the seeds. Tie the seeds inside a small muslin bag.

Combine the fruit, zest, seeds, water, ginger and chillies in a large saucepan. Bring to the boil and cook for 90 minutes, or until the liquid is reduced by three-quarters. Remove the bag of seeds.

Add the sugar and saffron strands to the mixture and stir until the sugar is dissolved. Do not allow to boil until the sugar is completely dissolved or the marmalade will crystallise.

Bring the mixture to the boil slowly, reduce the heat and simmer for 10 minutes, or until a teaspoon full of jam dropped onto a cold saucer sets. Pour into sterilised jars and seal. The chilli and saffron strands give the marmalade quite an attractive appearance.

Sambal Gerago

Grago are the tiny, almost microscopic prawns fished in the Melaka straits from kelong or deep-sea fishing platforms. With a series of lights and curved traps, fish are guided into nets that are hauled at intervals onto the kelong. It is quite scary to be on a kelong on a stormy night, and women are not normally welcome … not until my friend Annie's husband let us on his kelong one magic moonlit night. I will never forget the experience of cooking and eating fish and prawns almost as soon as they left the nets. Gerago may be substituted with dried or fresh prawns (shrimp).

Ingredients:

100 grams (3 1/2 oz) gerago, small krill or small prawns (shrimp)

1/2 cup (50 g / 2 oz) desiccated coconut or 1/2 cup (50 g / 2 oz) freshly grated coconut

1 tablespoon chilli black bean paste

1 tablespoon palm sugar, or to taste

1 tablespoon fish sauce

juice of 1 lime

4 kaffir lime leaves, rolled into cigar shapes and thinly sliced

pepper, to taste

Method:

Wash the gerago and lay out on absorbent paper to dry.

Mix all of the ingredients in a bowl. Tart or sweet flavours may be tailored to suit you, by adjusting the amount of chilli black bean paste, sugar, fish sauce and lime juice.

When mixed, add to a heated wok and dry roast on medium high until aromatic. You do not need to use any oil as the coconut contains some oil; this is enough to cook the entire dish.

Sambal Kang Kong

Kang kong is also known as water convolvulus, swamp cabbage,
ong choy or Asian spinach; it is a dark green vegetable
with arrow-shaped leaves and light green hollow stems.
It is rich in iron and is very tasty. It retains its
crunch even after cooking.

Ingredients:

1 tablespoon sambal oelek

2 red Asian onions, sliced

1/2 teaspoon shrimp paste, dry roasted

500 grams (1 lb) kang kong (water convolvulus)

1 tablespoon oil

1 tablespoon coconut cream

salt, to taste

Method:

Combine the sambal oelek, onions and shrimp paste together in a food processor or mortar and pestle until well blended. Pick off the tender leaves of the kang kong and break the thinner stems into 5 cm (2 in) lengths.

Heat the oil on medium high in a wok and sauté the blended mixture for 1 minute or until it loses its raw aroma. Add the kang kong a little at a time; it will soften and turn limp as it hits the pan so you can fit more in.

Add the coconut cream and salt and remove from the heat; the kang kong should not be allowed to overcook — it should stay crisp and tasty.

Back: Sambal Kang Kong
(recipe, this page); Front: Lily Bud Sambal
(Sambal Kim Chiam) (recipe, page 140)

Lily Bud Sambal
(Sambal Kim chiam)

Apart from the fact they were 'good for the blood' (most things were good for the blood!), my Amah used to add kim chiam or kum cham (lily buds) to soups and stir-fries because they gave an interesting texture and a smoky flavour to a dish. I enjoyed soaking the buds in water then tying them in knots for a cheerful salad.

Ingredients:

100 grams dried lily buds (kim chiam) or 200 grams (7 oz) watercress leaves

150 grams (5½ oz) medium, cooked prawns (shrimp)

½ small Spanish (red) onion, thinly sliced

1 Lebanese cucumber, chopped

¼ cup (60 mL / 2 fl oz) coconut cream

1 red chilli, seeded and sliced

80 grams (3 oz) Vietnamese mint

Dressing:

1 tablespoon palm sugar

1 tablespoon fish sauce or thin soy sauce

1 teaspoon sambal oelek

½ teaspoon shrimp paste, dry roasted

juice of 1 lime

Method:

The lily buds should resemble thick, brown string. Soak them in water for 30 minutes, rinse and boil in enough water to cover for 20 minutes, or until the water evaporates. When cool, tie the buds in knots.

Shell the prawns (shrimp), leaving the tails on. Soak the onion in water for 5 minutes. Drain.

Mix the sugar and fish sauce together until the sugar has dissolved. Blend together with the remaining dressing ingredients.

Place the lily buds in a bowl with the cucumber, coconut cream and salad dressing. Add the prawns (shrimp) and toss. Serve garnished with the onion, chillies and Vietnamese mint.

Pictured on previous page.

Pickled Limes

For our family, pickled limes were a must at lunch each day. Father ate them with some yoghurt, a sliced green chilli and a pickled lime — simple eating for a busy and a stressful life.

Ingredients:

1 kilogram (2 lb) limes

1¼ cups (300 g / 10½ oz) rock salt

2 tablespoons chilli powder

Method:

Cut the limes halfway through; do not cut all the way through.

Stuff each lime with 2 teaspoons of salt and a pinch of chilli powder. Place the limes one on top of the other in a sterilised, wide-mouthed jar with a tight-fitting lid. Cover and place in the sun for 10–15 days, shaking the jar daily to distribute the limes.

Put the jar in a cool place for about 6 months to allow the limes to gel; they will gradually turn into a beautiful golden syrupy-textured lime pickle.

These limes can be made into a hot pickle by bringing to the boil 1 cup (250 mL / 8 fl oz) mustard oil, some mustard seeds and some ground onions. When boiling, pour over the limes and marinate for 1 week. Use as desired.

The pickled limes are good with meats, as slivered pieces in salads or with any chicken or meat curries and sambals.

Pictured on page 130.

Mango Pachidi

This tasty dish goes well as a chutney with rice and hot curries. It can also be eaten as a salad or appetiser.

Ingredients:

2 hard green mangoes

1 tablespoon sambal oelek

½ teaspoon salt

½ cup (50 g / 2 oz) grated fresh or desiccated coconut, dry roasted until golden

2 stalks (20 g / 1 oz) curry leaves, chopped

1 medium Spanish (red) onion, peeled and finely diced

salt, to taste

Method:

Slice the unpeeled mango, shaving as close as possible to the seed.

Combine the sambal oelek, salt and coconut and pound roughly. Add the curry leaves to the mixture and continue pounding roughly in a mortar and pestle or, alternatively, mash roughly with a potato masher. The idea is to mingle the flavours but not to macerate everything completely.

Add the onion and mango. Toss and mix well. Season with salt if necessary. Serve chilled.

Mango Sambal

This sambal is eaten with Nasi Ulam (recipe, page 24).
Serving a number of relishes makes it possible for each
mouthful of food to taste different; a combination of
sambals can create a gastronomic feast.

Ingredients:

1 medium hard, green mango
6 large red chillies, seeded and chopped
1 cm ($^1/_2$ in) length shrimp paste, dry roasted then crumbled
3 red Asian onions, chopped or $^1/_2$ medium Spanish (red) onion, peeled and thinly sliced
juice of $^1/_2$ a lime (retain some of the zest, to taste)
salt, to taste

Method:

It is important to use a green mango, as ripe mangoes don't handle too well and will cause the salad to taste 'off'. Peel the mango and chop the flesh into small chunks, shaving close to the seed so that all of the pulp is used.

Pound the chillies with the shrimp paste. Add the onions, pounding until the mixture is semi-smooth. Add the lime juice and zest and salt.

Add the mango chunks to the mixture, pounding roughly to release some of the juices. Toss well and refrigerate. Serve with ulams or wild herb salads.

Pictured on page 134.

Mint Pachidi

This is a relish that goes well with Malaysian as well as
western-style lamb roasts. The curry leaves can be omitted,
or they can be substituted with rocket.

Ingredients:

1 bunch (125 g / 4 oz) mint
4 green chillies, seeded and sliced
1 Spanish (red) onion, chopped
2 cloves garlic, sliced
2 cm ($^3/_4$ in) length of ginger, cut into slivers
$^1/_3$ cup (30 g / 1 oz) grated fresh or desiccated coconut
1 tablespoon ghee or oil
1 bunch (125 g / 4 oz) curry leaves, chopped
juice of 1 lime
salt, to taste

Method:

Using only the whole leaves, wash the mint and drain on absorbent paper.

Heat the ghee on medium heat in a wok and stir-fry the onion, garlic and ginger until golden. Add the chillies, coconut and curry leaves and continue stir-frying until the coconut becomes dark and smells roasted.

Blend all of the ingredients together in a food processor or mortar and pestle. Remove and add the lime juice.

Season to taste and chill. Serve as a pachidi or mint purée on lamb or ham, or as a relish with rice or roti. It is also good with roast ham or beef.

Tomato Sambal

Tomatoes are not indigenous to Malaysia but, once
introduced, they became so popular that they are now
used almost daily in some form or another in Malaysian
cuisine. They originally came from South America
with Columbus' crew.

Ingredients:

1 tablespoon oil
1 teaspoon mustard seeds
2 Spanish (red) onions, diced
2 cloves garlic, chopped
8 firm green tomatoes or 8 ripe tomatoes, cubed
$^1/_2$ cup (90 g / 3 oz) sultanas
2 tablespoons sugar
1 teaspoon chilli powder (more if desired)
3 stalks (15 g / $^1/_2$ oz) curry leaves

Method:

Heat the oil on high in a saucepan and cook the mustard seeds until they pop. Add the onions and garlic and sauté until brown.

Add the tomatoes, reduce the heat and simmer until the liquid has reduced by half. Add the sultanas, sugar and chilli powder and simmer for 15–20 minutes or until the mixture thickens. Add the curry leaves, remove from the heat and cool. Use as a chutney or sambal.

Spinach Sambal

Try blending this sambal after cooking it to make a
fascinating dip or filling for a vegetarian quiche.
Interesting flavours develop when you experiment with food.

Ingredients:

1 cup (185 g / 6 oz) yellow split dahl

500 grams (1 lb) English spinach or
silver beet

1 tablespoon Maldive dried fish
(dried skipjack tuna)

2 green chillies

3 cups (750 mL / 24 fl oz) water

2 tablespoons vegetable oil

2 medium Spanish (red) onions,
halved and finely sliced

5 cloves garlic, pounded

$^1/_2$ cup (125 mL / 4 fl oz) water, extra

2 stalks (15 g / $^1/_2$ oz) curry leaves

$^1/_2$ teaspoon turmeric powder

$^1/_2$ cup (125 mL / 4 fl oz) coconut milk

salt, to taste

juice of 1 lime

Method:

Soak the dahl in enough water to cover
overnight. Drain. If using silver beet,
remove the stems. Clean and wash the
spinach (or silver beet) in running
water then finely shred. Break the dried
fish up into tiny pieces. Slit the chillies
right through, retaining the stems.

Cook the dahl and dried fish in the
water until the dahl is soft. Mash with
the back of a spoon.

Heat the oil on medium high in a
wok and sauté the onions and garlic
until golden and aromatic. Add the
spinach and extra water and, when the
water starts to boil and the spinach
breaks down, add the dahl, chillies,
curry leaves and turmeric and simmer
for 5 minutes.

Add the coconut milk and salt and
stir once. Before removing from the
heat, add the lime juice. This sambal
can be served cold or at room
temperature.

Back: Chilli Tempe Sambal (recipe, page 145);
Front: Spinach Sambal (recipe, this page)

Preserved Pickled Olives
(Sweet Kana Pickles)

*Malaysian children snack on soured and preserved olives
and lemons, tamarind with chilli, pineapple and green
mango with a smearing of thin soy sauce and chilli, and
unripe guava with powdered, salted olives. This pickle
is an adult extension of those childhood cravings and
makes a good relish to eat with hot Malaysian curries.
For this pickle you should use a variety of Asian
preserved olives and fruits, found in the confectionary
section of most Asian supermarkets.*

Ingredients:

2 tablespoons oil

2 tablespoons sambal oelek

2 cloves garlic, puréed

3 cups (750 mL / 24 fl oz) brown wine vinegar

salt, to taste

150 grams soft brown sugar

10 pickling onions or small red Asian onions

8 cloves garlic, extra, peeled and halved lengthwise

3 cm (1 in) length ginger, shredded

150 grams (5½ oz) preserved plums

100 grams (3½ oz) preserved olives (sometimes found twisted
in sweet wrappers)

100 grams (3½ oz) preserved mango

100 grams (3½ oz) moist sultanas

100 grams (3½ oz) preserved, pitted prunes

150 grams (5½ oz) preserved, seeded tamarind with chilli

Method:

The preserved fruit can either be crystallised or be absolutely dry.
To dry, place it in the bottom of a 100°C (210°F) oven for about
3 hours, or leave until dry in the sun.

The olives can be left unstoned provided you warn whoever
is eating the pickle that the stones haven't been removed.

Heat the oil on high in a wok and fry the sambal oelek and
garlic until aromatic. Add the vinegar and salt and bring to the
boil. When it is boiling, add the sugar, reduce the heat to low
and cook, stirring, until the sugar is dissolved.

Add the onions, extra garlic and ginger and stir. Add the
plums, olives, mango, sultanas, prunes and tamarind and stir over
a low heat with a wooden spoon so that the fruit gets thoroughly
coated with the hot syrup.

Raise the heat to medium and boil for 3 minutes. Remove
from the heat, cool and store in sterilised jars. Use with meats
and vegetable dishes as a relish.

Green Paw Paw Pickle

*This pickle can also be made using semi-ripe pineapple
if green paw paw (papaya) is unavailable.*

Ingredients:

1 small green hard paw paw (papaya) or 1 semi-ripe pineapple

⅓ cup (90 g / 3 oz) sugar

¼ cup (60 mL / 2 fl oz) vinegar

3 green chillies

½ tablespoon cumin, dry roasted

1 tablespoon coriander (cilantro) powder

5 cloves garlic, chopped

2 cm (¾ in) length ginger, chopped

1 tablespoon sambal oelek

1 teaspoon turmeric powder

½ cup (125 mL / 4 fl oz) oil

1 small Spanish (red) onion, sliced

3—4 stalks (15 g / ½ oz) curry leaves

salt, to taste

Method:

Peel the paw paw (papaya), seed and finely julienne and soak in
salty water for 10 minutes to remove the sticky pith. Drain. If
using pineapple, peel, core and chop. Dissolve the sugar in the
vinegar. Slit the chillies, retaining the stems.

Blend the cumin, coriander (cilantro), garlic, ginger, sambal
oelek and turmeric together in a food processor or mortar and
pestle.

Heat the oil on medium in a wok and cook the chillies and
onion until caramelised. Transfer to an enamel or heavy-based,
cast-iron pot.

Add the blended ingredients and cook on medium heat,
stirring frequently, until aromatic. Add the sugar and vinegar
mixture and paw paw (papaya) and slowly bring to the boil.

Lower the heat, add the curry leaves and simmer very slowly
for 1 hour, being careful that the mixture does not burn on the
bottom of the pot. Season with salt, remove from the heat
and cool.

Pictured on page 134

Satay Peanut Sauce

The sauce that has lunched a few million tourists. While to make an authentic peanut sauce you should really use dry roasted peanuts, you can also successfully make it with crunchy peanut butter.

Ingredients:

3 cloves garlic

2 medium Spanish (red) onions, roughly chopped

8 candlenuts or macadamia nuts

2 stalks lemon grass (white part only), chopped

1 tablespoon oil

$1/2$ tablespoon mixed Malaysian curry powder (see page 172)

$1^1/2$ tablespoons tamarind purée

2 tablespoons sambal oelek (more or less, according to taste)

1 cup unsalted, dry roasted peanuts, roughly ground or $1/2$ cup (130 g / $1/4$ lb) crunchy peanut butter (see note)

$1^1/2$ cups (375 mL / 12 fl oz) coconut milk

1 cup (250 mL / 8 fl oz) hot water

2 teaspoons sugar

salt, to taste

Method:

Blend the garlic, onion, candlenuts (or macadamia nuts) and lemon grass together in a food processor or mortar and pestle until a smooth paste forms.

Heat the oil on medium–high heat in a saucepan and saute the paste until it caramelises; this will take at least 7 minutes. Stir constantly and add a little extra oil if necessary so that the mixture doesn't stick to the bottom of the pan.

Add the curry powder, tamarind purée and sambal oelek to the mixture and stir well. Fry on medium heat for a few minutes. Add the peanuts or peanut butter, coconut milk and water. Simmer until the sauce is thick yet can be poured easily. The sauce will reduce very quickly so you will need to stir continuously. If the sauce is too thick add some hot water and stir well. Add sugar and salt to taste. Those who like a hot peanut sauce can add extra sambal oelek.

Note: If you grind the peanuts, make sure they are roughly ground so that large crunchy bits remain.

Chilli Tempe Sambal

Petai beans — large green beans that grow in black pods are used in this sambal. They have medicinal benefits and are reputed to cure diabetes.

Ingredients:

200 grams (7 oz) tempe, cubed deep fried

3 stalks lemon grass, chopped

3 cm (1 in) length galangal, peeled and chopped

1 cm ($1/2$ in) fresh turmeric or $1/2$ teaspoon turmeric powder

3 tablespoons oil

$1/2$ medium Spanish (red) onion, thinly sliced

2 cloves garlic, diced

125 grams (4 oz) canned petai beans, drained

juice of 2 limes

salt, to taste

pepper, to taste

3 kaffir lime leaves, shredded

mint

Method:

Blend the lemon grass, galangal and turmeric together in a food processor or mortar and pestle.

Heat the oil on medium–high in a wok and sauté the onion and garlic until golden. Add the blended ingredients and cook until aromatic. Add the tempe and cook on high until golden.

Add the petai beans and toss well. Add the lime juice and cook until the liquid has reduced by one-third. Season with salt, pepper and lime leaves. Serve garnished with the whole mint.

Variation:

The tempe can be substituted with 300 grams ($10^1/2$ oz) of prawns (shrimp) or squid. Peel and devein the prawns but leave their tails on. Clean the squid, halve, score the inside with a knife and cut into large triangles. Add to the wok in place of the tempe.

Pictured on page 142.

Mamak-style Prawn Sambal
(Udang Goreng)

The 'Mamak' are colourful characters from the west coast of India who have travelled far with their culinary skills. Mamak food is popular in Malaysia and is fiery chilli—hot.

Ingredients:

1 kilogram (2 lb) prawns (shrimp)

10 candlenuts or macadamia nuts

6 dried chillies, chopped or ½ tablespoon chilli powder

1 teaspoon shrimp paste, dry roasted and crumbled

½ cup (60 g / 2 oz) small red Asian onions, chopped or 2 Spanish (red) onions, chopped

2 tablespoons mustard or gingelly oil

1 cup (250 mL / 8 fl oz) thick coconut cream

sugar, to taste

salt, to taste

½ cup (125 mL / 4 fl oz) tamarind juice made from 2 cm (¾ in) length tamarind block and ½ cup (125 mL / 4 fl oz) water

1 tablespoon Malaysian-style curry powder (see page 172)

½ cup (50 g / 2 oz) desiccated coconut, toasted and finely pounded

2 peeled, cooked, chopped potatoes, fried until crisp on the outside

3 stalks (25 g / 1 oz) curry leaves

Method:

Shell and devein the prawns (shrimp), keeping the tails intact.

Blend the candlenuts, dried chillies, shrimp paste and onions together in a food processor or mortar and pestle until well ground.

Heat the oil on high in a wok and fry the ground ingredients until aromatic. Add the coconut cream, sugar, salt and tamarind juice and bring to the boil. Cook for 5 minutes or until the liquid reduces slightly, then add the prawns (shrimp) and curry powder.

Cook on medium heat until the prawns (shrimp) turn opaque. Add the desiccated coconut, potatoes and curry leaves and fry on medium heat, adding extra oil if necessary to prevent the ingredients from burning, until almost all of the liquid has disappeared. This is a dry curry dish.

Remove from the heat and serve with rice or roti or as a sandwich spread. The prawns (shrimp) in this dish, because they are cooked slowly, are quite sweet.

Pumpkin Sauce, Kerala Style

This is a brilliant way to serve pumpkin. With a microwave it takes only a few minutes to prepare.

Ingredients:

500 grams (1 lb) butternut pumpkin, diced

2 cm (¾ in) length ginger, shredded

2 cloves garlic, crushed

1 teaspoon chilli powder

½ teaspoon salt

½ cup (125 mL / 4 fl oz) water

1 tablespoon oil

2 teaspoons mustard seeds

3 stalks curry leaves, chopped

juice and rind of 2 limes

Method:

The pumpkin can be cooked in one piece in a microwave oven, then peeled and mashed. (Alternatively, you can place the pumpkin, ginger, garlic, chilli powder, salt and water in a pan and simmer, covered, on low heat for 15 minutes or until cooked and then mash.)

Place the pumpkin in a serving dish. Heat the oil on medium high and fry all of the remaining ingredients except the lime juice and rind until the mustard seeds pop. Sprinkle over the mashed pumpkin, stir in the lime juice and serve, garnished with the lime rind.

(This can be turned into a meat dish with the addition of crispy fried bacon.)

The Coconut

A nut that combines legend and fact with flavour and taste

The coconut is the fruit of the coconut palm, a tree that is intricately woven into the tradition and folklore of Asia.

The fruit is green when unripe and turns orange–yellow to brown when mature. Beneath the husk is a hard round shell containing thick white flesh. At the centre is the liquid known as coconut water.

The flesh, when scraped from the shell, grated and pressed, produces the thick, creamy liquid known as coconut 'milk'. The thick first pressing is a liquid with a high fat content. The fat rises to the top as coconut cream and is used — just as cream from cow's milk is used in Western cooking — to finish a dish or as a thickener for a sauce.

The second and third pressings produce successively thinner 'milk'. This liquid, being less creamy, is used as a cooking medium for vegetables, fish and rice dishes. Being a meat tenderiser, it is used in stews. It is also used in drinks and soups.

The liquid in the centre of the coconut — the coconut water — is fairly sweet and rich in vitamins. It is used in India for 'women's problems' and in rural areas of Asia it has been used in medical emergencies when saline for a drip is unavailable. While still in the shell, coconut water is clean, germfree and pure.

Asians use coconut milk and cream in the same way that Westerners use cow's milk and cream. Coconut milk — like cow's milk — goes rancid easily, especially when it is unrefrigerated; it boils over and curdles when cooked on a rolling boil; separates when covered with a lid after cooking; and needs to be stirred and cooked on low to preserve its shape and texture.

Grated coconut can be used as a dressing, as a garnish, and when sroasted and blended it gives texture to Rendangs and Southeast Asian salads.

The white flesh of the coconut is pure and untainted, symbolic of purity in life. Asians have for countless generations used coconuts in religious ritual. Hindus ceremoniously break coconuts at birthdays and weddings for good luck. When a coconut is broken at a wedding it is important that the break is smooth and even so the marriage is smooth and not fraught with jagged events which would upset the even temper of life. Malays plant a coconut tree when a baby is born and count the rings on the trunk to calculate that person's age

Roast Pork Sauce

To be served with roast belly of pork or with the ready-made roast pork with brown crackling that you can find in most Chinatowns throughout the world. The pork should be sliced and still have its crackling attached.

Ingredients:

2 teaspoons oil

2 cloves garlic

2 teaspoons sambal oelek

1 teaspoon red Szechwan pepper, dry roasted then ground to a paste

$1/2$ teaspoon cinnamon powder

1 star anise, pounded

$1/2$ teaspoon thick soy sauce (kecap manis)

1 teaspoon palm sugar

Method:

Heat oil in a wok and sauté garlic and sambal oelek, then add spices, soy and sugar. Lower heat till all ingredients start to cook, and simmer for 1 minute.

Remove the sauce from the wok and brush it on the pork pieces. Grill the basted pork, allowing it to heat through for a few minutes.

Serve the pork with pickled Japanese radish and Vinegared Cucumber Pickle (page 133).

Home-made Sambal Oelek

This is a staple for the freezer or the refrigerator. I make it in large batches and use as necessary in curries and sambals. Oelek is the term for grinding, so Sambal Oelek merely means ground chilli sambal.

Ingredients:

500 grams (1 lb) red chillies

150 grams ($5^1/2$ oz) garlic, peeled and chopped

150 grams ($5^1/2$ oz) young, tender ginger, peeled and chopped

2 stalks lemon grass bulbs, thinly sliced

$3/4$ cup (180 mL / 6 fl oz) vinegar

1 cup (250 g / 8 oz) sugar

salt, to taste

1 tablespoon lime zest, shredded

Method:

Pick the stems off the chillies. Blend the chillies, garlic, ginger and lemon grass bulbs together slowly in a food processor or mortar and pestle. Gradually drizzle in the vinegar during the processing.

Place the puréed mixture in a saucepan and bring to the boil. Reduce the heat and simmer for 3 minutes.

Add the sugar and stir until dissolved. Add the salt and lime zest and stir. Remove from the heat, cool and bottle in sterilised jars.

An alternative is to heat 1 tablespoon of oil in a frying pan and sauté 1 teaspoon of dry roasted and crumbled shrimp paste for 1 minute. Add this to the mix before removing from the heat and cool in sterilised jars.

Pictured on page 130.

Squid in Lime
(Sambal Limau Sotong)

Once you have finished cleaning and scoring the squid in neat checks, then it takes only a minute or two to cook this refreshing Sambal.

Ingredients:

½ Spanish (red) onion, thinly sliced

½ cup (125 mL / 4 fl oz) lime or lemon juice

1 kilogram (2 lb) baby squid (about 8 cm / 3 in tubes)

1 teaspoon turmeric powder

2 tablespoons oil

2 cloves garlic, chopped

1 teaspoon sugar

salt, to taste

Method:

Marinate the onion in ¼ cup (60 mL / 2 fl oz) of the lime juice for 20 minutes. Discard the liquid. Clean and skin the squid tubes and slice them in half. Open them out flat and score in close-set diamond shapes on the inside of the skin with a sharp knife. Brush with the turmeric.

Heat the oil on medium high in a wok and sauté the garlic until browned. Remove the garlic from the wok. Turn the heat up to high and fry the squid in small batches, taking them out as soon as they show signs of curling. (If you put too much in the wok at one time the squid will merely stew.)

Replace all of the squid in the wok and stir briskly. Add the garlic, sugar, salt and a little of the lime juice. Cook on high heat, briskly stir-frying until aromatic and very little liquid remains.

Remove from the heat and add the remaining lime juice. Put the squid on a serving dish with the onions in the centre.

Tamarind Pickle

Large tamarind trees used to grow by the side of my primary school and I remember using sticks and poles to dislodge the green fruit before flying foxes and bats got to them. When pickled they make a crunchy, tart snack that western children should find very unusual.

Ingredients:

150 grams (5½ oz) tamarind block, well ground

1 cup (250 mL / 8 fl oz) water

80 grams (3 oz) pitted dates, chopped or 50 grams (2 oz) pitted dates, chopped and 30 grams (1 oz) whole raisins combined

2 teaspoon fennel seeds, dry roasted and finely ground

1 tablespoon sambal oelek

2½ tablespoons palm sugar

salt, to taste

1 tablespoon oil

½ teaspoon mustard seeds

6 green chillies, slit and seeded

Method:

Make a purée from the ground tamarind block and the water — you need about 1 cup (250 mL / 8 fl oz). Blend with the dates, ground fennel, sambal oelek, sugar and salt.

Heat the oil on high heat in a wok or saucepan and cook the mustard seeds until they pop. Add the chillies and date mixture and bring to the boil.

After about 4 minutes, when the mixture starts to thicken, lower the heat and simmer for 2 minutes. Stir well, remove from the heat and cool.

Bottle in sterilised jars. This relish goes well with either curried or roasted lamb, or with slices of cold chicken or ham.

Iced Kacang (recipe, page 160)

Mango Fool
(Mango Lassi)

*A fool is something made for fun, and is not meant to be
taken seriously. This drink, blended with milk and
green mangoes, is very fresh and appeals
to most people's tastebuds.*

Ingredients:

9 hard or semi-ripe green mangoes

1 cup (250 g / 8 oz) sugar

pinch of salt

2 cups (500 mL / 16 fl oz) chilled milk

zest of 1 lime, grated

Method:

Peel and dice the mangoes and cover with water in a small
saucepan. Add the sugar and cook on medium heat, stirring, until
it dissolves. Bring to the boil and simmer for 2 minutes or until
the pulp of the mango is soft and mushy. Add the salt.

Remove from the heat and push through a sieve with the
back of a spoon. Discard the pulp. The remaining syrup should
be thick but should not contain any stringy parts of pulp. Chill in
the refrigerator. Blend the mango syrup with the milk and serve
garnished with the lime zest.

NOTE: Milk should only be used in this recipe with green
mangoes. If ripe mangoes are used the tart flavour is lost so you
should use yoghurt instead of the milk.

Ghee Balls

*My friend Radha's special recipe for ghee balls is easy and
uncomplicated. Make some and freeze for the New Year
or for a birthday party.*

Ingredients:

$^1/_3$ cup (50 g / 1 oz) rice flour

1 cup (125 g / 4 oz) greenpea flour (hoenkwe)

1 cup (220 g / 7$^1/_2$ oz) icing (powdered) sugar

1 tablespoon chopped, roasted cashew nuts

1 tablespoon chopped raisins

$^1/_2$ cup (100 g / 3$^1/_2$ oz) icing (powdered) sugar, sifted, extra

$^2/_3$ cup (150 g / 5$^1/_2$ oz) ghee

Method:

Combine the rice flour and greenpea flour. Roast on high in a
microwave for 3 minutes or dry roast on medium heat in a clean
and dry wok, tossing and turning the flour for about 10 minutes
or until it smells roasted.

Combine the flours with the icing (powdered) sugar, cashews
and raisins. Place the extra icing (powdered) sugar on a flat dish.

Heat the ghee on medium heat in a saucepan until boiling,
then pour over the flour mixture and mix well and rapidly with a
wooden spoon. Form the mixture into small, walnut-sized balls
and roll in the extra icing (powdered) sugar. The balls will set
firmly as they cool.

It helps to have two people working on this dish — one to
roll the balls initially and one to roll the balls in the icing sugar as
they set.

Pictured on page 162.

Malaysian Pineapple Tarts

*These pineapple tarts, made with a very short pastry,
are a special Nonya delicacy.*

Ingredients:

2 cups (500 g / 1 lb) butter

2 eggs

6 cups (750 g / 1$^1/_2$ lb) plain (all purpose) flour

$^3/_4$ cup (250 g / 8 oz) Pineapple Jam (recipe, page 153)

$^1/_2$ cup (125 mL / 4 fl oz) milk

Method:

Beat the butter and eggs together until creamy. Fold in the flour
until a soft dough forms. Refrigerate for 1 hour.

Roll the pastry out into a sheet 1 cm (½ in) thick. Use a small
petit four mould or tart cutter to cut shapes from the pastry.

Place a small ball of pineapple jam in the centre of the pastry,
using only enough to fill the centre and leaving a ring around the
edge of the tart. Brush with the milk.

Place on greased oven trays and bake at 200°C (400°F) for
8–10 minutes. Remove from the oven and cool. The tarts are
very brittle so they should be stored carefully in airtight
containers. (They will keep for one week.)

Pineapple Jam

Serve as a jam or use to make Malaysian Pineapple Tarts
(recipe, page 152).

Ingredients:

2 large pineapples or 6 small Mauritian or Hawaiian
pineapples
8—10 cups (2—2¹/₂ kg / 4—5 lb) granulated sugar
2 cinnamon sticks

Method:

Remove the skin and eyes from the pineapples. Grate the flesh,
discarding the core. Place the pulp in a large sieve over a bowl and
squeeze out the juice from the pulp. Reserve the juice to use for
Pineapple Syrup (recipe, below). The pulp should be fairly dry.

Measure the pulp into a large saucepan and add 1 cup (250 g /
8 oz) of sugar for every 1 cup (250 g / 8 oz) of pulp. Add the
cinnamon sticks and bring to the boil slowly over a medium
heat, stirring constantly until the sugar has dissolved. Do not stir
once the sugar has dissolved or the jam will crystallise.

Simmer for approximately 1 hour or until the jam is a deep
golden colour and has thickened and caramelised. Stir with a
wooden spoon occasionally so that the jam does not catch on the
bottom of the pan. The cinnamon sticks can be left in the jam.

Cool and store in sterilised jars. Cover only when completely
cold.

Pineapple Syrup

Mixed with water and topped with a mint sprig,
this makes a deliciously refreshing drink. It can be made
using the leftover pulp from Pineapple Jam (above).

Ingredients:

2 large pineapples or 6 small Mauritian or Hawaiian
pineapples
4—5 cups (1—1¹/₂ kg / 2—3 lb) sugar
2 cinnamon sticks
mint sprigs

Method:

Remove the skin and eyes from the pineapples. Grate the flesh,
discarding the core. Place the pulp in a large sieve over a bowl
and squeeze out the juice from the pulp. Reserve the pulp to use
for Pineapple Jam (recipe, above).

Place the pineapple juice in a saucepan and add ½ cup
(125 g / 4 oz) of sugar for each cup (250 mL / 8 fl oz) of juice.
Bring to the boil, add the cinnamon sticks and cook, stirring
constantly, until the sugar has dissolved.

When the sugar has dissolved, remove the scum from the
surface. Reduce the heat and simmer for 5—7 minutes or until
thickened. Remove the cinnamon sticks. Cool and chill in
the refrigerator.

To serve, half-fill a glass with the syrup and top with water to
taste. Add ice and a mint sprig.

Coconut Créme Brûlée

This recipe developed quite by accident when I needed to
make up a dessert for a Frenchman I knew, Jerome.
I assumed a brûlée would appeal and the coconut was an
inspired decision. Most commercial kitchens have
blowtorches for quick searing; a similar effect can be
achieved with a very hot grill.

Ingredients:

¹/₃ cup (90 g / 3 oz) palm sugar
2 tablespoons water
7 egg yolks
1 cup (250 mL / 8 fl oz) coconut milk
1 pandan leaf or vanilla bean, split
1¹/₂ cups (375 mL / 24 fl oz) coconut cream
¹/₄ cup (30 g / 1 oz) glacé ginger, shredded
2 teaspoons green ginger wine
zest of 1 lime
1 tablespoon fresh lime juice
4 tablespoons palm sugar, extra
ginger, shredded

Method:

Preheat the oven to 175°C (340°F). Place the sugar and water in
a saucepan and cook on medium heat until the sugar is dissolved.
Cool.

Beat the egg yolks into the sugar mixture. Add the coconut
milk and continue beating until light and fluffy.

Shred the pandan leaf by running a fork through its length,
then tie it in a knot and add to egg mixture.

Place the coconut cream, pandan leaf, ginger and ginger wine
in the top of a double saucepan over a medium heat. Gradually
add the egg mixture, but do not allow the mixture to boil.
Remove from the heat.

Remove the pandan leaf and stir in the zest and lime juice.
Place in wetted moulds (½ cup / 125 mL / 4 fl oz capacity) in a
baking dish half-filled with boiling water. Bake for 40 minutes or
until the custard is firm. Cool the custards and refrigerate.

To make the brûlée, sprinkle 2 teaspoons of the extra sugar
over each custard and heat with a blowtorch or under a hot grill
until the sugar caramelises. Refrigerate until ready to serve.

Masala Coffee by the Yard
(Kopi Tarek)

To make this coffee well you will need two jugs, as it should be poured
repeatedly from one to the other until froth is produced — a sort
of hand-made cappucino.

Ingredients:

2 tablespoons freshly ground coffee

2 cups (500 mL / 16 fl oz) milk

2 tablespoons sugar or rock sugar

2 cm (³/₄ in) length ginger

4 cardamom seeds, pounded

1 cinnamon stick

Method:

Place milk and sugar in a saucepan and bring to the boil.

Dry roast the ginger under a grill then pound a little in a mortar and pestle to release the juices. Add to the milk, then add the cardamom, cinnamon and coffee. Cover and allow the coffee to steep in the heat for 3 minutes.

Strain off the dregs, and pour the coffee from one jug to another in a steady stream. You need to hold the jugs far apart and repeat the process until the coffee begins to froth.

Singapore Sling

This drink was created for the Raffles Hotel by a Chinese barman,
Mr Ngiam, early this century, when the Raffles Hotel was synonymous
with Singapore and gracious living. It would have been drunk to the
accompaniment of singing mosquitoes at the famous long bar —
when air-conditioning was non-existent but dedication and
old-fashioned service more than compensated for it.

Ingredients:

1 cup (250 mL / 8 fl oz) gin

¹/₂ cup (125 mL / 4 fl oz) cherry brandy

¹/₄ cup (60 mL / 2 fl oz) fresh lime juice

4 cups (1 litre / 32 fl oz) unsweetened pineapple juice

¹/₃ cup (80 mL / 2¹/₂ fl oz) Grenadine

dash Benedictine Dom

dash Triple Sec

few drops angostura bitters

3 slices orange, halved

Method:

Combine all of the ingredients together in a large pitcher filled with ice cubes. Strain into tall glasses over ice. Garnish each glass with an orange slice half. This recipe serves 6.

Preparing Masala Coffee by the Yard

Makan-lah!

Red Bean Ice-cream

Malaysians, like most Asians, use beans and potatoes in desserts, a texture and taste sensation that comes as quite a surprise for many westerners.

Ingredients:

1 cup (185 g / 6 oz) red (adzuki) beans

3 cups (750 mL / 24 fl oz) water

1 cup (250 g / 8 oz) sugar

1 teaspoon mixed spice

1 cup (250 g / 8 oz) sour cream

$1/2$ cup (125 mL / 4 fl oz) cream

zest of 1 orange, grated

Method:

Cover the beans in water and soak overnight. Drain. Place in a saucepan with 3 cups of water and boil, uncovered, for 40 minutes or until soft when mashed with the back of a spoon.

Add the sugar and mixed spice and boil, stirring occasionally, for a further 20 minutes or until the beans are soft enough to squash between your fingers. Cool and purée in a food processor or mortar and pestle.

Slowly fold all of the remaining ingredients except the orange zest into the puréed beans. Add the zest, reserving a small amount for garnish.

Freeze in an ice-cream machine or pour into a plastic–lined tin and freeze, beating occasionally to break up any ice crystals. The ice-cream is ready to serve when it is firm and smooth. Serve with the reserved orange zest sprinkled on top.

Ginger Ice-cream

Ginger is used medicinally in Malaysia as well as being used as a spice for cooking. It is good for stomach upsets, and a ginger tea always cures my colds. This ice-cream is tasty and does not have the cloying sweetness of commercial ginger ice-creams.

Ingredients:

$1/3$ cup (80 mL / $2^1/2$ fl oz) milk cream (using equal parts of dairy cream and coconut milk)

$3/4$ cup (185 g / 6 oz) palm sugar

2 eggs, separated

4 cm ($1^1/2$ in) length ginger, finely shredded

juice and grated zest from 1 lime

$1^3/4$ cups (425 mL / 14 fl oz) coconut milk

pinch of salt

ginger flakes or glacé ginger

green ginger wine

Method:

Place the milk cream and palm sugar in a saucepan. Heat on medium, stirring, until the sugar dissolves. Place in a bowl with the egg yolks, ginger, lime juice and rind and coconut milk.

Beat the egg whites with the salt until firm but not dry. Fold the whites into the bowl with the milk cream mixture. Freeze in an ice-cream machine or pour into a plastic-lined tin and freeze, beating every 30 minutes until smooth.

Serve with the ginger flakes or glace ginger and green ginger wine.

Ceylon—Malay Pudding

Although this sweet, coconut-flavoured pudding originated in Sri Lanka, it is typical of Malay sweets and desserts. The Malays who live in Sri Lanka were transported there by the Indonesian Dutch. The dish uses the green colour typical of Malaysian cooking and jaggery, a local sugar from Sri Lanka.

Ingredients:

2 tablespoons custard powder

3 tablespoons cornflour (cornstarch)

2 cups (500 mL / 16 fl oz) coconut milk

2 cups (500 mL / 16 fl oz) coconut cream

3 tablespoons sugar

2 tablespoons semolina

1 vanilla bean

2 tablespoons finely chopped crystallised ginger or pineapple

3 tablespoons palm sugar or jaggery

2 tablespoons chopped pistachio nuts

1 pandan leaf, shredded

pale green food colouring

Method:

Combine the custard powder with a small amount of cold water and whisk with a fork to break up any lumps. Combine the cornflour (cornstarch) with a small amount of water.

Combine the coconut milk and coconut cream. Measure out 2 cups (500 mL / 16 fl oz) of this mixture into a small saucepan and add the sugar, semolina and vanilla bean. Bring to the boil, stirring constantly.

Add the custard powder and stir, using a whisk. Simmer for 2 minutes or until thick and the semolina is cooked. Add the ginger, remove from the heat and pour into a wet serving dish or mould. Allow to set. This layer of the pudding will be pale yellow in colour.

Heat the remaining coconut milk and cream with the palm sugar. Add the cornflour (cornstarch). Bring to the boil and, when it thickens, add the pistachio nuts, pandan leaf and food colouring. Pour carefully over the yellow layer of custard. Chill overnight. Turn out of the mould and serve.

Doing the Purple Congo
(Ubi Chacha)

Another recipe that I adapted from a yam recipe we make in Malaysia. I was very happy to discover that the yams mash well and make a spectacular dessert.

Ingredients:

400 grams (13 oz) purple yam or purple Congo potatoes
1 cup (250 mL / 8 fl oz) water
1/4 cup (60 grams /2 oz) white or rock sugar
1/2 cup (125 g / 4 oz) castor sugar
1 pandan leaf, shredded and tied in a knot
2.5 cm (1 in) length ginger, roughly pounded
2 tablespoons coconut cream
pinch salt
butter

Method:

Peel and slice the potatoes, and steam for 10 minutes or until tender. When cooked, mash well and set aside.

Place the water, sugars and pandan leaf in a saucepan and cook, stirring, on high heat for 4 minutes or until the sugars dissolve and the liquid thickens slightly. Remove the pandan leaf.

Fold in the mashed potatoes and cook on medium heat for 5–7 minutes. Add the ginger, coconut cream and salt, stirring constantly until the liquid has thickened and the mixture is almost dry. Remove any remaining ginger.

Place in a greased pie dish and smooth the top with a little butter. Chill in the refrigerator.

When cold, cut into 4 x 4 cm (1½ x 1½ in) squares and serve. It can also be served as a scoop on top of ice-cream.

Avocado Mousse

The Dutch colonials in Indonesia used avocados as a dessert fruit instead of using it in salads.

Ingredients:

6—8 cinnamon sticks
1/2 cup (125 mL / 4 fl oz) rum
1 tablespoon lemon juice
3 ripe avocadoes, halved
1/2 cup (125 mL / 4 fl oz) condensed milk
1/4 cup (60 mL / 2 fl oz) cream
1 tablespoon Creme de Cacao
2 tablespoons Kahlua or 1 teaspoon powdered instant coffee
1/2 cup (60 g / 2 oz) chopped pistachio nuts

Method:

Soak the cinnamon sticks in the rum for 10 hours or overnight. Drain. Sprinkle the lemon juice over the avocado halves, then scoop out the flesh into a bowl. Mash with the condensed milk and cream. Add the Creme de Cacao and Kahlua.

Serve with the rum-soaked cinnamon sticks and pistachio nuts. This dish is best made just before serving, but if you wish to keep it for a short time leave the avocado seed in the mix, cover with plastic wrap and remove the seed just before serving.

Coconut Custard
(Seri Kaya)

The Malaysian egg custard has a similar name to its close cousin the Thai Sangkaya, though the Malaysian version relies on the flavour of pandan, not rose water. It is also spread on a blue and white sticky rice cake at Nonya functions.

Ingredients:

1 cup (250 g / 8 oz) palm sugar
1/2 cup (125 mL / 4 fl oz) water
6 eggs
1 cup (250 mL / 8 fl oz) thick coconut cream
1/4 cup (60 mL /2 fl oz) evaporated milk
vanilla
1/4 teaspoon nutmeg

Method:

Place the sugar and water in a saucepan and cook on low until the sugar is dissolved. Cool.

Beat the eggs by stirring well but do not allow them to froth. Beat the sugar into the eggs, then add the coconut cream. Strain the mixture. Add the nutmeg and vanilla.

Pour into a greased pudding bowl and steam for 1½ hours in a bamboo steamer, carefully wiping down the steamer lid occasionally to prevent condensed water from dripping into the steamer.

When the custard has thickened and a knife slices easily into it (approximately 20 minutes), remove from the steamer and chill. Serve cold with Black Rice Pudding (Pulut Hitam) (recipe, page 166).

Chendol

Chendol is a drinkable palm sugar and cold coconut milk dessert.
The texture of chewy bits inside this dessert is something westerners
have to get used to, as Malaysian desserts rely on texture
as much as western desserts rely on sugar and cream.

Ingredients:

6 pandan leaves, chopped

¹/₂ cup (125 mL / 4 fl oz) water

1 packet (100 g / 3¹/₂ oz) of greenpea flour (hoenkwe)

¹/₃ cup (100 g / 3¹/₂ oz) palm sugar

¹/₂ cup water, extra

2 cups (500 mL / 16 fl oz) coconut milk

¹/₂ teaspoon salt

¹/₂ cup (125 mL / 4 fl oz) coconut cream

Method:

Blend the pandan leaves with the water to make a liquid. Strain off the dregs and add enough water to make up 3 cups (750 mL / 24 fl oz) of liquid.

Stir into the greenpea flour and smooth out any lumps in a blender or by sieving the mixture directly into a saucepan. Cook on medium heat until the mixture starts to boil, then continue stirring until the mixture becomes a thick and almost transparent custard/jelly. Cool slightly.

Place a large-apertured grater or sieve over a basin of water containing ice cubes. Press the warm greenpea mixture through the sieve. The mixture will form teardrop-shaped pieces (chendol) that, as they fall into the ice water, will firm up and maintain that shape.

Drain off the water and keep the chendol pieces refrigerated until needed.

Place the palm sugar and extra water in a saucepan and cook on medium heat until the sugar dissolves. Remove from the heat.

Pour the coconut milk into a jug and add the salt. Add 1 cup (250 mL / 8 fl oz) of water to the milk and stir well.

To serve as a dessert or as a textured drink, half-fill bowls or tall glasses with the coconut milk, add 2 tablespoons of chendol and top with 1–2 tablespoons of the palm sugar syrup and 2 tablespoons of the coconut cream. Fill with crushed ice and serve immediately.

Chendol

Iced Kacang

The iced kacang is probably Malaysia's national dessert. Nuts and gelatine are built up layer on layer, then a mountain of crushed ice topped with a snowcap of evaporated milk completes the picture. It is easier to use an ice crusher to make the crushed ice for this dessert, otherwise wrap the ice in a tea towel and crush with a hammer.

Ingredients:

2 cups (450 g / 14 oz) red beans (adzuki)
4 cups (1 litre / 32 fl oz) water
15 grams (1/2 oz) clear agar agar
3 cups (750 mL / 24 fl oz) boiling water
2 cups (450 g / 14 oz) castor sugar
1 1/2 cups (375 g / 12 oz) sugar
2 pandan leaves, shredded with a fork then knotted
red food colouring
1 1/2 cups (300 g / 10 1/2 oz) whole sweet corn kernels
150 mL (5 fl oz) canned attap palm seeds, halved
12 dark cherries, seeded and halved or 12 blueberries
6 rambutans or lychees, peeled and halved
seeds from 1/2 pomegranate
1 x 375 mL (12 fl oz) can evaporated milk

Method:

Place the beans and water in a saucepan and soak overnight. Bring to the boil and cook for 20–30 minutes or until soft enough to mash with the back of a spoon. Drain and cool.

Wash the agar agar, which will soften and become pliant in the process. Squeeze out any excess water. Place in a deep saucepan with the boiling water and 1 cup (225 g / 7 fl oz) of the castor sugar and boil for 10 minutes or until the threads all melt and there are no bits floating in the water.

Add the sugar, pandan leaf, red food colouring (enough drops for a deep pink or light red colour depending on your preference) and remaining castor sugar, reduce the heat and simmer until the sugars have melted. Take out the pandan leaf.

Sieve the agar agar onto a wet pie dish. Allow to cool and harden at room temperature. Cut into 5 cm (1 in) cubes.

To serve, place 2 tablespoons of the mashed beans and 1 tablespoon of the corn on the bottom of an ice-cream compote dish. Pile the attap palm seeds, agar agar bits, cherries, rambutan and pomegranate seeds into a pyramid shape on top. Finish with crushed ice — to do this, put ice in a tea towel (dish towel) and crush with a hammer — then add 2 tablespoons of the evaporated milk and some of the red syrup.

Pictured on page 150.

Rice and Coconut Custard Layer Cake
(Seri Muka)

Seri Muka *means beautiful and smooth. In my past life as an English teacher, a student once referred to his mother's face as being as smooth as* **Seri Muka** *(which is very odd, as* **Seri Muka** *is traditionally coloured green) but the simile has stuck in my mind and I am never able to make* **Seri Muka** *without wondering about a smooth- and green-faced woman walking around somewhere in Malaysia.*

Ingredients:

1 1/4 cups (250 g / 8 oz) glutinous rice (pulut)
1 1/2 cups (375 mL / 12 fl oz) coconut milk
1 pandan leaf, shredded (optional)
1 tablespoon sugar
salt, to taste

Coconut Custard:

4 pandan leaves, chopped or a few drops of rose essence and yellow food colouring
6 eggs
1 1/2 cups (375 mL / 12 fl oz) thick coconut cream
1 cup (220 g / 7 1/2 oz) sugar
salt, to taste
2 tablespoons rice flour

Method:

Cover the rice with water and soak for 3 hours. Drain. Place in a round cake tin with the coconut milk, pandan leaf, sugar and salt.

Cover the tin and steam for 20 minutes by placing it on top of a platform in a wok a quarter-filled with water, or in a bamboo steamer. Carefully remove the lid of the wok, making sure that none of the drops that have collected on the lid fall into the rice. Pat the rice down with a piece of greaseproof paper to even out the layer.

Pound the chopped pandan leaves in a mortar and pestle to make juice. Strain and discard the pith.

Beat the eggs lightly, so they don't froth. In another bowl, mix the coconut cream, pandan juice, sugar, salt and rice flour and beat until the sugar has melted. Fold into the eggs.

Roughen the top layer of rice to create a few ridges so that the egg custard will easily adhere to the rice. Pour the egg mixture slowly onto the rice layer and steam for 15–20 minutes or until the custard is firm when a knife is placed in it. Again, make sure that any liquid accumulated on the underside of the lid does not fall into the custard. Cool, cover and refrigerate until ready to serve.

Butter Coconut Cake

Coconut cream or milk adds a rich and buttery flavour to a simple cake. The icing can be made with powdered coconut milk, icing (powdered) sugar and a hint of coconut cream, blended and spread on the cake.

Ingredients:
1 cup (250 g / 8 oz) butter
3/4 cup (185 g / 6 oz) castor sugar
1/4 cup (60 g / 2 oz) palm sugar, pounded
5 — 6 eggs
pinch of salt
2 cups (250 g / 8 oz) self-raising flour
2 tablespoons coconut cream
2 pandan leaves, shredded and pounded to make juice or
1 teaspoon rose essence

Method:
Cream the butter and sugars until smooth. Add the eggs, one at a time, with the salt, using a whisk or a mixer to inject some air into the mixture.

Sift the flour three times. Add alternately with the coconut cream, folding slowly with a metal spoon until well blended.

Add the pandan juice, which will turn the cake a light green colour. Use rose essence if this doesn't appeal to you.

Line the bottom of a greased 25 cm (10 in) round or square cake tin with greased paper. Coat with flour, dusting off any excess. Bake for 25 minutes at 170°C (340°F) on the middle shelf of the oven. The cake is ready when it shrinks away from the side of the tin. Cool for a few minutes on a wire rack before turning out.

Rainbow Kueh Lapis Cake

The colours in this typical Malaysian layered cake are very enticing.

Ingredients:
3/4 cup (180 mL / 6 fl oz) coconut milk
1 cup (125 g / 4 oz) rice flour
1/4 cup (30 g / 1 oz) greenpea flour (hoenkwe)
1/4 cup (30 g / 1 oz) tapioca starch flour
3/4 cup (200 g / 7 oz) sugar
salt, to taste
red, green and yellow food colouring

Method:
Add enough water to the coconut milk to make 2 cups (500 mL / 16 fl oz) of liquid. Combine the three flours, then stir the coconut milk into the mixture. Put in a saucepan with the sugar and salt and stir, over low heat, until the sugar has dissolved.

Divide the batter into three portions and add a little red colouring to one, green to the second and yellow to the third.

Grease a 20 x 20 cm (8 x 8 in) square dish, pour in a thin layer of one of the batters and steam for 3 minutes. Add a different coloured layer and steam for 3 minutes. Continue adding layers until all the batter is used up. Steam the final layer for 3 minutes and remove. If this cake has been steamed well the layers will be clearly defined and can be peeled apart when eating. Cool and chill.

To serve, cut diagonal slices with a sharp, oiled knife, turn and cut diagonal slices the other way to form diamond shapes.

Sago and Palm Sugar Pudding
(Sago Gula Melaka)

This dessert used to be the standard post-curry dessert in every club or government rest house in Malaysia. Chilled sago is an excellent refreshing palate cleanser and tongue soother.

Ingredients:
3 cups (500 g / 1 lb) sago
2 egg whites
1/2 teaspoon salt
2 pandan leaves
1 1/4 cups (300 g / 10 1/2 oz) palm sugar
1 cup (250 mL / 8 fl oz) water
1 cup (250 mL / 8 fl oz) coconut cream
palm sugar, flaked, extra (optional)

Method:
Bring a saucepan (capacity 4 litres / 7 pints) full of water to the boil. Pour the sago into the water, stirring, then reduce the heat. Do not allow the sago to boil without stirring or it will become lumpy. When all of the grains of sago are transparent, remove from the heat. Drain.

Wash the sago in cold running water to remove the starch, then drain it in small batches in a colander. You may have to wash the sago a few times to remove the bulk of the starch.

Beat the egg whites and salt until stiff peaks form. Fork the egg whites through the sago to separate the grains. Place into a pre-wetted mould and chill.

Shred the pandan leaves and tie into a knot.

Place the pandan leaves, palm sugar and water in a saucepan and bring to the boil. Cook over low heat for 5 minutes or until fairly thick. Be careful not to overboil or it will caramelise and solidify. Remove the pandan leaf and cool.

To serve, half-fill small bowls with the sago and top with a spoonful each of the palm sugar and coconut cream. Garnish with the flaked palm sugar.

Pictured on page 166.

Sweet Yam Dessert Soup
(Bubor Cha Cha)

This Nonya dessert soup is best served cold.

Ingredients:

500 grams (1 lb) sweet potatoes

500 grams (1 lb) yam (taro)

200 grams (7 oz) tapioca or starch flour

6 tablespoons cold water

500 mL (16 fl oz) boiling water

1/2 cup cornflour (cornstarch)

red, green and yellow colouring

200 grams (7 oz) rock sugar (crystallised sugar from Asian grocers)

400 grams (13 oz) white sugar

750 mL (24 fl oz) water

1 litre (32 fl oz) coconut milk

1/2 teaspoon screwpine essence or 3 pandan leaves shredded then tied in a knot

500 mL (16 fl oz) coconut cream

Method:

Cut the sweet potato into 1 cm (½ in) cubes, and the yam into diagonal shapes of a similar size. Steam for 5 minutes or until soft but not mushy. Drain then cool. Set aside.

Mix the tapioca flour with the 6 tablespoons of cold water in a wide saucepan to form a paste. Pour in the 500 mL (16 fl oz) of boiling water, stirring to make a thick starch. Cook on high heat till it becomes transparent. Cool. Knead cornflour into the paste to make a soft dough (you may need more cornflour).

Divide the dough mixture into three. Colour one part red, one green and one yellow. Roll the coloured dough into strips and cut it into different shapes.

Bring a pan of water to the boil, then throw shapes of one colour into the water and cook. They will rise when cooked. Scoop out and plunge in cold water. Cook the other colours one at a time.

Place the sugars in a small pan with 750 mL (24 fl oz) of water, bring to the boil over a medium heat. Stir until sugars dissolve. Allow to simmer 3 minutes without stirring, to form a syrup.

Add coconut milk to the syrup, bring to a gentle boil, add screwpine essence (or pandan leaves) and remove from heat. (If allowed to boil further it will curdle.) Chill the coconut syrup.

To serve, place the sweet potato and yam into bowls with starchy coloured shapes.

Half fill each bowl with some coconut syrup and top with coconut cream.

Back: Ghee Balls (recipe, page 152)
Front: Sweet Yam Dessert Soup (Bubor Cha Cha) (recipe, this page).

Rich Suji Semolina Cake
(Suji Cake)

While called Suji (semolina) in Malaysia, a similar cake made by my aunts in Sri Lanka is called the love cake. We use almonds and the Sri Lankans use cashews in the batter. This is often made for weddings, where a thin marzipan layer seals the cake for a heavy fondant finish.

Ingredients:

1 teaspoon cinnamon
1 teaspoon nutmeg
$^1/_2$ teaspoon cardamom powder
500 grams (1 lb) small-grained semolina (suji)
3 cups (750 g / $1^1/_2$ lb) butter, chopped
7 egg whites
$^1/_2$ cup (60 g / 2 oz) plain (all purpose) flour
$1^3/_4$ cups (220 g / $7^1/_2$ oz) self-raising flour
12 egg yolks
$3^3/_4$ cups (750 g / $1^1/_2$ lb) castor sugar
$1^3/_4$ cups (200 g / 7 oz) ground almonds (almond meal)
pinch of salt
$^1/_2$ cup (155 g / $5^1/_2$ oz) honey
2 tablespoons brandy
25 mL (1 fl oz) vanilla essence
1 teaspoon rose essence
2 teaspoons almond essence

Method:

Grind the cinnamon, nutmeg and cardamom well then put through a sieve. Dry roast the semolina over medium heat in a wok or saucepan for 10 minutes or until golden and aromatic. Add the ground spices halfway through to strengthen the flavours. Remove from the heat.

Make a well in the centre of the semolina and put the butter into the well. Cover with more semolina so the butter melts into it. Leave for at least 2 hours, or overnight if possible.

Beat the egg whites with the salt until stiff peaks form. Sift the flours together twice. Whisk the egg yolks and sugar until thick and creamy.

Add the egg yolk mixture to the semolina. Fold in the sifted flour, ground almonds and egg whites alternately with the honey, brandy and essences. Fold slowly until the mixture is well amalgamated.

Set aside the cake mix for 1 hour. Line a greased 30 x 25 cm (12 x 10 in) cake pan with two layers of greased greaseproof paper. Dust with flour and shake off the excess. Give the cake mixture a couple of good twirls with a spoon before spooning into the pan.

Cook in a moderate oven (175°C / 340°F, or 150°C / 300°F for a fan-forced oven) for $1^1/_2$–2 hours. If the cake browns too fast, cover with brown paper. You can also use two 20 x 20 cm (8 x 8 in) cake tins lined with three thicknesses of brown paper. This quantity makes about 2 kilograms (4 lb) of cake. Store in an airtight tin.

Mung Bean Diamonds

I find that roasting the small, green mung beans makes them brittle, but tastier and easier to grind.

Ingredients:

1 cup (200 g / 7 oz) mung beans
$1^1/_2$ cups (375 mL / 12 fl oz) water
2 cm ($^3/_4$ in) length ginger, shredded
$^3/_4$ cup (185 g / 6 oz) palm sugar
$^3/_4$ cup (75 g / $2^1/_2$ oz) desiccated coconut
$^1/_2$ cup (60 g / 2 oz) pistachio nuts, chopped

Method:

Place the mung beans in a microwave and cook on high for 3–4 minutes or until brown, or dry roast on medium heat in a clean, dry wok until golden. Place the beans in a pudding bowl, cover with 5 cm (2 in) of water and soak overnight.

Place the beans and water in a microwave-proof bowl and cook on high for 20 minutes. You can also place the beans and water in a saucepan, bring to the boil and cook until soft. Drain off any remaining water. Add the ginger and mash with a potato masher.

Add the sugar and coconut. Continue to cook on high heat for a further 10 minutes, stirring occasionally, until the beans thicken and the liquid reduces almost totally; the dish will be hard to stir. Remove from the heat.

Place into an oiled pie plate and sprinkle the pistachio nuts over. Flatten the mashed beans firmly with the back of a buttered wooden spoon. Refrigerate overnight. To serve, cut the mixture into diamond shapes.

Rich Ceylonese Fruit Cake

The recipe for this Sri Lankan Christmas cake came to my family via my Sri Lankan aunts. There is only enough flour in it to hold the fruits, butter and semolina together. The cake takes several days to prepare, so read through the instructions before starting to make it.

Ingredients:

2 cups (350 g / 12 oz) sultanas

1½ cups (250 g / 8 oz) mixed rind and peel

1⅓ cups (250 g / 8 oz) glacé cherries

4 tablespoons flour

⅓ cup (60 g / 2 oz) currants

¾ cup (300 g / 10½ oz) ginger preserve

⅔ cup (250 g / 8 oz) candied sweet melon preserve

¾ cup (180 mL / 6 fl oz) brandy

1½ cups (250 g / 8 oz) semolina

1 teaspoon cinnamon powder

1 teaspoon cardamom powder

1 teaspoon nutmeg powder

1 teaspoon cloves

1 star anise

1¼ cups (300 g / 10½ oz) butter

2½ cups (300 g / 10½ oz) mixed cashew nuts and almonds

13 eggs

3 cups (500 g / 1 lb) brown sugar

3 tablespoons vanilla or vanilla essence

2 tablespoons rose essence

grated rind of 1 small lemon

juice of 1 small lemon

pinch of salt

¾ cup (250 g / 8 oz) apricot or plum jam

½ cup (155 g / 5½ oz) honey

Method:

A few days before cooking the cake: Chop the sultanas and mixed rind and peel very finely. Chop the cherries separately and dredge with 2 tablespoons of the flour. Soak the sultanas, mixed rind and peel, currants, ginger preserve and sweet melon preserve in the brandy. Cover with plastic wrap and allow to marinate for 2 days. Drain, reserving the brandy.

The day before cooking the cake: Roast the semolina in a dry frying pan over a low heat until golden and aromatic. Mix in ½ teaspoon each of the cinnamon, cardamom, nutmeg and cloves and ½ of the star anise. Place the butter in the centre of the semolina to melt with the spices. Mix well then store overnight.

Blend the mixed nuts in a food processor or mortar and pestle in short bursts making sure that it does not powder or turn mushy. Mix in the remainder of the spices and store overnight.

On the day of cooking the cake: Separate the egg yolks and egg whites, setting aside 5 of the whites. Whip the yolks until fluffy. Gradually whisk in the brown sugar until it dissolves. Add the semolina mixture to the egg mixture with the vanilla and rose essence, lemon rind and lemon juice. Set aside. Beat the reserved egg whites with a pinch of salt until stiff.

Mix the drained fruit, jam, honey and preserves into the yolk mixture alternately with the egg whites and remaining flour, mixing slowly with a 'cutting' motion. The mix should be of a dropping consistency. Set aside for 30 minutes.

Line two 22 cm (8½ in) square cake tins with five sheets of greased greaseproof and one sheet of greased brown paper. Line the sides of the tin with four sheets of greased greaseproof paper and one sheet of greased brown paper. Dust with flour.

Spoon the mixture into the prepared cake tins so that the tins are no more than three-quarters full.

Bake in the centre of a 150°C (300°F) oven for 40–50 minutes or until the surface of the cake has set. Reduce the heat to 120°C (250°F), cover the cakes with brown paper to reduce moisture loss and prevent burning and bake for a further 2–3 hours. Test by inserting a skewer diagonally through the cake centre; if the cake is cooked it will come out clean.

When cool, remove the paper, prick holes in the cake with a skewer and pour 3 tablespoons of the reserved brandy into each cake. Wrap well in foil and store until needed.

Before serving, cut the cake into 6 cm x 3 cm (2½ in x 1 in) rectangles, wrap in cellophane paper, twist the ends like tiny Christmas bonbons and serve with port or sherry.

Black Rice Pudding
(Pulut Hitam)

I am often amused by the look on the faces of my western friends when I serve this dessert, and have learnt to watch that gradual hesitation turn to absolute delight at the subtle fragrance and the wonderful chewy texture of the glistening black rice topped with a dollop of white coconut cream. This variety of rice still only grows in Southeast Asia.

Ingredients:

2½ cups (500 g / 1 lb) black rice (pulut), rinsed

2 cm (¾ in) length ginger, roughly pounded

2 pandan leaves, shredded

1 cup (250 g / 8 oz) sugar

salt, to taste

Method:

Place the rice, ginger and pandan leaves in a saucepan and cover to 4 cm (1½ in) above the level of the rice with water. Bring to the boil and cook until the rice is soft and sticky and the grains have broken up. Add water if necessary to maintain the level of liquid in the saucepan.

This dish can be made into a thick custard by simmering for another few minutes until the rice is very thick and holds its shape.

Add the sugar and stir over a medium heat until dissolved. Add the salt and remove from the heat.

Serve hot as a custard with a dollop of coconut cream on top, or serve cold in timbale moulds and top with a scoop of ice-cream or Coconut Custard (recipe, page 157).

Back: Sago and Palm Sugar Pudding (Sago Gula Melaka) (recipe, page 161)
Front: Black Rice Pudding (Pulut Hitam) (recipe, this page)

Layer Cake
('Spekkoek', Kueh Lapis)

This rich Indonesian cake is grilled in individual layers (lapis). I have included it because of its butter-rich and spicy flavours that are so unusual and so evocative of the East. Do not begin unless you have a day to yourself.

Ingredients:
1 cup (250 g / 8 oz) castor sugar
15 egg yolks (from 55 g / 2 oz eggs)
1³/₄ cups (400 g / 13 oz) butter, slightly softened
1 cup (120 g / 4 oz) plain (all purpose) flour
¹/₂ teaspoon baking powder
10 egg whites
pinch of salt
2 tablespoons rose essence

Mixed Spice:
1¹/₂ teaspoons nutmeg
15 cloves
1 teaspoon cinnamon
1 star anise
3 cardamom pods, seeded

Method:
Line a 22–24 cm (8½–9 in) cake tin with greased greaseproof paper. Dust the paper with flour and shake off the excess.

Divide the sugar in half and beat one lot with the egg yolks until fluffy. Cream the remaining sugar with the butter until light. Combine the two sugar mixtures until well amalgamated.

Sift the flour and baking powder twice. Whisk the egg whites with the salt until soft peaks form. Fold the flour, rose essence and egg white mixture alternately into the egg yolk mixture, cutting it through until well mixed.

Grind the mixed spice ingredients together and sift; you need 3 teaspoons of mixed spice.

Divide the cake mix into two. Add 2 teaspoons of the mixed spice into one half, and the remaining teaspoon into the other.

Heat the oven to 175°C (340°F) then warm the empty cake tin in the oven for 3 minutes. While it is warming, turn the grill on to medium heat.

Using a soup ladle, pour one ladleful of the first mixture into the warmed tin, spreading the mix evenly by tilting the tin. Place under the grill for 4 minutes, during which time the cake should cook and some bubbles should form on the surface.

Remove the pan from the heat and prick the bubbles with a skewer. Press down firmly on the cake with a flat-surfaced object like the bottom of a glass so that the layers are even and do not puff up.

Pour in a layer of the second mixture and cook under the grill as above. Alternate layers until both mixtures are used up and about 10 layers are formed. Place the cake in the oven for 10 minutes to cook completely. When the cake is cooked, turn out onto a wire rack to cool.

The cake is very rich and spicy so serve in thin wedges.

Sweet Coconut Milk Rosettes
(Thoddu)

These Indian cakes resemble the traditional stud earrings with six diamonds that most Malaysian women wear as part of their wedding jewellery. You need a special rosette mould on a long handle that allows it to be dipped in hot oil for this recipe.

Ingredients:
1¹/₂ cups (185 g / 6 oz) rice flour
¹/₄ cup (60 g / 2 oz) sugar
pinch of salt
1 cup (250 mL / 8 fl oz) coconut milk
1 egg
8 cups (2 litres / 64 fl oz) oil, approximately

Method:
Season the rosette mould by standing it in boiling oil for at least 1 hour. Leave it in the oil to cool.

Combine the rice flour, sugar and salt in a bowl. Make a well in the centre and add the coconut milk and egg. Beat the coconut milk and egg together, then slowly incorporate the flour into this wet mixture to form a smooth batter. The batter should be thicker than standard pancake batter.

Half-fill a small wok with the oil and heat gently until the oil is hot but not smoking. Dip the prepared mould into the oil to heat then dip it into the batter, ensuring the batter comes only three-quarters of the way up the sides of the mould.

Immerse the mould in the oil. As it cooks the batter will pull away from the sides of the mould; if this does not happen, use a satay skewer to lever or push the cooked batter away until it falls off into the oil. (If the batter pulls away from the mould and flattens out the oil is too hot. In this case, cool the oil and start again).

Allow the rosette to cook in the oil for a few more seconds, then remove and drain on absorbent paper. Cool and store in an airtight container. The rosettes will keep for 1 week.

Halva
(Dodol)

Dodol, a festive Malay dessert, is traditionally made with glutinous rice and coconut milk, stirred slowly in a large vat until it thickens into a dark and moist mixture that is wrapped in banana leaves. This microwave recipe, which I developed for my television program in Malaysia, saves time and effort and tastes just as good if wrapped in banana leaves.

Ingredients:

3 cups (750 g / 1½ lb) palm sugar

1 cup (250 g / 8 oz) castor sugar

½ cup (125 mL / 4 fl oz) water

4 cups (500 g / 1 lb) glutinous rice flour

4 cups (1 litre / 32 fl oz) coconut milk

2 pandan leaves, shredded and tied in a knot

Method:

Place the palm sugar, castor sugar and water in a Pyrex or ceramic microwave-proof bowl. Microwave on high for 10 minutes until the sugar melts.

Blend the rice flour and coconut milk to form a smooth, lump-free batter. Strain if necessary. Pour into a large microwave-proof bowl and cook on low for 5 minutes. Whisk well, then whisk into the sugar mixture.

Add the pandan leaves and cook on low for 10 minutes. Stir well then cook on high for 8 minutes and then on medium low for 35 minutes, whisking every 10 minutes to prevent lumps from forming. The mixture will gradually become thick and darken and cluster together into a paste that is wobbly while hot but firm when cool.

Place the dodol paste in some plastic wrap and roll into a fat sausage shape. Cool and slice into thin pieces. Serve with hot black coffee.

Semolina Halva
(Khesari)

This is an Indian dessert and, in the tradition of Indian desserts, can be very sweet. The ghee that is used to fry the semolina is quite rich and fattening, but do not be tempted to use vegetable oil — the aroma and flavour produced by ghee can never be reproduced.

Ingredients:

1 cup (250 mL / 8 fl oz) milk

1 cup (250 mL / 8 fl oz) water

¾ cup (185 g / 6 oz) sugar

1 teaspoon cardamom seeds, pounded

½ cup (125 g / 4 oz) ghee or butter

1 cup (185 g / 6 oz) large-grained semolina

¼ cup (50 g / 1 oz) sultanas

¼—½ cup (60—125 mL / 2—4 fl oz) golden syrup (or to taste)

2 tablespoons almonds, slivered then roasted

Method:

Butter a 22 cm (8½ in) pie plate.

Place the milk, water, sugar and cardamom in a saucepan. Bring to the boil, stirring, until the sugar melts. Pour into a jug and allow to cool slightly.

Melt the ghee over medium heat in a wok and pour in the semolina. Stir-fry until the semolina is golden brown and smells roasted. Do not allow the wok to get too hot or the semolina will burn.

Add the sultanas and fry for 1 minute. Lower the heat, pour in the golden syrup and stir well to mix. Pour the milk mixture into the wok and, while it is boiling, stir quickly for 4—5 minutes or until the liquid has reduced.

Pour the halva into the prepared plate, smooth with the back of a buttered spoon then cut into 3 cm (1 in) slices diagonally one way then 3 cm (1 in) slices diagonally the other way to form a diamond pattern. Decorate each slice with an almond sliver.

Serve either cold or warm.

Glossary

Agar agar: A setting agent that does not require refrigeration. Extracted from seaweed, it is available in the form of strands or as a powder from Chinese grocers or health food stores.

Amchur: *See* Dried mango powder.

Asafoetida: The dried, powdered resin obtained from giant fennel. It is generally purchased as a powder or in waxlike pieces and while it has a very unpleasant smell, this is not carried over into the food. It is used in very small quantities to enhance the flavour of food and aid in digestion.

Assam glugor: Thin slices of dried tamarind.

Basil (Daun kemangi or Daun selaseh) (bot. *Ocimum basilicum*): Either sweet basil or Thai basil can be used in Malaysian cooking.

Bean sprouts (Nga choy or Taugay) (bot. *Glycine max*): The sprouts of soya beans have long, white tails with oval-shaped yellow beans on top. Salt should never be added to them until after they are cooked or they will wilt and lose their crunchy texture. For this reason Malaysians use light soy sauce instead of salt when cooking bean sprouts.

Beanthread Noodles (Glass noodles or Suhoon): Very fine, transparent noodles made from mung bean flour. They need to be soaked in warm water before use.

Beehoon noodles (Mei fun): Needle-thin rice noodles that take only 2 or 3 minutes to cook; they are usually added to soups or dishes with plenty of sauce.

Belacan: *See* Shrimp Paste.

Betel leaf (Daun kadok) (bot. *Piper sarmentosum*): A small, deep green, glossy, heart-shaped leaf. It has a slightly bitter taste and is chewed together with betel nut but can also be used in Malaysian cooking as a wrapping for food. It is soaked in sugared water before use to remove any bitterness.

Bittermelon (bot. *Momordica charantia*): Light green, ridged vegetable with red seeds and pithy insides. The bitterness of the flesh can be reduced by soaking the melon in salt water before cooking.

Bok choy (bot. *Brassica chinensis*): Dark green cabbage with fleshy, white stems. Both the stems and leaves are used; it is best suited to stir-frying.

Candlenut (bot. *Aleurites moluccana*): Used to thicken curries, these hard, oily nuts were also once used as candles. If candlenuts are unavailable, macadamia nuts can be substituted though they have a sweeter flavour.

Chilli (bot. *Capsicum annuum*, *C. frutescens*): Malaysians use many varieties of chilli. In general, the smaller the chilli the hotter it is. The hottest type, the bird's eye chilli (chilli padi), is common in Malaysia, as are the anaheim and serrano chilli. When using dried chillies look for the dark, fairly straight-shaped chillies from India and China.

Chinese Sausages (Lap Cheong): Spicy, red, dried sausages containing pork meat and fat.

Choy sum (bot. *Brassica chinensis* var. *parachinensis*): Large mustard greens with yellow flowers. The stems and leaves can be used; it is best suited to stir-frying.

Cloudear fungus (bot. *Auricularia polytricha*): Wrinkled, ear-shaped, dark black fungus said to be good for reducing blood pressure; it must be soaked in boiling water and trimmed before use. It adds a crunchy texture to stir-fries.

Coriander (Ketumber or Cilantro) (bot. *Coriandrum sativum*): All parts of this plant can be used in cooking, depending upon the recipe. Its small, round, beige-coloured seeds are nutty in taste and are used as the base for most curries.

Cumin (Jintan puteh) (bot. *Cuminum cyminum*): Similar in shape to caraway seeds, cumin seeds are added to food for their flavour and aroma.

Curry leaves (Karipincha or Daun kari) (bot. *Murraya koenigii*): Small, tear-shaped leaves similar in appearance to the leaves of the Orange Blossom tree; they add a strong, aromatic flavour to Indian curries.

Dried fish (Ikan kering and Ikan bilis): The most common type used is the dried kurau, sometimes known as the Siamese mergui fish. Malaysians also use tiny dried whitebait called *ikan bilis*. All dried fish needs to be soaked in water then pounded for use in stocks, dahls and curries.

Dried mango powder (Amchur): A green-grey powder made from ground, dried, unripe mango.

Dried prawns (Udang kering): Used in many Malaysian dishes, dried prawns can be bought in packets — choose those that are large, regular shapes and are bright orange/pink in colour.

Fennel seeds (Jintan manis) (bot. *Foeniculum vulgare*): Essential for Malaysian cooking, fennel seeds are similar in shape to caraway seeds, and have a sweet taste and an aromatic quality.

Galangal (Laos or Lengkuas) (bot. *Alpinia galanga*): This spicy, aromatic rhizome is a pinky-yellow colour and has a delicate and distinctive flavour. Though it is woody it is easily ground in a food processor or mortar and pestle.

Garlic chives (Kuchai) (bot. *Allium tuberosum*): Same in appearance as normal chives, but with a strong garlic aroma and taste; older plants can be tough, so choose young shoots.

Hoisin sauce: A thick, red-brown Chinese sauce which is both sweet and spicy; it is made from fermented black beans, soy beans, garlic and a number of spices, and is used for barbecuing.

Jackfruit (Nangka) (bot. *Artocarpus heterophyllus*): A very large ovoid-shaped fruit with a rough, green, spiny skin. Do not confuse it with the durian, which has sharper spikes on its skin. When cutting, use oil-smeared gloves to prevent the rubbery sap from sticking to your fingers.

Kaffir lime leaf (Daun limau purut) (bot. *Citrus aurantifolia*): Aromatic leaf of the kaffir lime tree; fresh leaves are best but dried leaves are more widely available.

Kang kong (Water convulvulus, Swamp cabbage or Ong choy) (bot. *Ipomoea aquatica*): Dark green arrow-shaped leaves with hollow stems; suited to stir-frying with sambal belacan and/or dried prawns.

Koey Teow Noodles: Broad, flat white rice noodles used in stir-fries and soups.

Lemon grass (bot. *Cymbopogon citratus*): Commonly used in Southeast Asian cooking, this lemon- and lime-flavoured grasslike plant is good in curries and salads. Only the thick bulbous stems of the fresh plant should be used; it is also available dried or in brine.

Mango (bot. *Mangifera indica*): When ripe, the skins of mangoes are yellow or red in colour; they can be eaten fresh or used in desserts, but green mangoes (or mango powder (amchur)) can be used to give a sour flavour to curries and when barbecuing fish.

Palm sugar (Gula jawa or Gula malacca): Caramelised sugar in cake-form, made from the sap of the coconut palm. It is easily reconstituted into syrup when chopped and microwaved on High for 2 minutes or boiled in a little water (100 grams (3½ oz) with 60 mL (¼ cup/2 fl oz) water makes a good working quantity for most recipes).

Pandan leaf (Screw pine leaf or Daun pandan) (bot. *Pandanus latifolia*): The long, thin leaf of the pandanus plant, which has a subtle aroma. It is used to flavour and colour rice and desserts. If fresh leaves are unavailable use the dried leaf (packaged as 'Rampe', a Sri Lankan name).

Pickled radish (tangchai): Available in Asian grocery stores in plastic packets or in jars, pickled radish is added for its texture as well as its flavour; wash before use to remove the salt.

Red Asian onions (bawang) (bot. *Allium rubrum*): Sometimes known as red or Asian shallots or purple onions, they are small onions that grow in clumps and are used exclusively in Asia in curries, salads and soups. If you can't find red Asian onions, the closest substitute is the larger Spanish (red) onions, which are sweeter and more flavoursome than brown and white onions.

Red Vinegar: An orangey-red Chinese vinegar that is tart and slightly salty in flavour.

Rice: Long- and medium-grained rices are usually favoured with curries. In Malaysia, the most commonly used long-grained rice is Mahsuri. Basmati is an aromatic, long-grained rice from Pakistan; the grains do not stick together when cooked. Jasmine rice originates in Thailand, is very fragrant and is used for everyday cooking. Glutinous rice and black glutinous rice are used when making desserts.

Rojak paste (Haekoe): A sweetish, dark black shrimp paste. It has a very fishy flavour and should be used sparingly.

Salted cabbage (Kiam chye): Salted mustard greens or cabbage, not to be confused with the Korean 'Kim chee' which is made from a similar cabbage but has a heavier flavour of chilli and garlic. Kiam chye is sold in large earthenware containers or in plastic bags. It should be washed before use to remove excess salt.

Salted turnip (Tung chye): Brined turnip sold in small, squat jars with plastic lids, available from Chinese grocery stores. It is used in soups, stocks or fried rice and should be washed before use.

Shao Hsing wine: Made from fermented rice, this golden-coloured, pungent Chinese wine is good in stews, soups and marinades.

Shrimp paste (Belacan): Small shrimp that have been salted, fermented and left to dry slowly in vats, shaped into balls or bricks then left to dry in the sun. It comes in many varieties – the lighter the paste the less impurities.

Snake beans (Kacang panjang or Long beans) (bot. *Vigna unguiculata*): A very long, thin bean used in stir-fries, fried rice, fish cakes and omelettes.

Snowpeas (Hor lan dow, Kacang kapri or Mangetout): Both the flat pod of the snowpea and the tiny peas inside are eaten, usually whole, after the strings have been removed.

Soy sauce: There are three varieties of soy sauce: dark, light and thick (kecap manis). Dark soy is used when you wish to add colour to a dish, while the saltier light soy is used when you want to avoid discolouring the food. The thick Malaysian soy sauce (kecap manis) caramelises, sweetens and colours food.

Star Anise (Bunga Lawang) (bot. *Illicium verum*): Aromatic and imparting a slightly tingly taste to food, it is a very small, dried, star-shaped fruit with eight points.

Starfruit (Carambola): Tropical fruit which forms a star shape when sliced. The large, light green starfruit is used in Malaysia for its juice while the smaller, harder starfruit (belimbing) is used to sour curries.

Sweet Black vinegar: A dark brown, thick Chinese rice vinegar which looks (but doesn't taste) a little like dark soy sauce. It has a rich aroma and is flavoured with the Chinese spices cassia and star anise.

Szechwan Pepper (Fagara) (bot. *Xanthoxylum piperitum*): Small, red seeds which resemble red-coloured peppercorns. It has a spicy and tingly taste, similar to that of star anise. It should be lightly roasted before use.

Tamarind (bot. *Tamarindus indica*): A fruit with a sweet/sour taste, it adds an acidic flavour to fish curries and is essential to the flavour of many Malaysian dishes. It is available in compacted brick form, with or without seeds, or as purée.

Taucheo: Salted black beans with a smoky, nutty, salty flavour; they add depth to pork and chicken dishes. Before use they need to be washed and pounded into a paste. Salted yellow beans and miso are similar in flavour and may be substituted if taucheo is unavailable.

Tempe: Fermented tofu; high in vitamins and protein.

Tofu: Unfermented soya bean curd, tofu is available in many forms: small, fried puffy pillows called tofupok; thick fresh tofu blocks; pickled tofu; creamy custard-like tofu; tofu milk (tofu-chui); and fuchuk. The latter is made by drying the thin skin that rises to the top when tofu milk is boiled. It is brittle but, when wet, it becomes pliable and can be used as a wrapper around other food.

Turmeric (Daun kunyit) (bot. *Curcuma domestica*): A member of the ginger family. The yellow rhizome of the turmeric plant is one of the main ingredients in Malay cooking; the plant's long, broad leaves, similar in shape to that of the canna lily, are used in Rendangs and Malay curries and shredded as a garnish.

Vietnamese mint (Daun kesum) (bot. *Polygonum* var.): Used in Assam Laksa and as a garnish, Vietnamese mint is not actually a member of the mint family and tastes more like coriander (cilantro) than mint. It has long, arrow-shaped leaves with faint red, serrated markings.

Water chestnut: The sweet, white flesh of the water chestnut is added to Malaysian food because of its crunchy texture. While it can be purchased fresh, in a brown, papery skin, it is more commonly available canned.

Yam bean: A light brown legume that is shaped like a top and has a thin papery skin. If unavailable, substitute Chinese cabbage.

Yellow mee noodles (Hokkien mee): Long, thick wheat noodles that are available both fresh and dried and that range in shape from flat ribbons to thin strips. They are not made from durum wheat as Western-style pasta is, so they will become gluggy when soaked in warm water; for best results, blanch in cold water before use.

Malaysian Ingredients and Techniques

Curry powder

Malaysians usually get their curry spices ground in the markets each morning or use a curry powder blended at home from different spices. The most common blend for general use in curries is: 2 tablespoons dried, ground coriander seeds; 1 tablespoon dried, ground cumin seeds; ¼ tablespoon dried, ground fennel seeds; ½ tablespoon chilli powder (more or less, according to taste); ½ teaspoon turmeric powder, ¼ teaspoon cloves, ¼ teaspoon cinnamon, ¼ teaspoon cardamom and ¼ teaspoon pepper. This will make enough powder to curry 600 to 800 grams (1 lb 5 oz − 1 lb 12 oz) of beef, lamb or chicken. For fish curries, omit the fennel and use 1 teaspoon of fenugreek seeds (halba) instead, after first heating them in a dry pan for 1 minute on a medium heat, then pounding roughly in a mortar and pestle.

Fresh coconut

When choosing a fresh coconut it is important to go by the weight rather than the size. A good coconut is heavy and when shaken one should be able to hear liquid sloshing about inside. (If you cannot hear liquid it may mean that it is too old and dry, and contains oil rather than milk.) Break the coconut at its equator with a machete or chopper, then drain out the coconut water, which can be used in drinks. Prise the coconut apart with a cleaver to reveal the white flesh, which should smell fresh. In Malaysia a manual coconut grinder – a low bench with a serrated blade sticking out of one end – would be used, but you can prise the flesh out of the shell with a sharp knife and blend it in a food processor.

To obtain coconut cream, add 1 cup (250 mL / 8 fl oz) of water to the ground coconut flesh and squeeze it with your fingers, or put it through the blender, extracting as much cream as you can. Strain it and store in the refrigerator. To obtain coconut milk, add another ½ cup (125 mL / 4 fl oz) of water to the coconut flesh, squeeze through the fingers or put through a blender and strain. You can repeat this process a number of times, until the liquid becomes too thin and watery. One large coconut yields about 1 cup (250 mL / 8 fl oz) of coconut cream and 2 to 3 cups (16−24 fl oz) of coconut milk, depending on the number of times you add water.

When refrigerated, coconut cream and milk will last for up to 2 days. Should it begin to turn sour, boil it, stirring slowly, for about 5 minutes, then leave to cool and refrigerate. It will keep for a few days but won't be as tasty as the fresh product. Canned coconut milk is a good substitute for fresh. It usually looks greyish in the can − beware of coconut milk or cream that is blue-white as whiteners may have been added.

Dry roasting

Dry roasting heightens the flavours of ingredients and is essential for many Malaysian dishes. If a recipe calls for a dry roasted ingredient, it should be heated in a saucepan or wok with no oil or water added. When dry roasting spices, heat them until the aroma is noticable, but be careful not to let the spices burn.

Dry roasted shrimp paste (belacan)

Mould a tablespoon of shrimp paste (belacan) into a marble-sized ball with your fingers and skewer the ball with a fork or place it onto a piece of foil. Hold it over a medium flame and dry roast it until it crumbles. If you prefer to use a microwave oven, place the shrimp paste (belacan) in a small dish and cook it on High for 1½ minutes.

Dry roasted coconut (krisek)

Dry roasted coconut (krisek) is used as a thickener in curries and in salads and pickles. Place 1 cup (90 g / 3 oz) of grated or desiccated coconut in a dry wok or saucepan on medium heat and toss continuously until it turns golden brown, approximately 8−10 minutes. Blend the coconut in a mortar and pestle or in a food processor until the coconut oil is released.

Sambal Belacan

Before you begin to make Sambal Belacan you will need to dry roast your shrimp paste (belacan), as described above. While Sambal Belacan is best made using a mortar and pestle, it can also be prepared in a food processor.

Smoke 2 fresh chillies by holding them over a low flame. Place 2 or 3 small red Asian onions or 1 chopped medium-sized Spanish (red) onion into a mortar and pound well with a pestle until mashed. Add 1 teaspoon or a 1 centimetre (½ in) long piece of dry roasted shrimp paste (belacan) and the 2 smoked chillies, and pound until the onion and shrimp paste are well combined and the chilli is in small chunks. Add the juice of half a lime and ½ a teaspoon of salt, pound gently to combine and remove from the mortar and pestle. Sambal Belacan can be stored, covered, in the refrigerator for up to a week.

Rice

Rinse the rice in several changes of water until the water runs clear − this removes the preservatives and the cornflour or starch used to whiten the rice. For each cup (220 g / 7 oz) of rice you should use 2½ cups (625 mL / 20 fl oz) of water. Malaysians, however, use the very effective knuckle method: place the rice in the pot and cover it with water up to the level of the middle joint of your index finger (with the tip of your finger resting on the top of the rice), or 3.5 centimetres (1½ in) above the rice, regardless of the quantity of rice or the size of the saucepan.

Place the saucepan, uncovered, on a high heat and bring to the boil. When boiling, partly cover with the lid and turn the heat down to medium. When the rice has absorbed all of the water cover the saucepan fully, turn off the heat and allow the rice to steam for about 10 minutes. Run a fork through the rice to fluff it up before serving.

Tamarind purée

Tamarind is available in brick-like blocks of compacted flesh, with or without seeds. The lighter, toffee-coloured tamarind is better than the darker variety. To prepare it for use, mix approximately 3 tablespoons of tamarind with 1 cup (250 mL / 8 fl oz) of water, then either stir well with a fork or work through with your fingertips to release the thick pulp. Strain, discard the dregs and use the puree as directed. The puree can be refrigerated for up to a week.

Crispy Fried Onions

Thinly slice the onions across or lengthways. Quarter fill a saucepan with oil and place onto a medium-high heat. When the oil is hot, add the onions and stir well until they start to brown.

Keep a close watch so that they only brown, but do not burn. Remove the onions from the oil and drain on kitchen paper. To make crispy fried onions in the microwave oven, half fill a microwave-safe bowl with oil, add the sliced onions (the oil must cover the onions) and cook for approximately 10 minutes on High. Remove the onions from the oil and drain on kitchen paper as soon as they turn golden, otherwise they will continue to cook in the oil and burn. They can be used as a garnish or as a topping for soup.

Using a wok for the first time

Before using a new wok you will need to season it, as many new woks are coated with machine oil. Wash the wok well with warm, soapy water and dry. Pour a little cooking oil into the wok and wipe it off with paper towels. This will remove some of the machine oil. Place 2 cups (180 g / 6 oz) of desiccated coconut into the wok and heat, tossing, until the coconut is brown. Discard the coconut and start again. Repeat this procedure several times, until the coconut stops absorbing oils and dirt. The wok will have taken on a patina of oil that will prevent food 'catching' on it during cooking.

Where to Buy Ingredients

Australia

In the larger cities, Coles, Woolworths, Franklins, Action and Safeway Supermarkets generally have Asian food sections.

Australian Capital Territory

Dickson Asian Food
16–18 Brooley Street
Dickson ACT 2602

New South Wales

In Sydney you will find Asian grocery stores in Cabramatta, Chatswood and Chinatown.

Burlington Centre Supermarket
285 Penshurst Street
Willoughby NSW 2068
Ph: (02) 9417 2588

Graeme's spices
9 Angus Crescent
Yagoona NSW 2199
Ph: (02) 9644 5506

Queensland

In Brisbane, you will find many Asian grocery stores in Fortitude Valley and West End.

Royal Foods
248 Heming Road
Hemmant QLD 4174
Ph: (07) 3890 3100

South Australia

In Adelaide, try the markets for fresh Asian produce.

Capital Foods
28–32 Kintore Lane
Mile End SA 5031
Ph: (08) 8234 0170

M&J Supplies
39–47 Holland Street
Thebarton SA 5031
Ph: (08) 8234 8011

Victoria

In Melbourne, head for Box Hill or Richmond to find Asian grocery stores.

Store 70
422 Summerville Road
Footscray West VIC 3012
Ph: (03) 9314 2288

Western Australia

In Perth, try the suburb of Northbridge for Asian grocery stores.

Central Fine Foods
6 Granite Place
Welshpool WA 6106
Ph: (09) 350 6766

United Kingdom

M. and S. Patel
372–382 Romford Road
London, E7 8BS
Ph: (0181) 472 6201

Rafi's Spice Box (mail order)
c/o 31 Schoolfield
Glemsford
Suffolk CO10 7RE

The Spice Shop
115–117 Drummond Street
London NW1 2HL
Ph: (0171) 387 4526

United States of America

Arizona

G&L Import-Export Corporation
4828 East 22nd Street
Tuscon, Arizona 85706
Ph: (602) 790 9016

Manila Oriental Foodmart
3557 West Dunlap Avenue
Phoenix, Arizona 85021
(602) 841 2977

California

Indian Food Mill
650 San Bruno Avenue East
San Bruno, California 94014
Ph: (415) 583 6559

Connecticut

India Spice and Gift Shop
3295 Fairfield Avenue
Fairfield, Connecticut 06605
Ph: (203) 384 0666

Florida

Grocery Mahat and Asian Spices
1026 South Military Trail
West Palm Beach, Florida 334436
Ph: (407) 433 3936

Illinois

Indian Groceries and Spices
7300 St Louis Avenue
Skokie, Illinois 60076

Maryland

India Supermarket
8107 Fenton Street
Silver Springs, Maryland 20910
Ph: (301) 589 8423

Massachusetts

India Groceries
Oak Square
Boston, Massachusetts 02111
Ph: (617) 254 5540

New Jersey

Maharaja Indian Foods
130 Speedwell Avenue
Morristown, New Jersey 07960
Ph: (210) 829 0048

New York

Indian Groceries and Spices
61 Wythe Avenue
Brooklyn, New York 11211
Ph: (718) 963 0477

Ohio

Crestview Market
200 Crestview Road
Columbus, Ohio 43202
Ph: (614) 267 2723

Pennsylvania

Gourmail Inc.
Drawer 516
Berwyn, Pennsylvania 19312
Ph: (215) 296 4620

Texas

MGM Indian Foods
9200 Lamar Boulevard
Austin, Texas, 78513
Ph: (512) 835 6937

Index